Between the Old and the New
Mid Century Black and White Photography by a GI Stationed in Europe

Photos by Chris Shaw
Text by Robert Gould Shaw

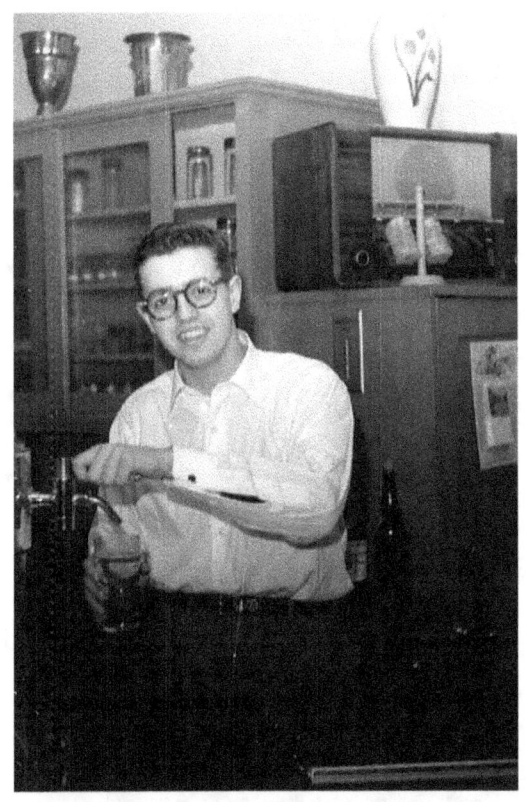
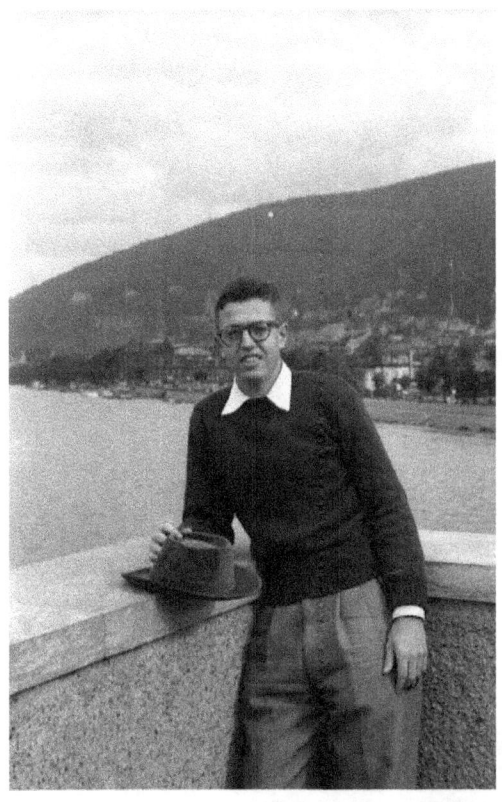
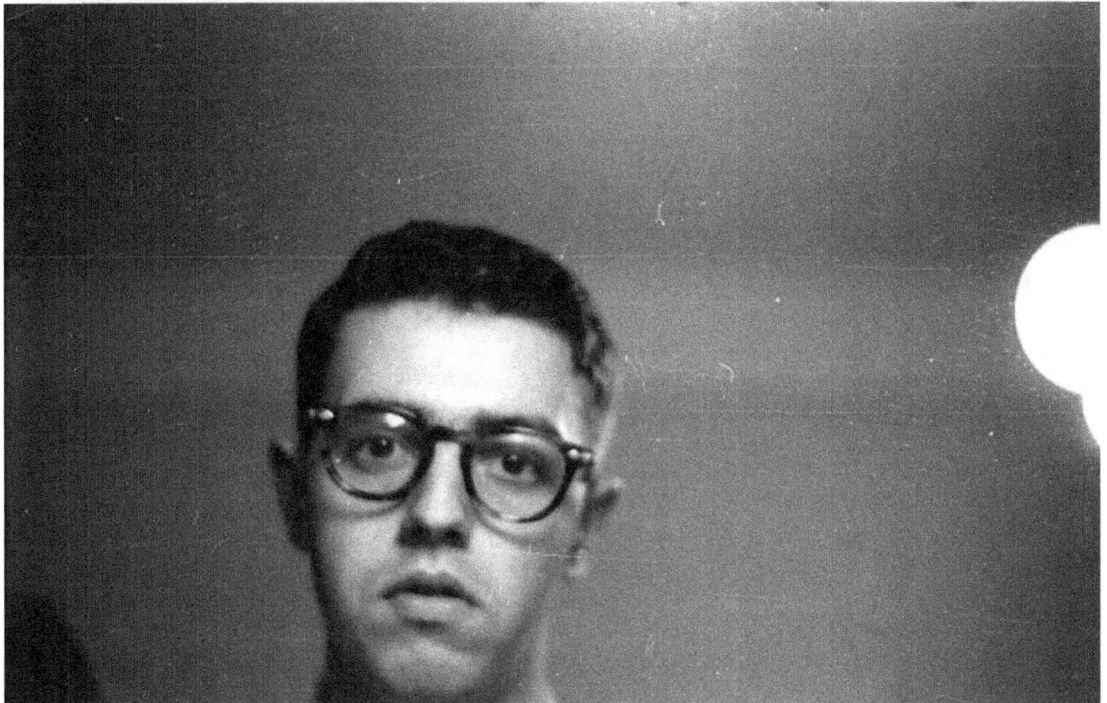

Chris Shaw

Between The Old and the New

In 1954, West Germany was in the midst of its *Wirtschaftswunder*, or economic miracle, and their soccer team had won the World Cup that summer for the first time. Purchasing power was rising dramatically, while cities, that had been bombed to rubble a decade earlier, were rebuilding, often in a new style. Modern housing blocks were quickly built to house displaced persons. Commercial buildings and factories were built to accommodate the growing demand for goods and services. Austria was in the last year of occupation and in the midst of its own *Wirtschaftswunder*.

Germany and Austria were halfway between the old and the new. In some cities, like Nuremburg, the ancient city center was recreated so that the new buildings resembled the old. Heidelberg, an ancient city with a ruined castle and the oldest university in Germany, was not bombed and was filled with Medieval, Renaissance, and Baroque buildings. Mannheim. was heavily bombed, destroying 80 percent of its city center. After the war, Mannheim was rapidly rebuilt but often in a new style. Salzburg, an ancient city that was ruled by a Prince Bishop for centuries and then annexed by Austria in 1805, was bombed but many of the building facades remained standing at the end of the war and many were rebuilt to resemble their former selves.

In 1954, the Second World War might have seemed long past when Chris arrived in Germany. Germany was prospering. The people were friendly and the girls were attractive. Heidelberg was beautiful and quaint while Mannheim, which also hosts a major university, was a construction site and more a city of commerce than a city for the young. Many younger adults in 1954 would have been in the Hitler youth before and during the war. A twenty-year-old soldier in 1944 would have been thirty and junior officers might be forty in 1954.

A new society was being created in Germany and Austria by the booming economy, different political situation, and a new generation growing up in far different circumstances than those of a decade earlier. Rock and roll was in its infancy and was making only the tiniest of impact through American GIs and Armed Forces Radio. Bill Haley's *Rock Around the Clock* was released in April 1954 and Elvis Presley was just starting his career. Popular music was largely cabaret songs, popular songs, and novelty numbers.

People in the photos are dressed in *Trachten*, traditional clothing still worn today, in suits and dresses that were similar to those worn in the 1930s, and girls dressed as bobbysoxers, one of them sporting a leather flight jacket, possibly borrowed from a boyfriend. There is a horse cart and Volkswagen Beetles. There are also photos of Carnival parades in Heidelberg and Salzburg.

In the 1950s, there were many US military bases between Mannheim and Heidelberg. Chris Shaw was stationed at a base near enough to Heidelberg that he spent the majority of his time off-duty there. As a university city with an intact old town, its night life would have been a major attraction to a young American serviceman.

Chris' monthly pay was likely between $85 and $122 per month, which in 2020 dollars equals between $821 and $1179 per month. Chris lived on base, which meant that his basic daily needs of food and lodging were taken care of. In 1954, one dollar was worth 4.2 Marks. According to the 1957-58 Fielding's Travel Guide to Europe, "$1.50 will buy a good meal in almost any routine establishment." A mug of beer cost between 10 and 20 cents.

During the winter of 1954/1955 Chris visited Munich, Germany and Salzburg, Austria, an hour and a half southeast of Munich. He also visited Zurich, Switzerland, possibly on the way to Paris and Nice, France. Chris' color photography from this era, including photos of Germany, Austria, Paris and Nice, are collected in a separate volume titled *On Leave: Mid Century Color Photography by a GI Stationed in Europe*.

Chris was documenting his present. With more than 60 years' perspective, they document a world largely, but not completely gone. When I visited Heidelberg with Chris in 1999, we looked for a basement nightclub that he had frequented, presumably the one captured in some of the photos. The nightclub was no longer there and we couldn't find where it had been. If you visit Heidelberg today, in most cases, you can see the same buildings and they will look very much the same, with the exception of commercial signage. It's rare to see people dressed in suits and fedoras and homburgs, but you can still see nuns dressed as they were and Germans, especially in Bavaria, and Austrians, dressed in *Trachten,* especially on the weekends. We live amongst the past surrounded by old buildings, ghost signs, and the memories, either personal or collective. As Wordsworth wrote, "The child is the father of the man."

--

The photos have not been edited. To the best of my ability, I have identified the locations.

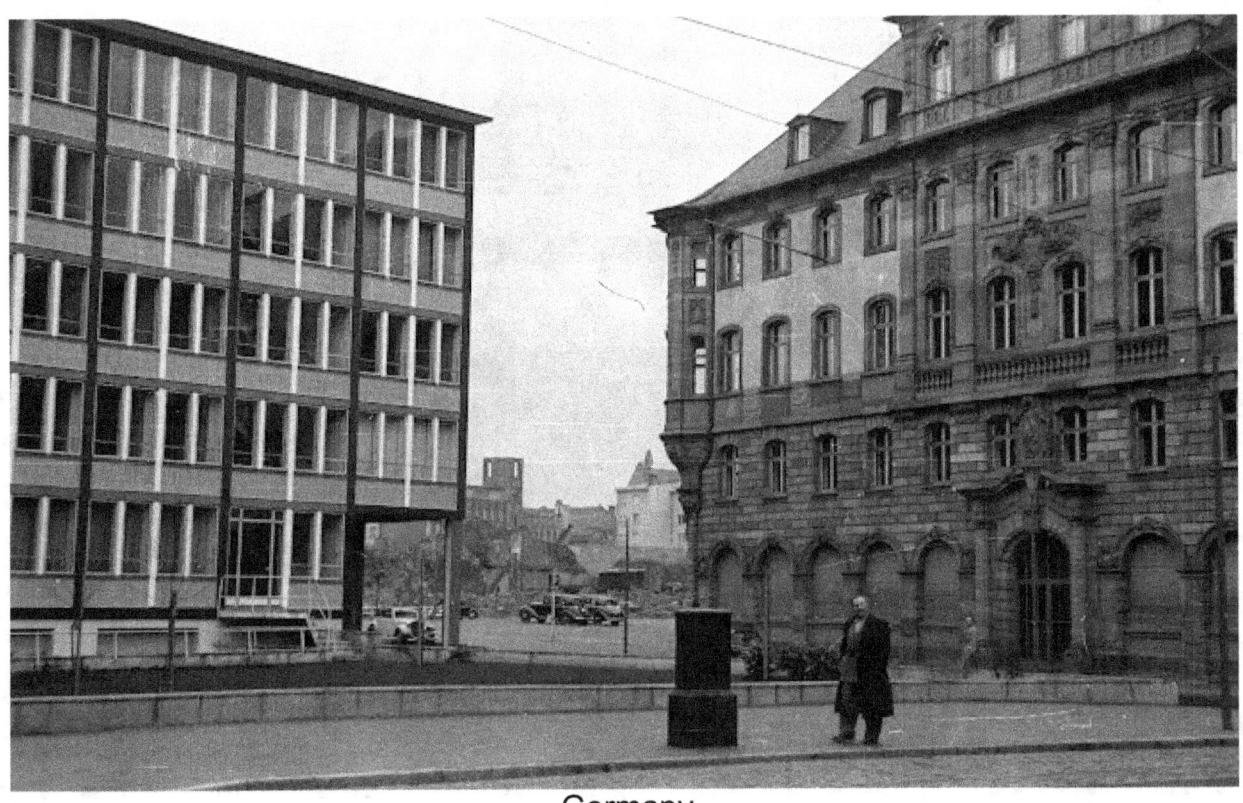
Germany

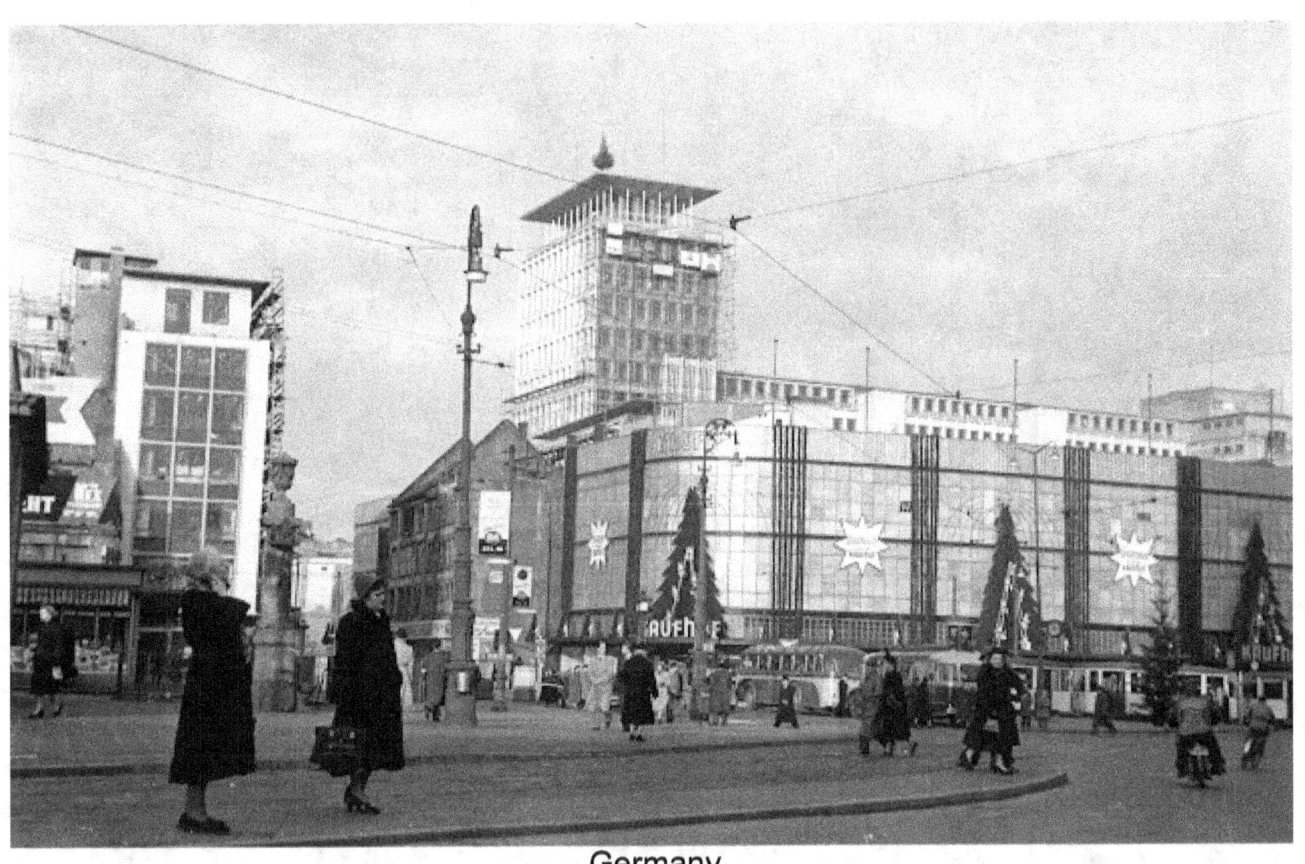
Germany

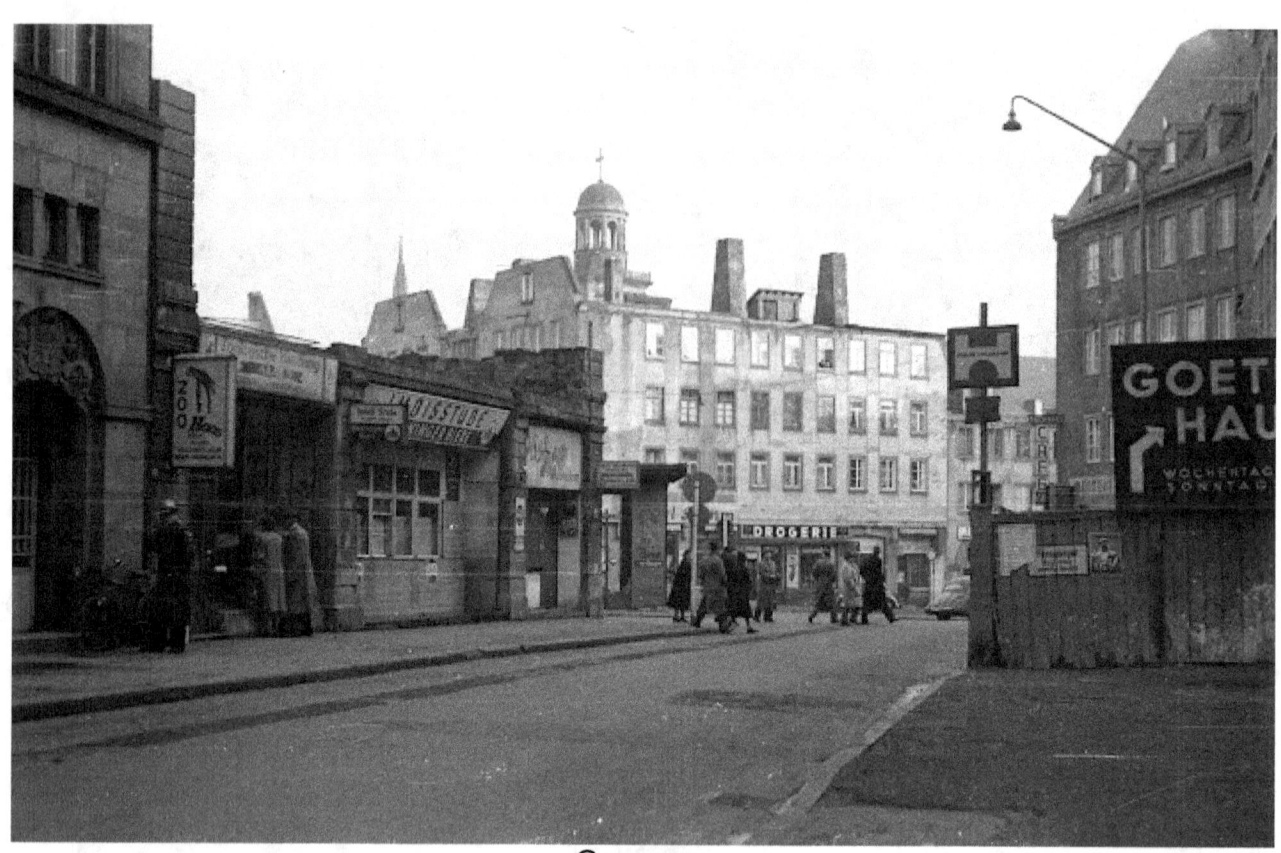
Germany

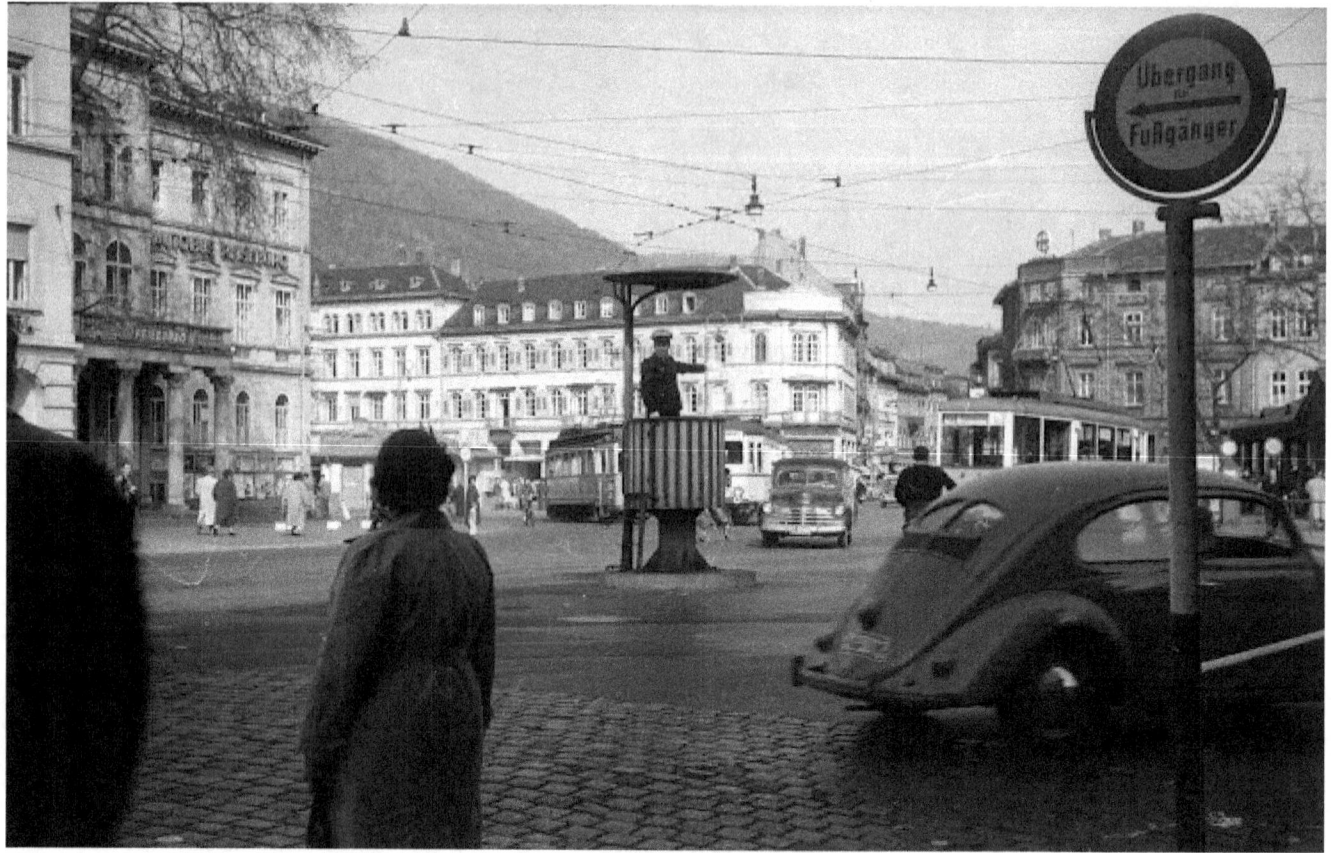
Germany

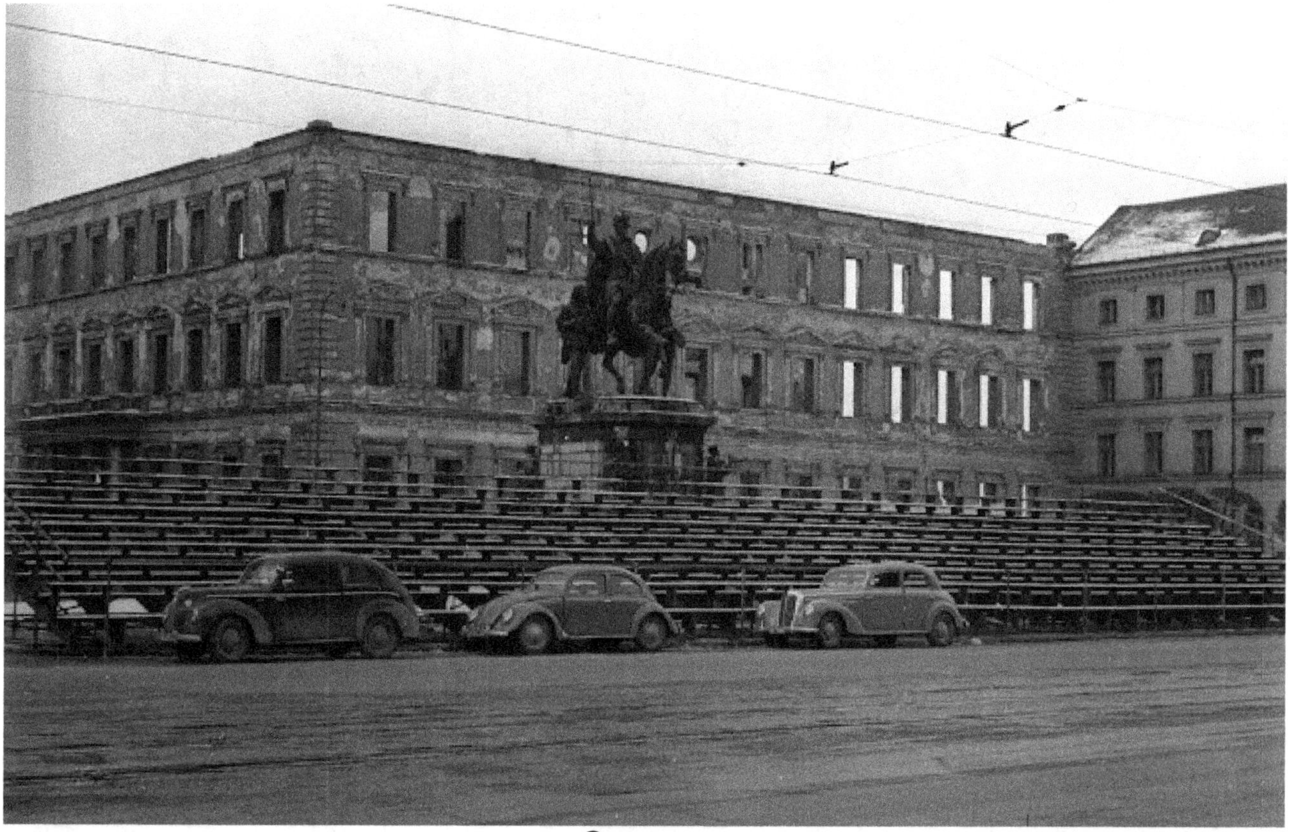

Germany

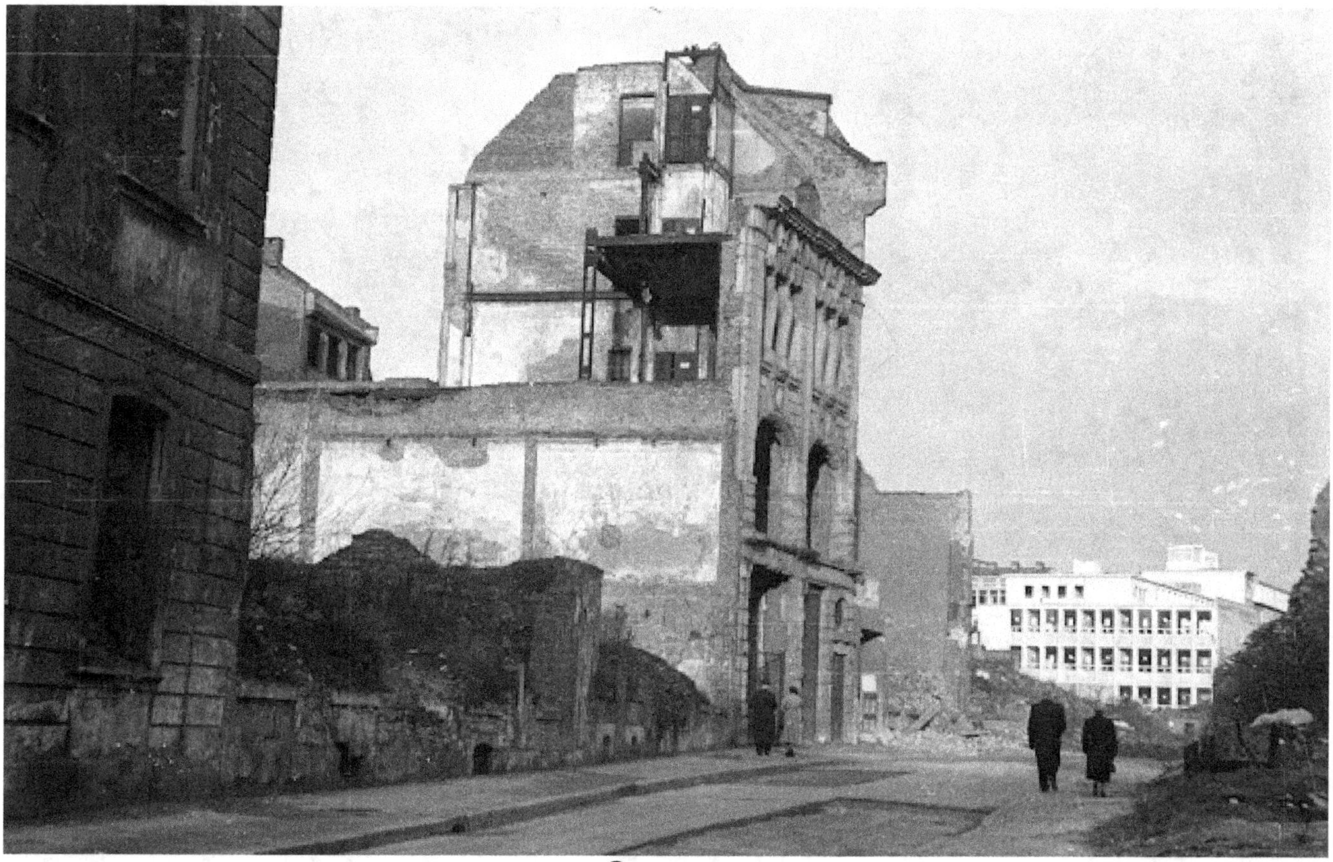

Germany

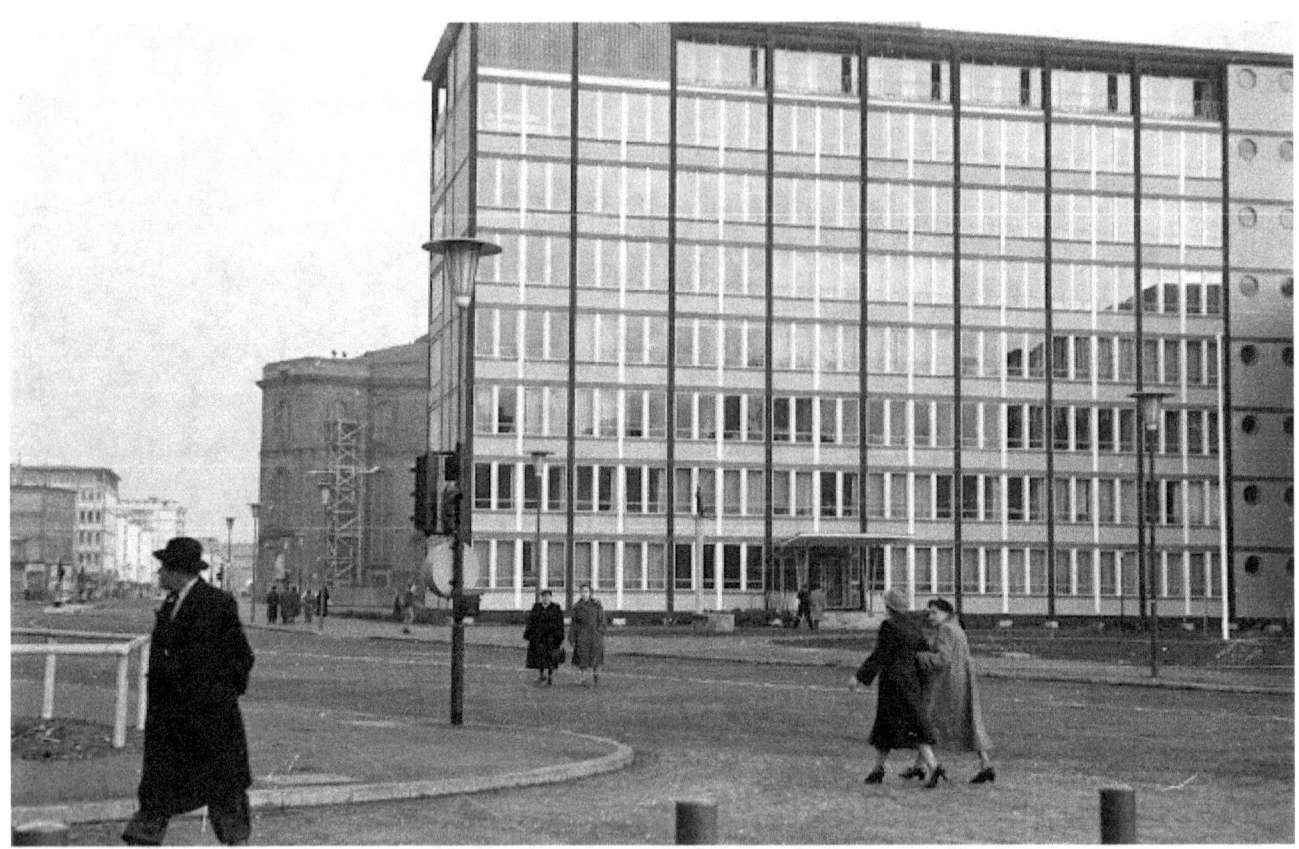
Germany, Possibly Mannheim

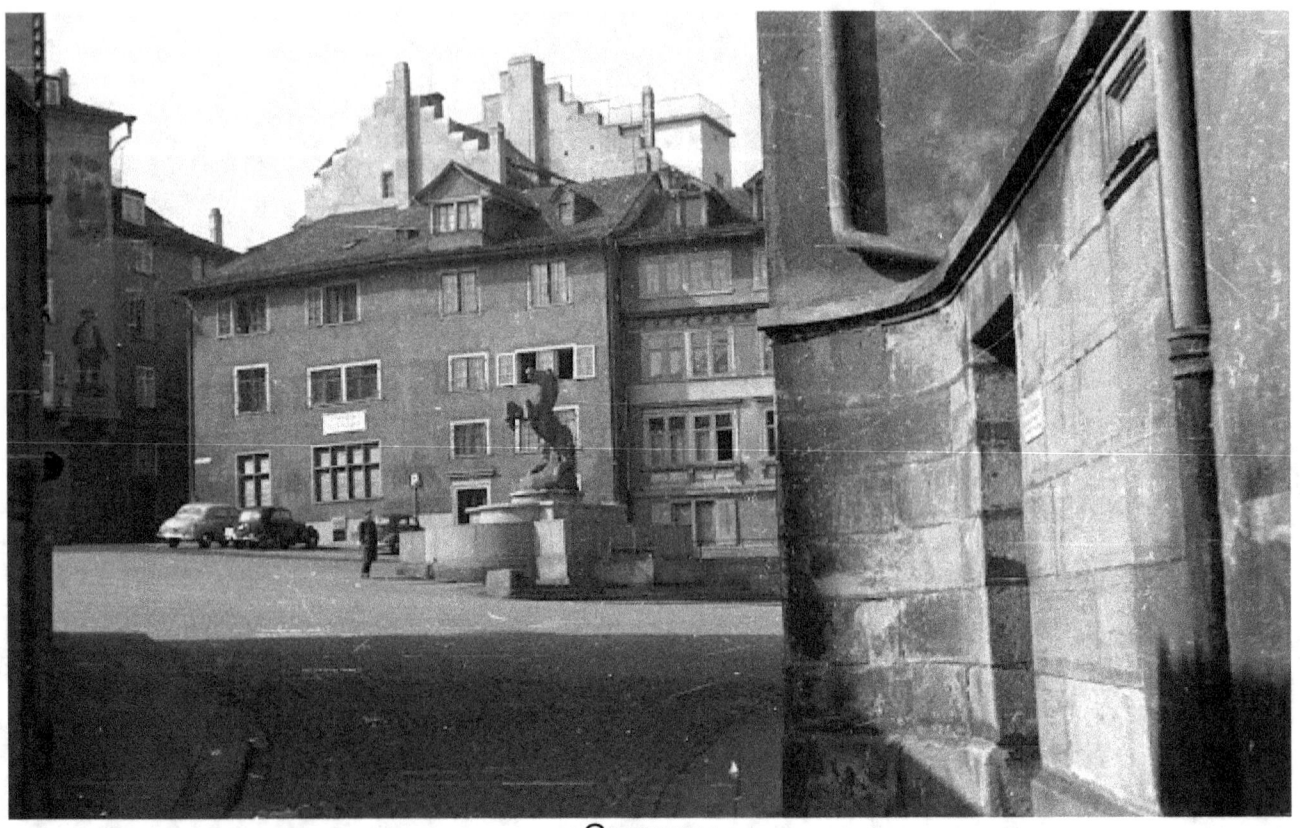
Germany

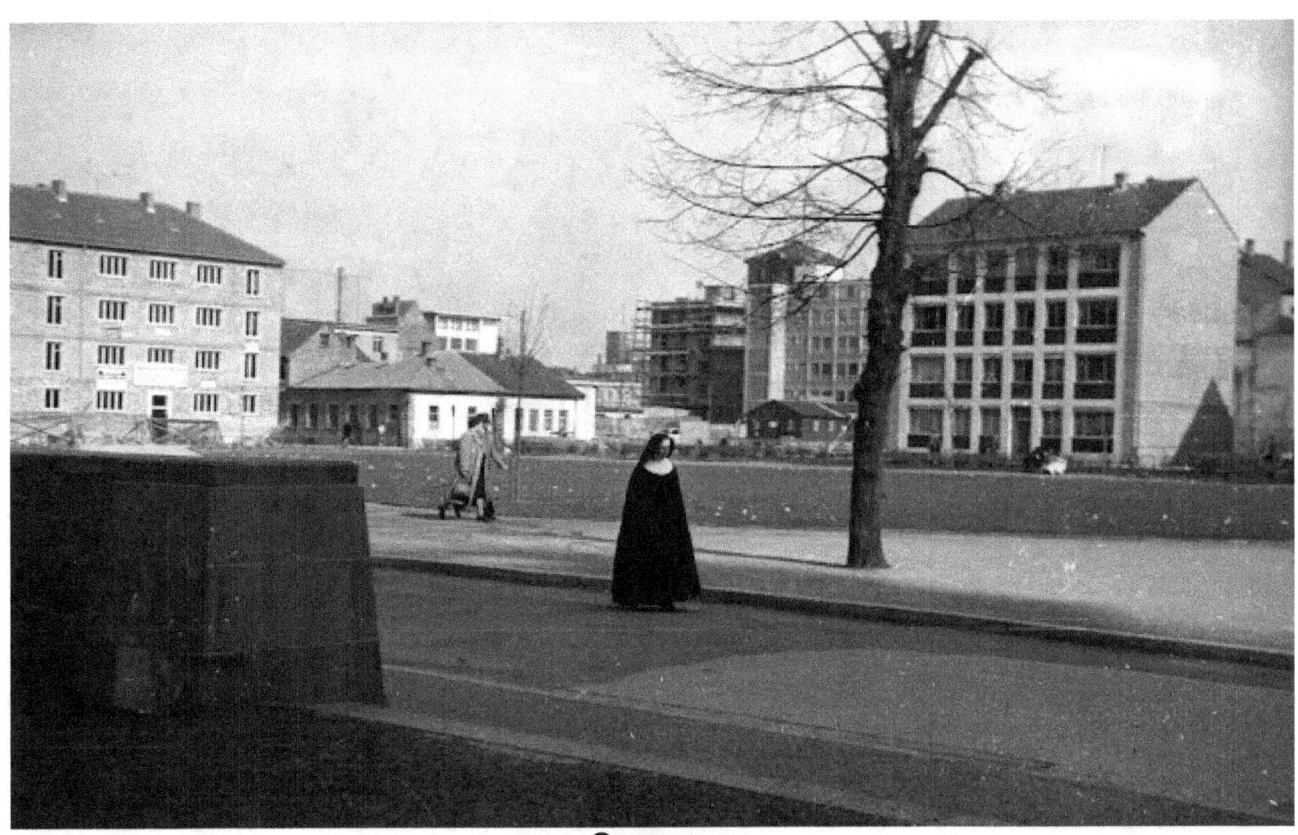
Germany

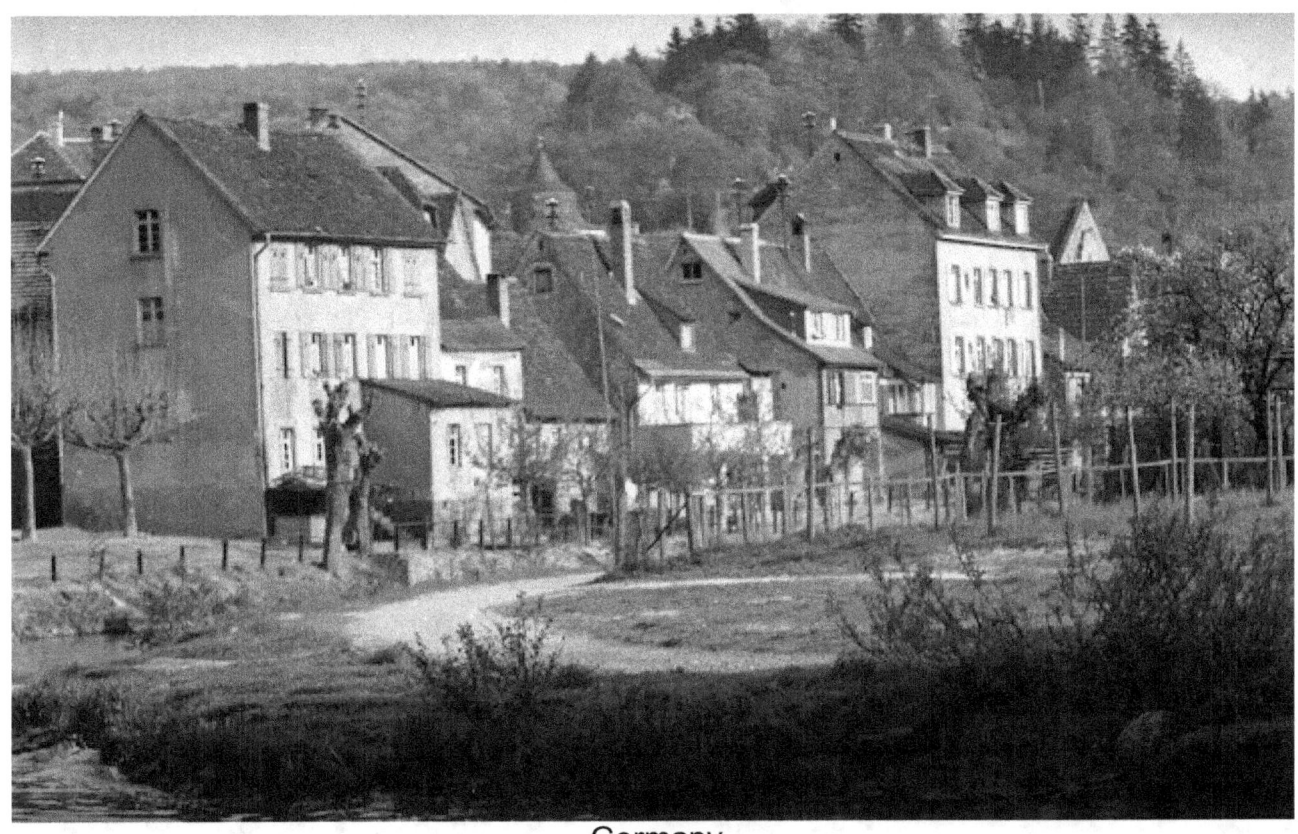
Germany

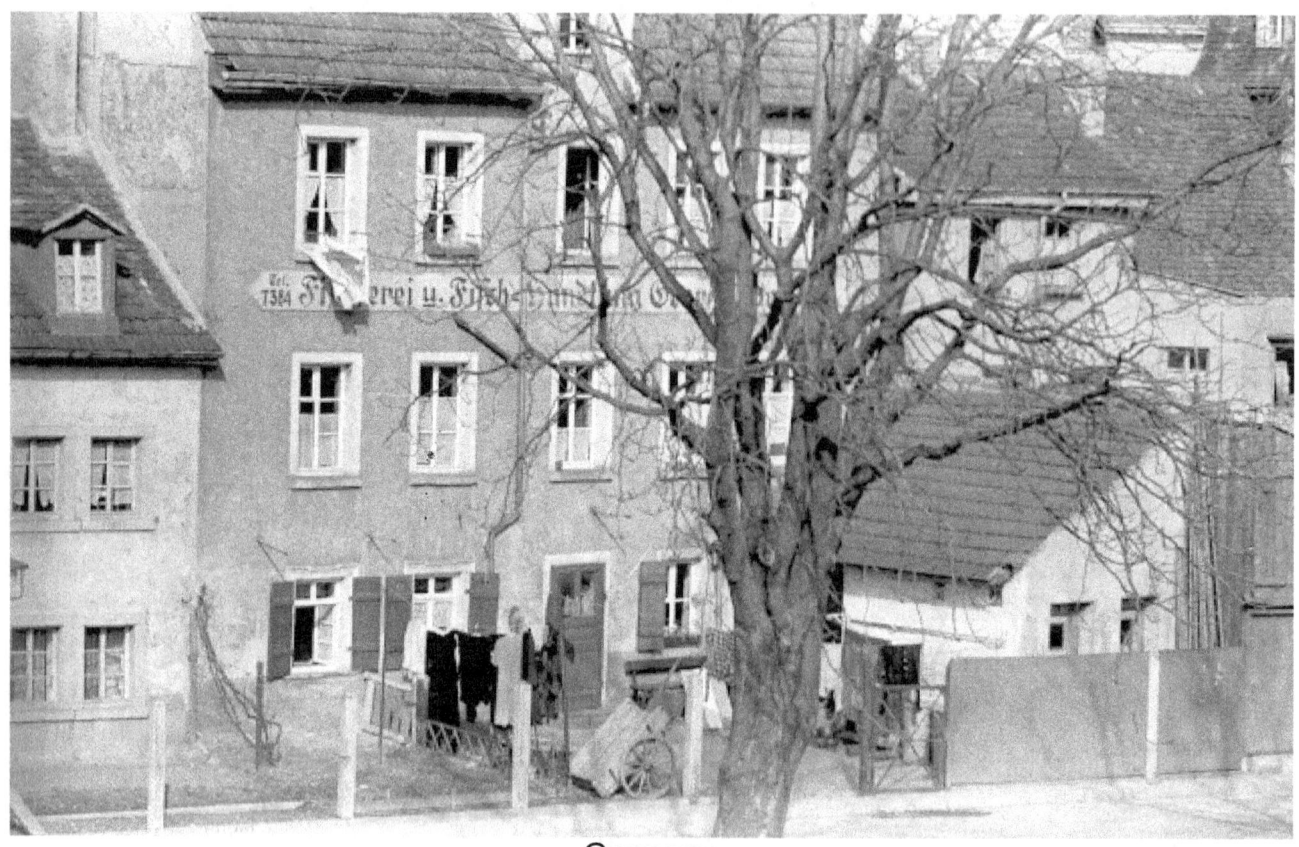

Germany

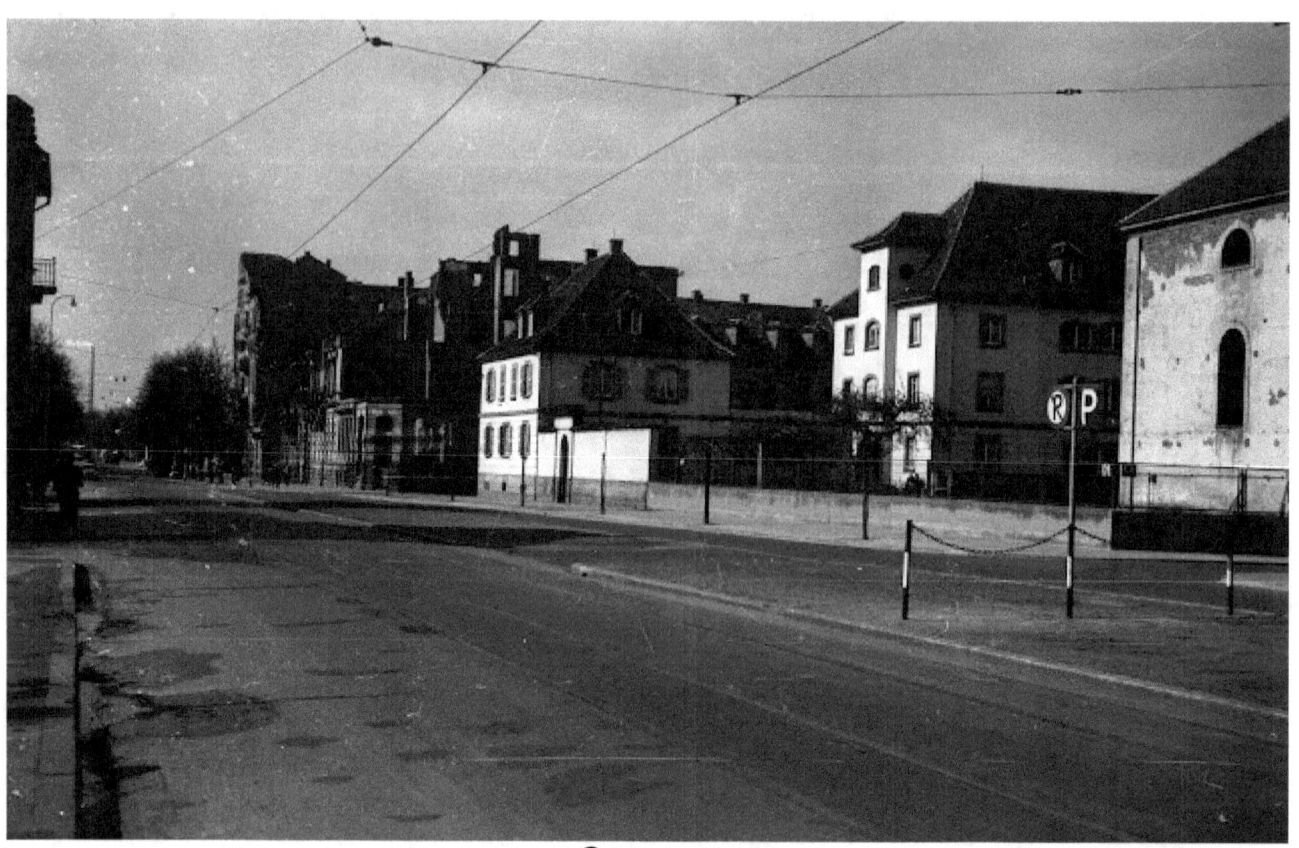

Germany

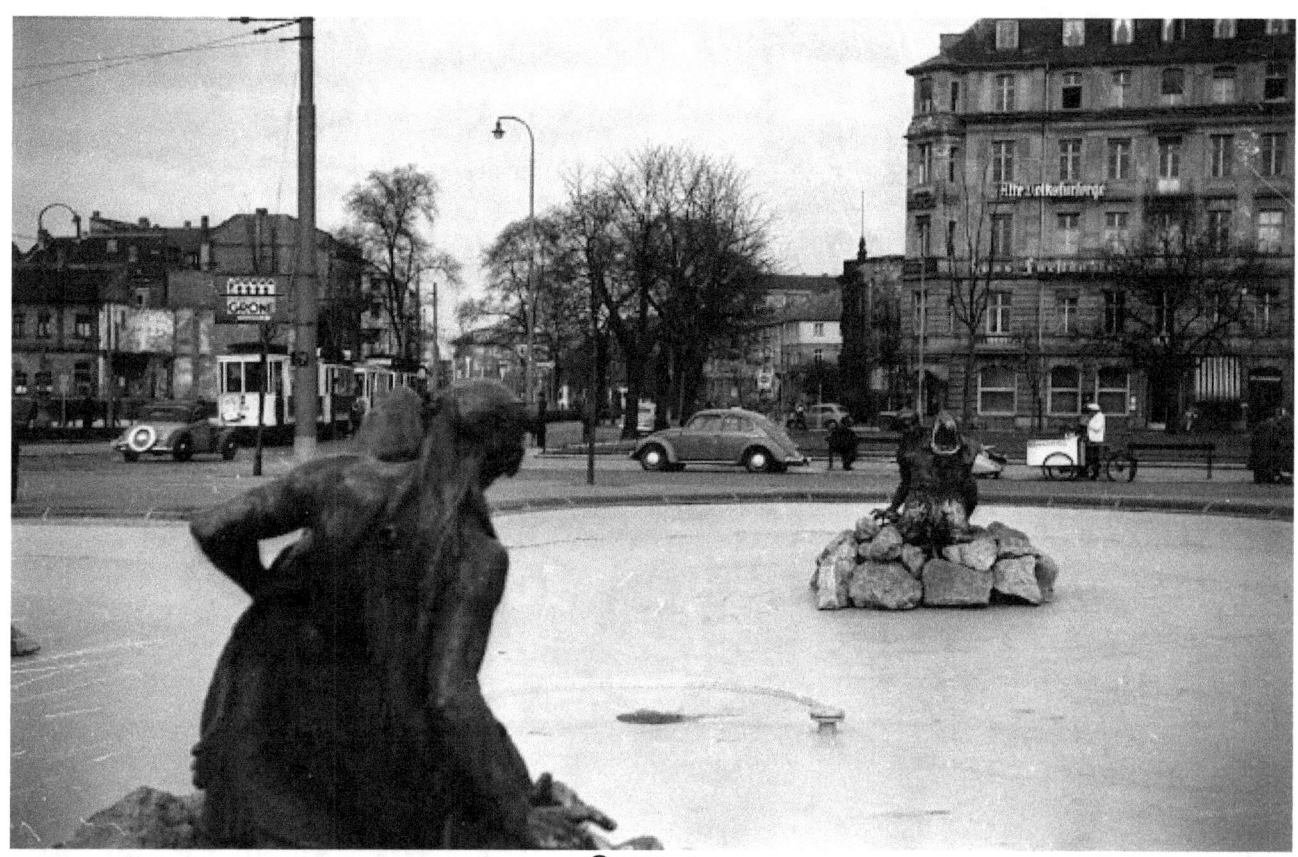
Germany

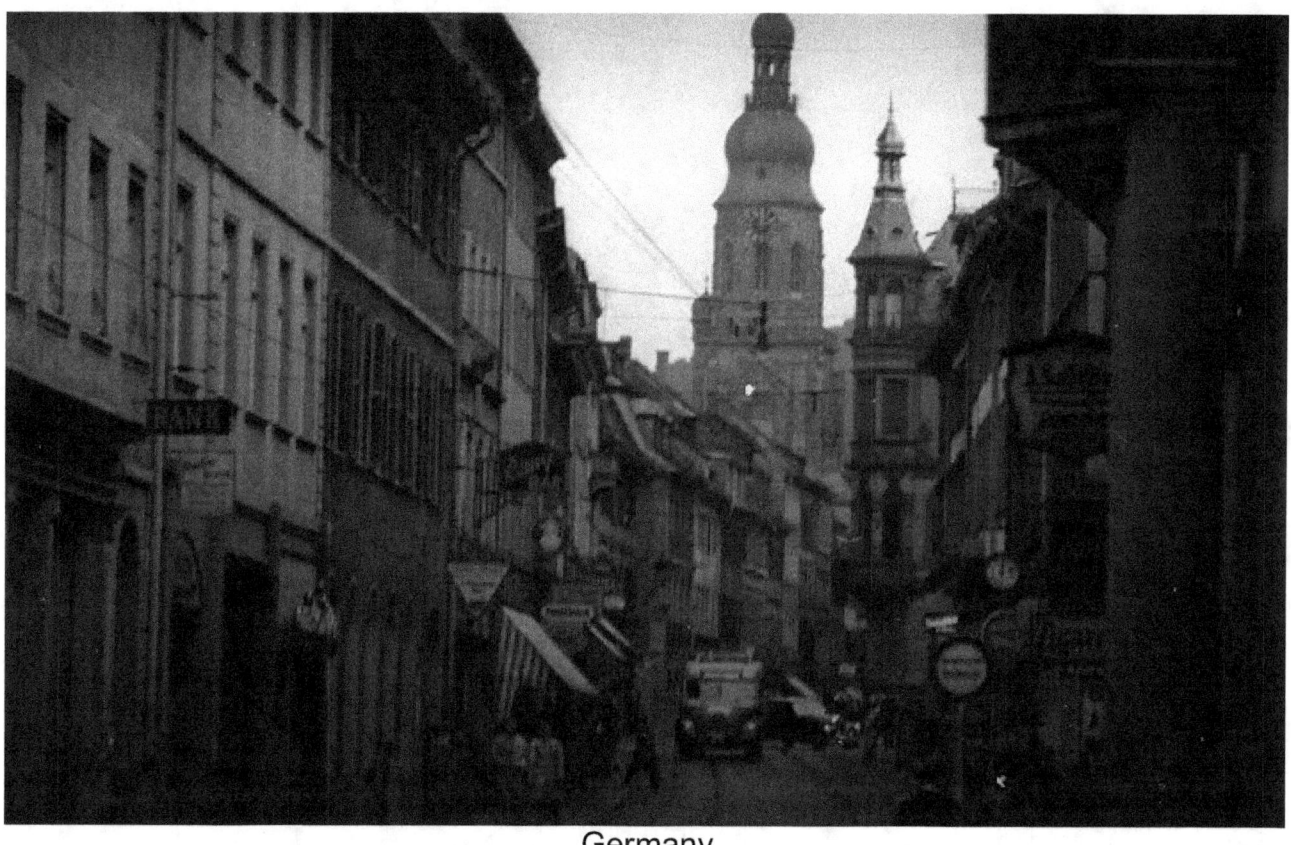
Germany

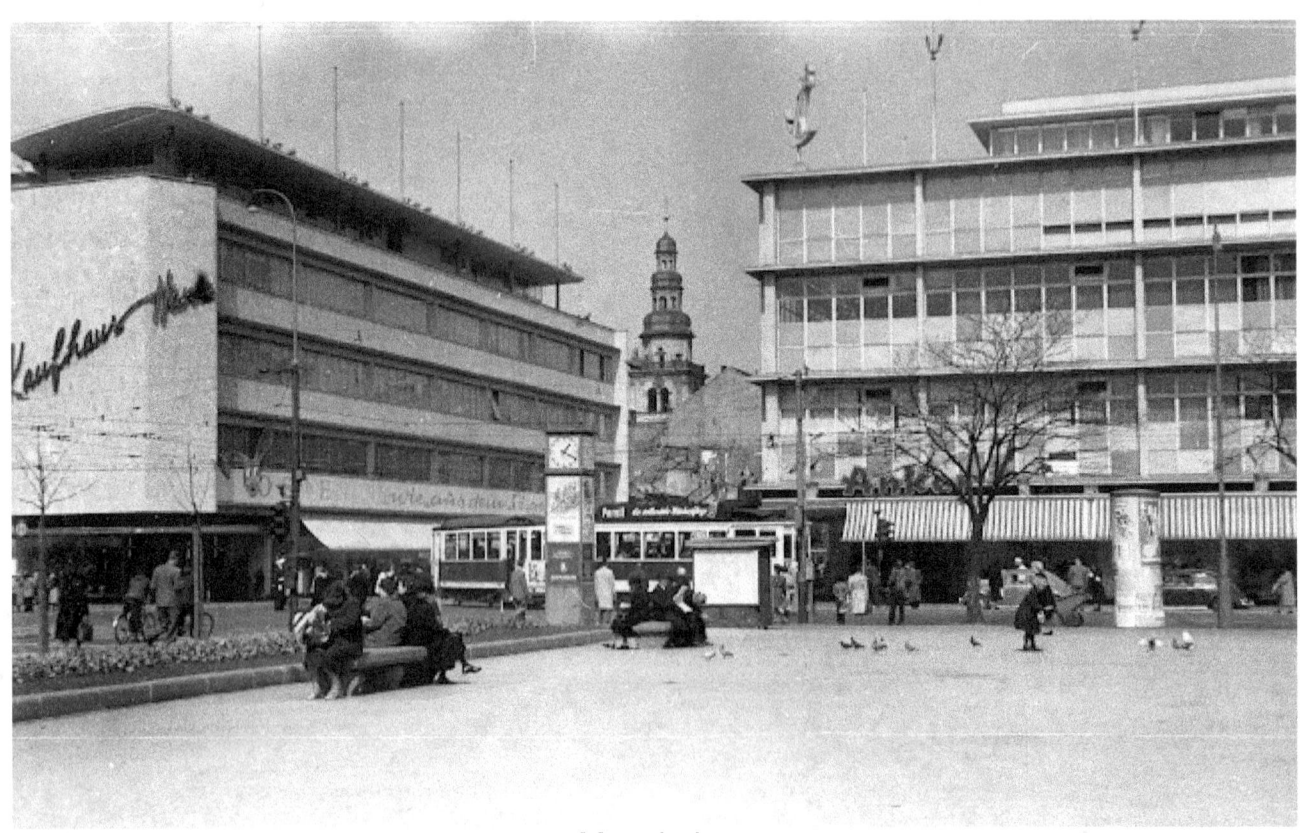

Mannheim

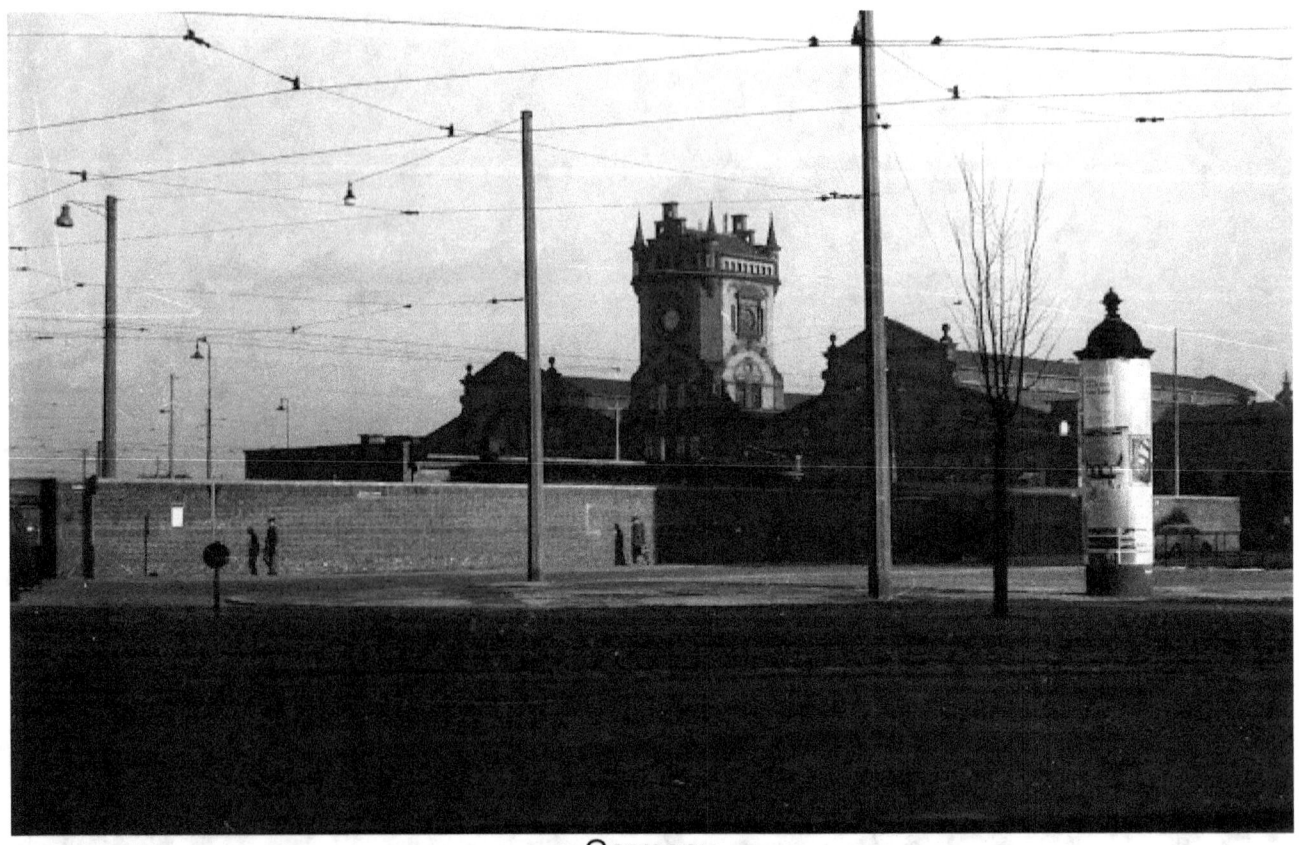

Germany

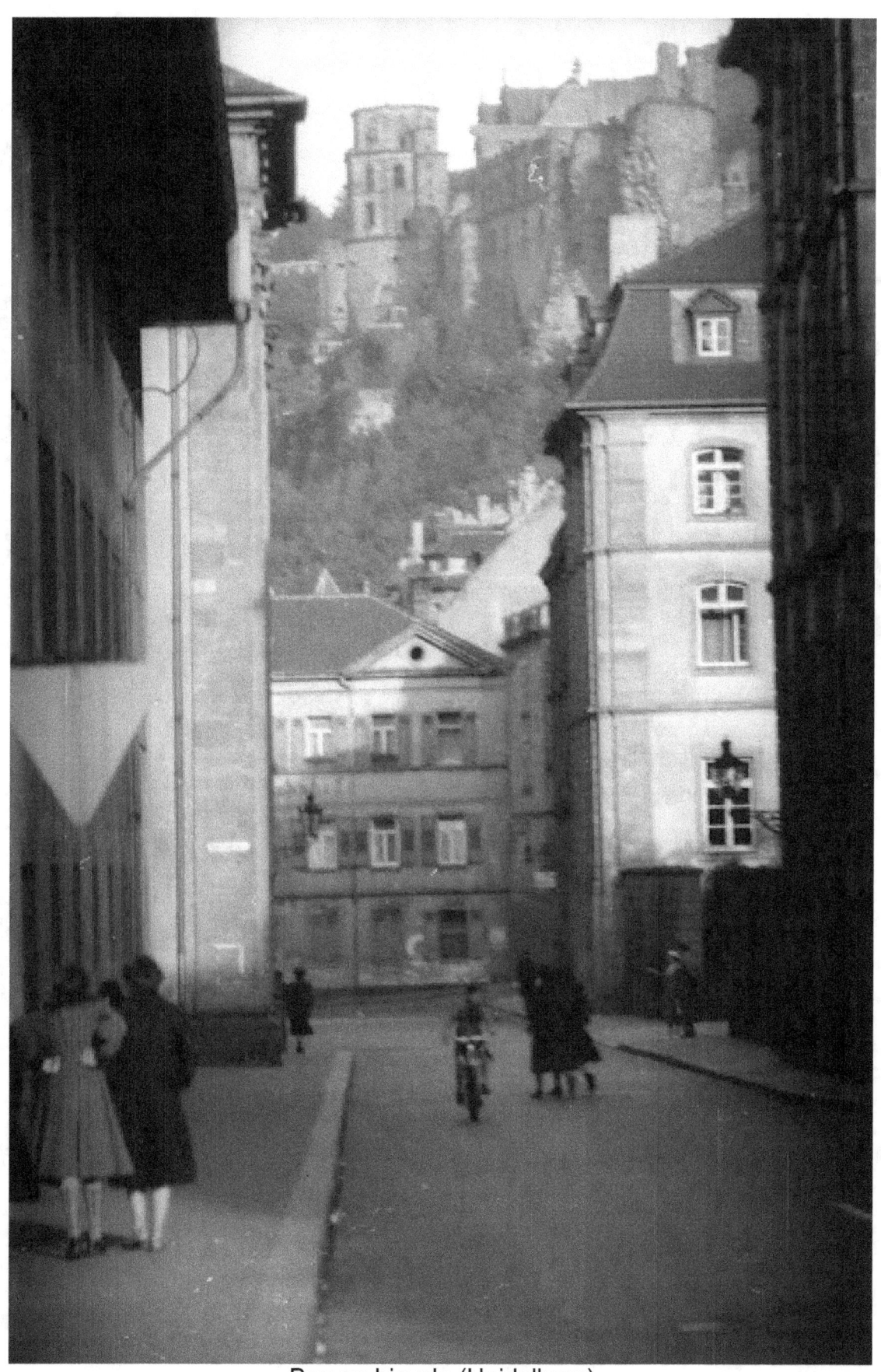
Boy on bicycle (Heidelberg)

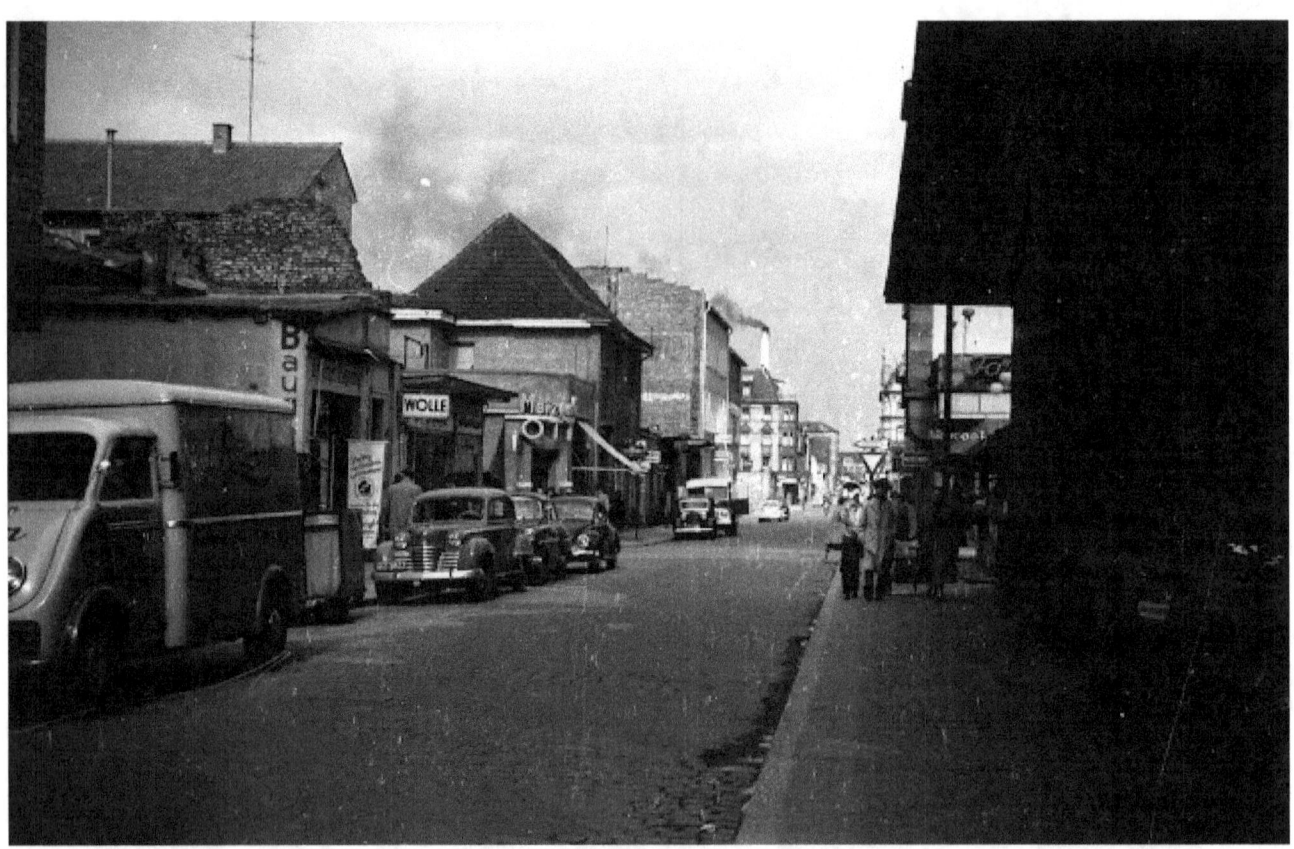
Germany

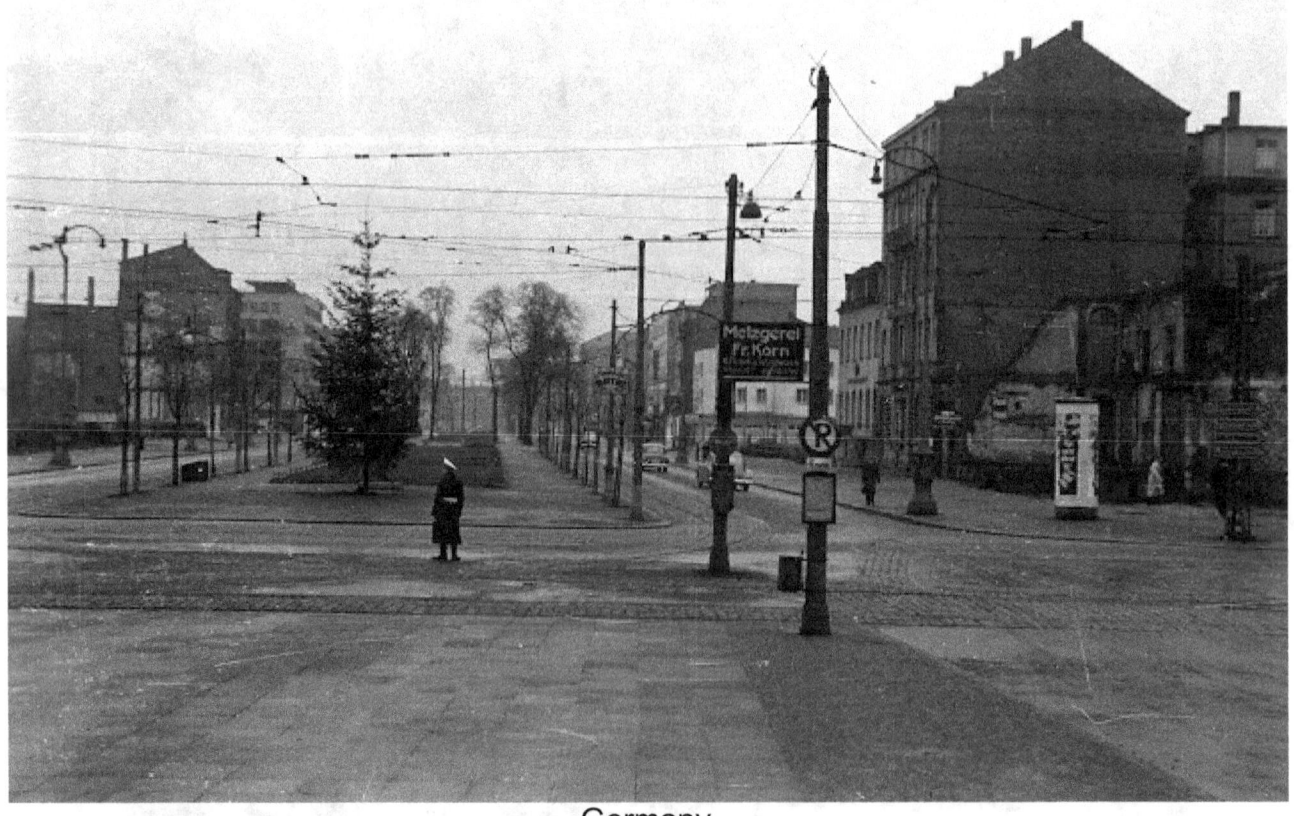
Germany

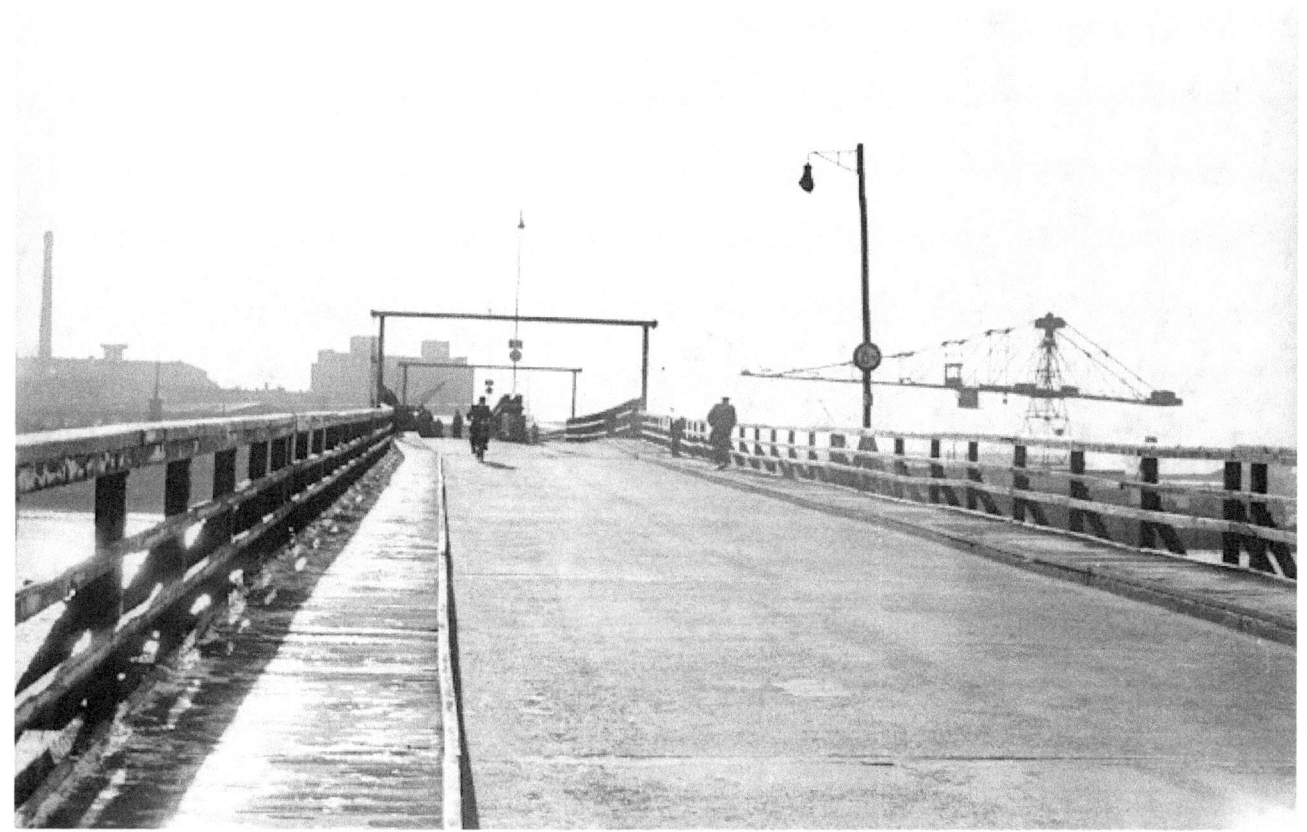
Germany

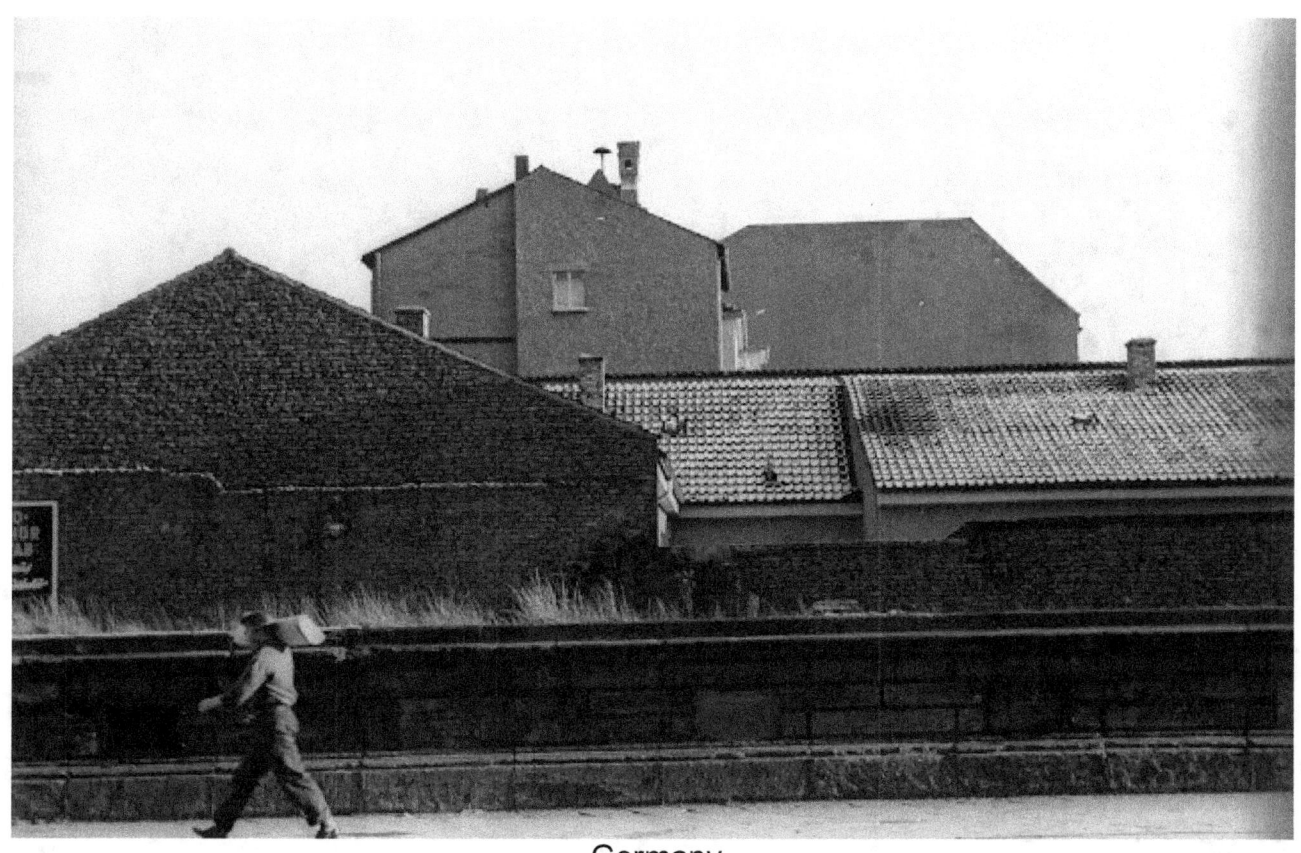
Germany

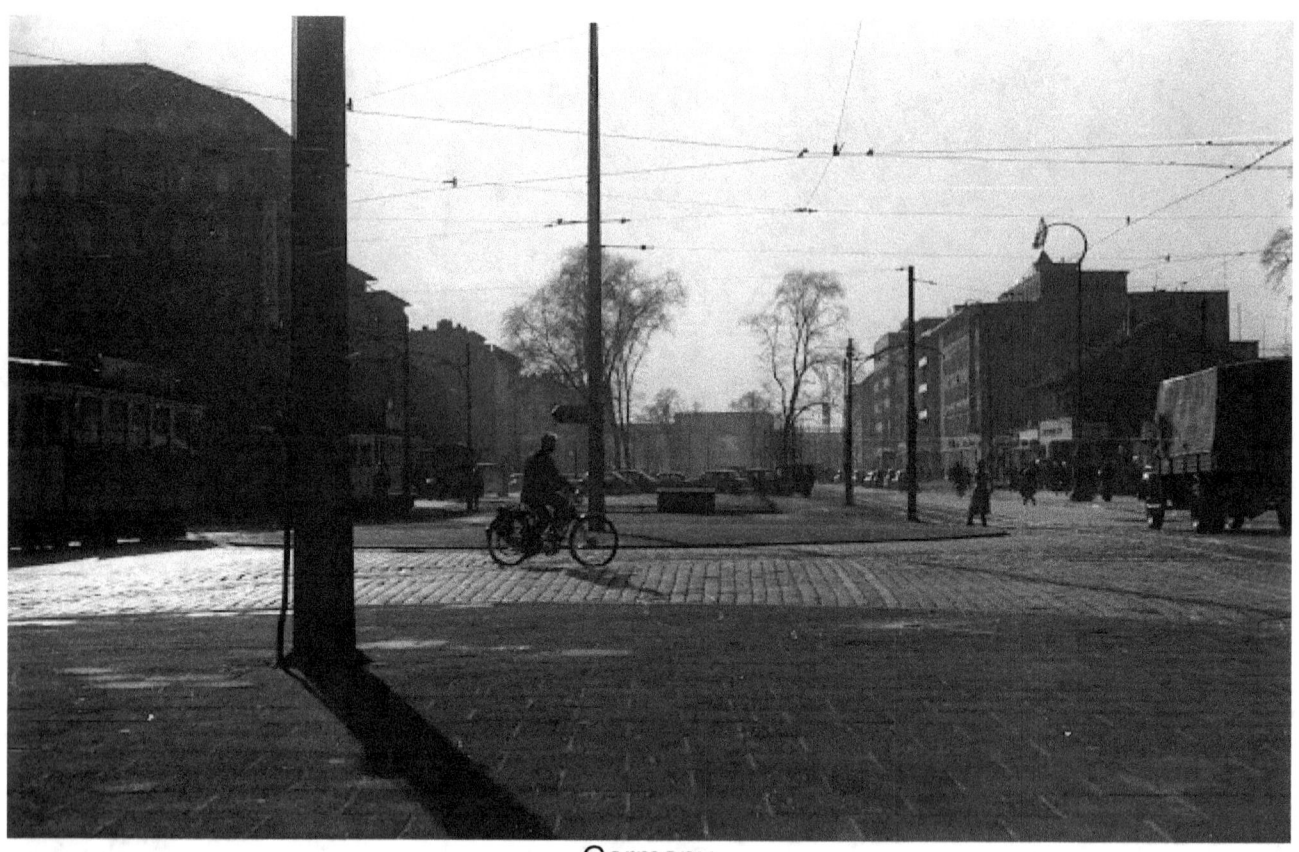
Germany

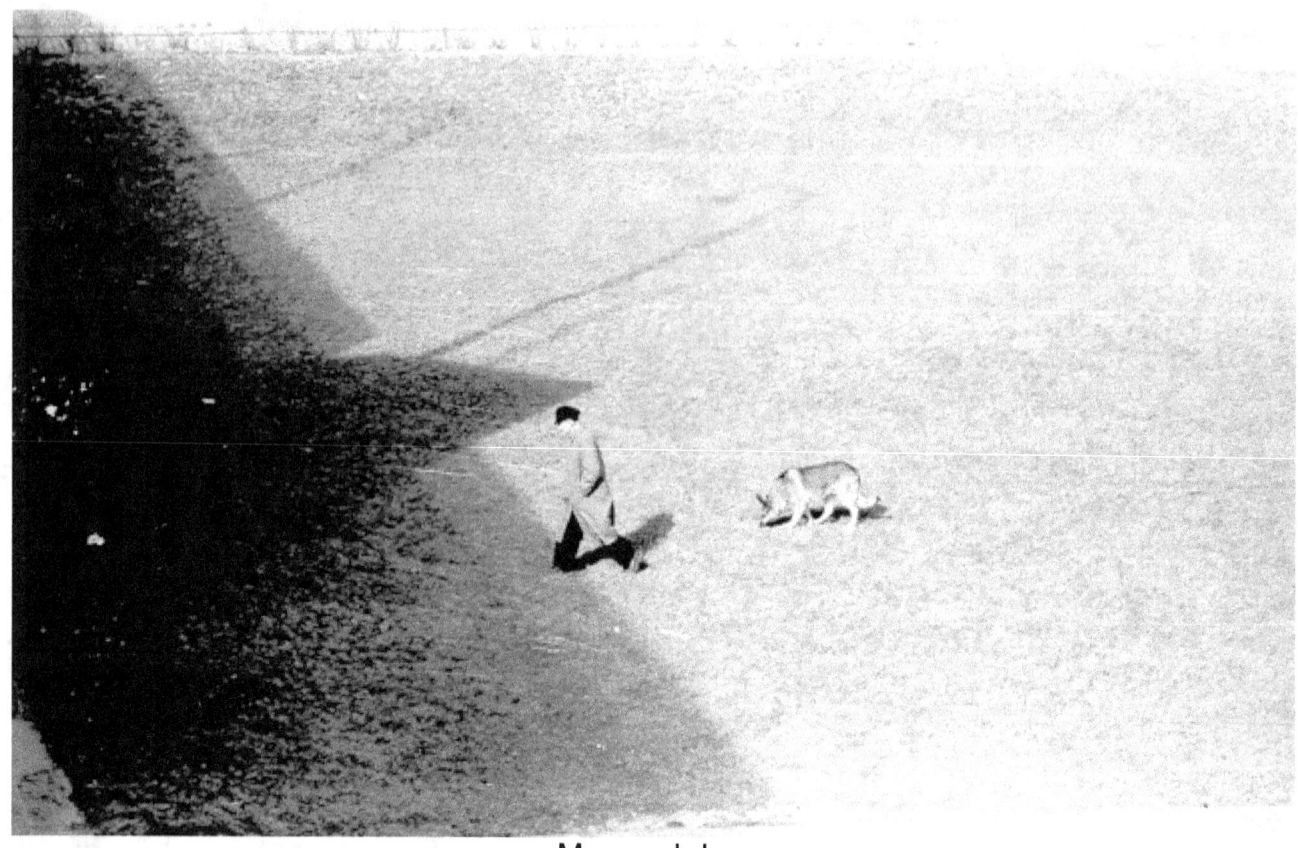
Man and dog

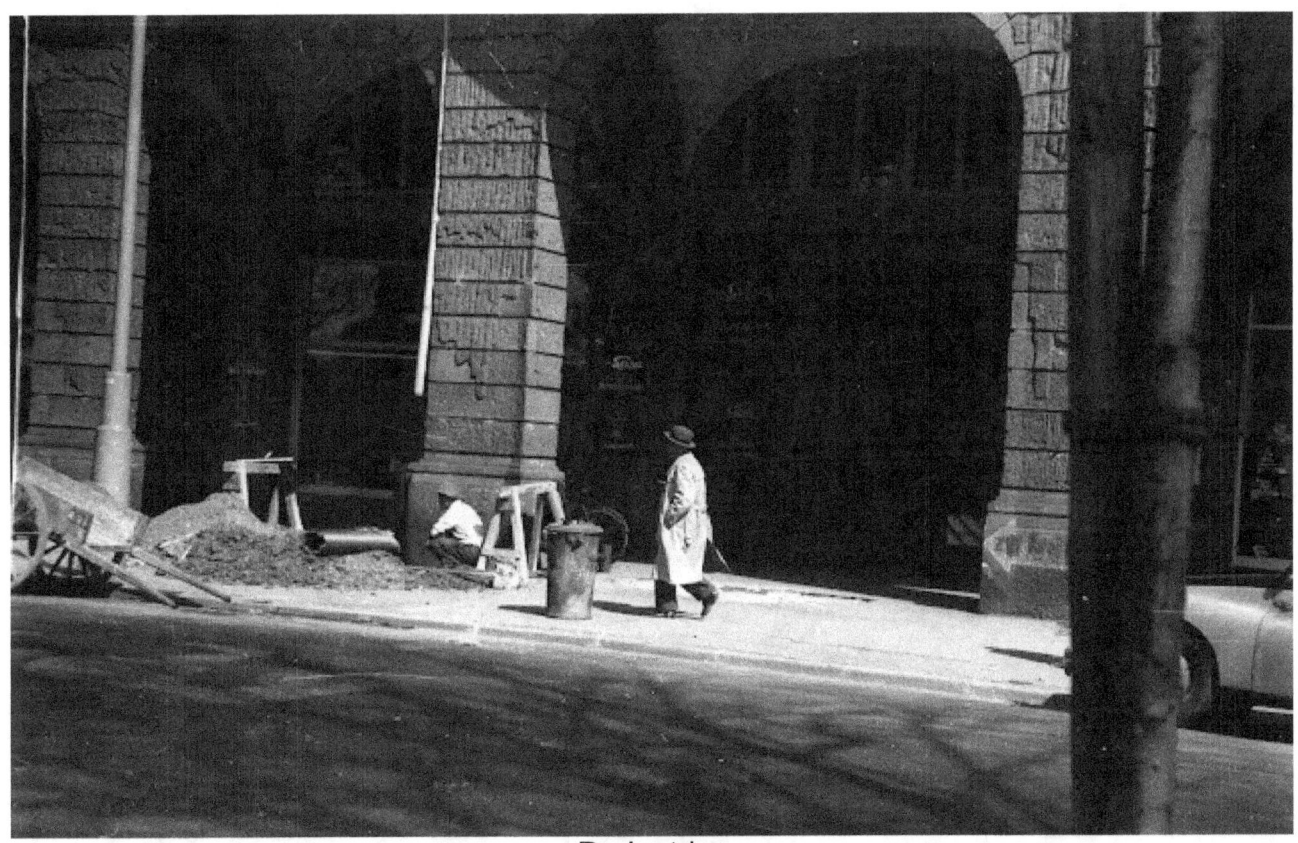
Pedestrian

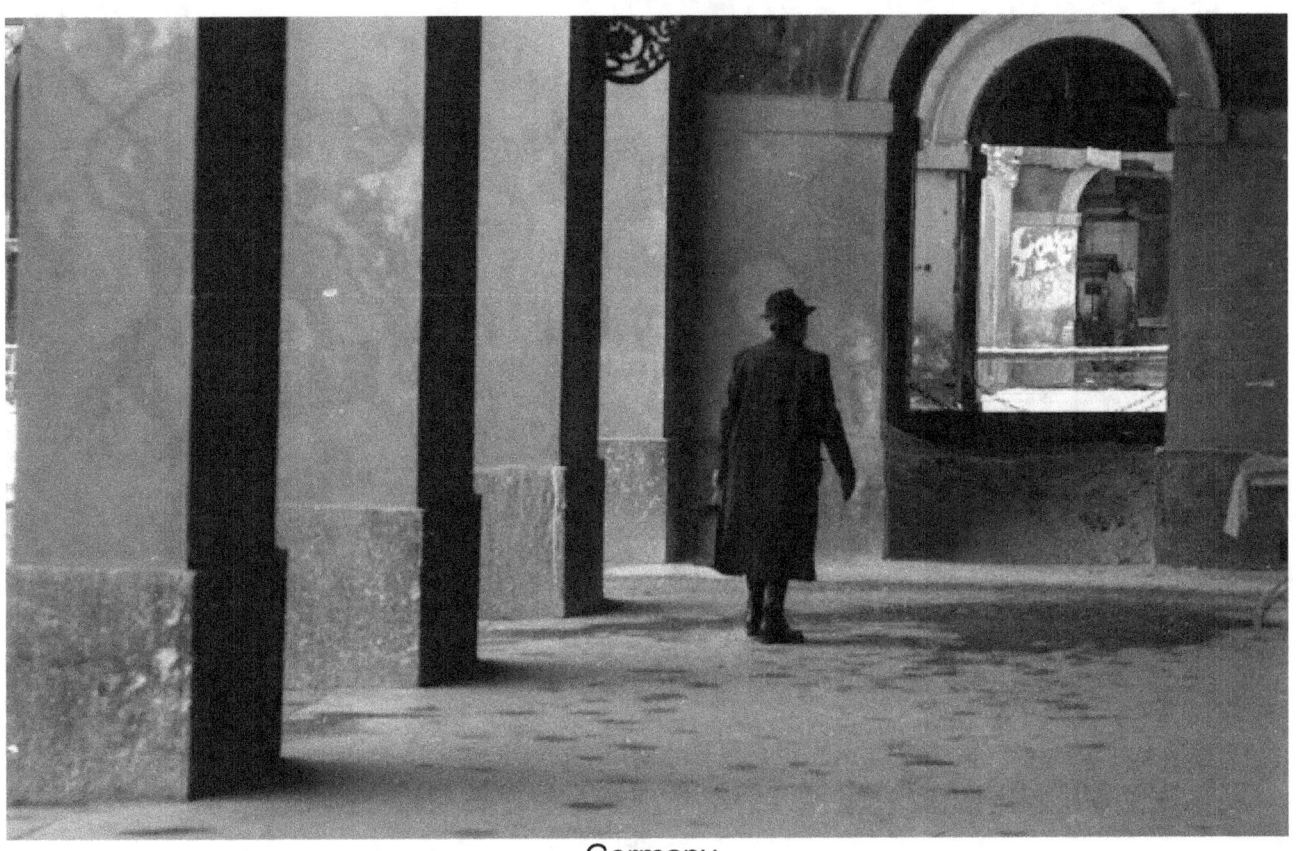
Germany

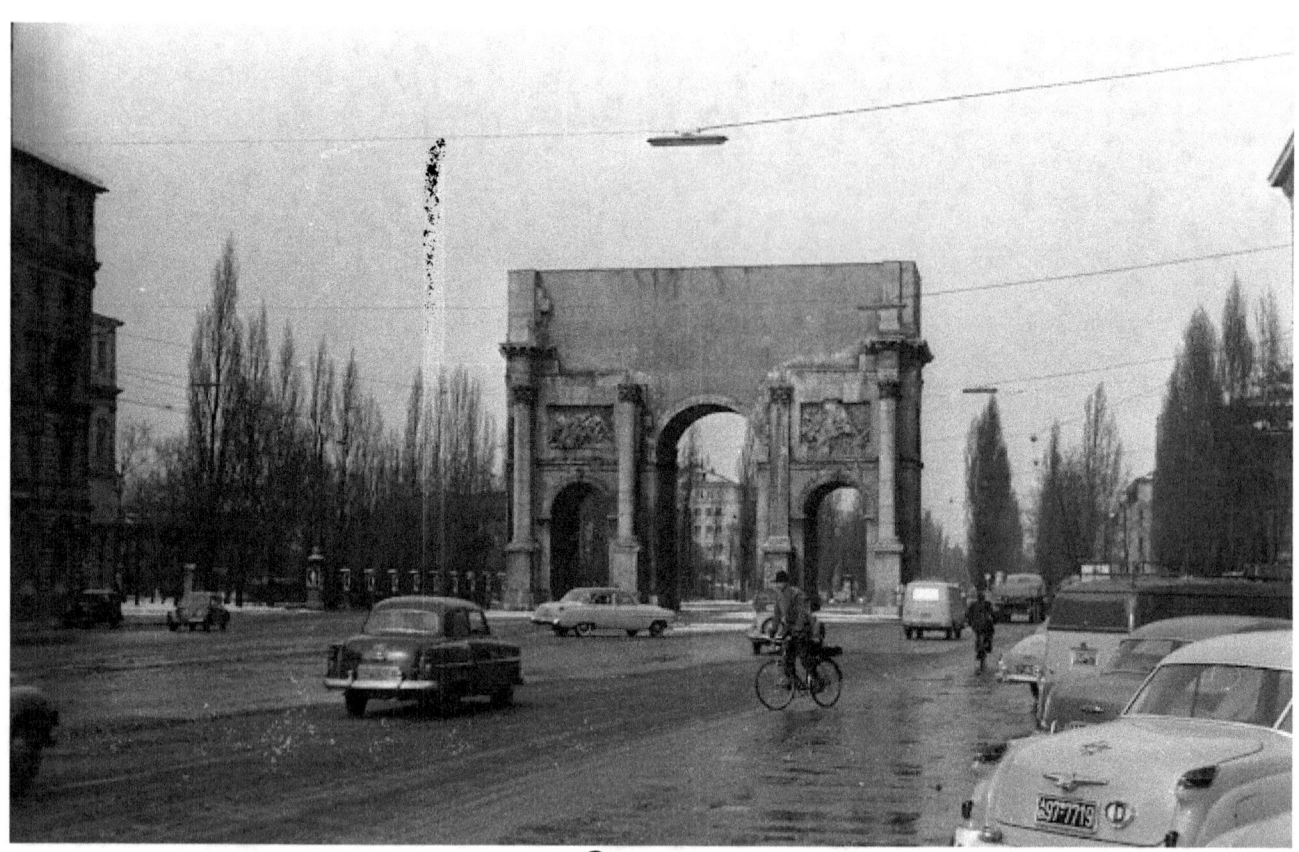
Germany

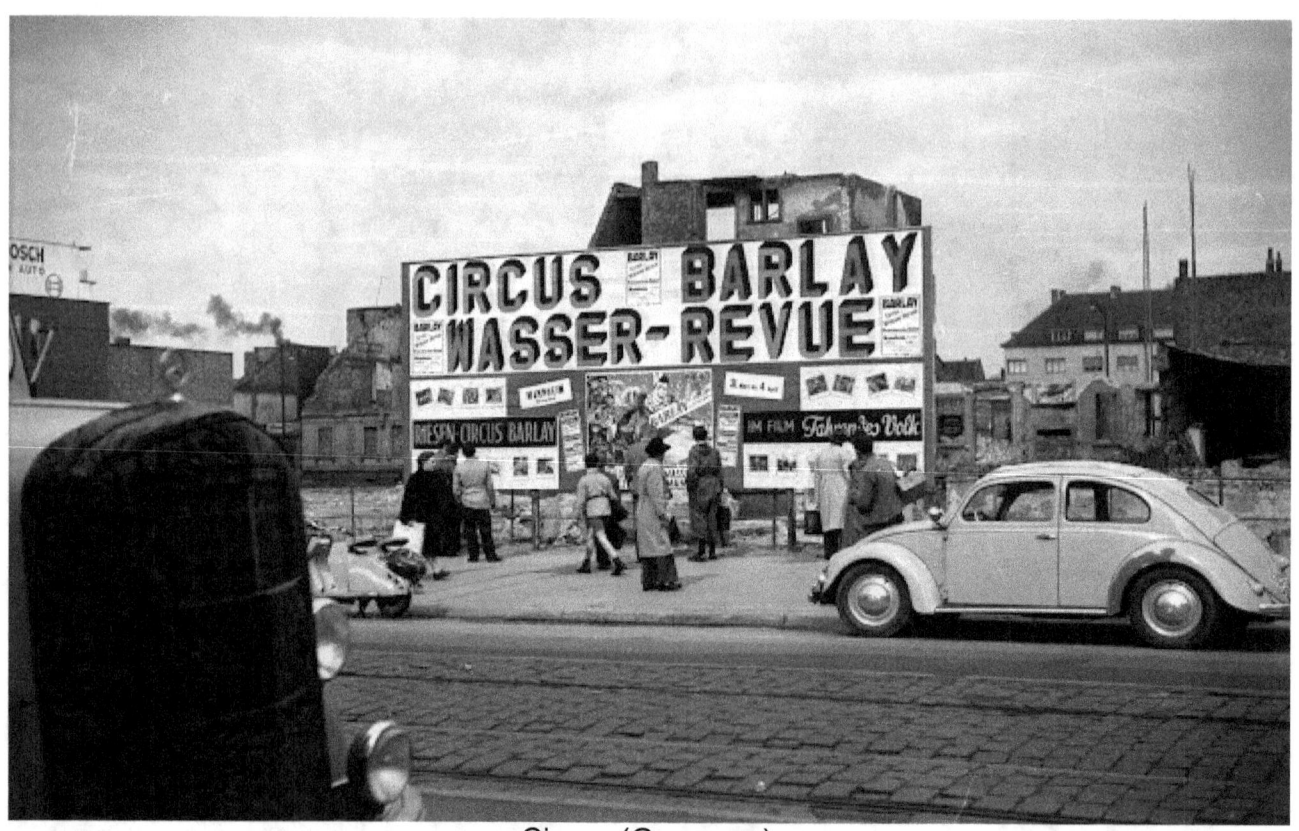
Circus (Germany)

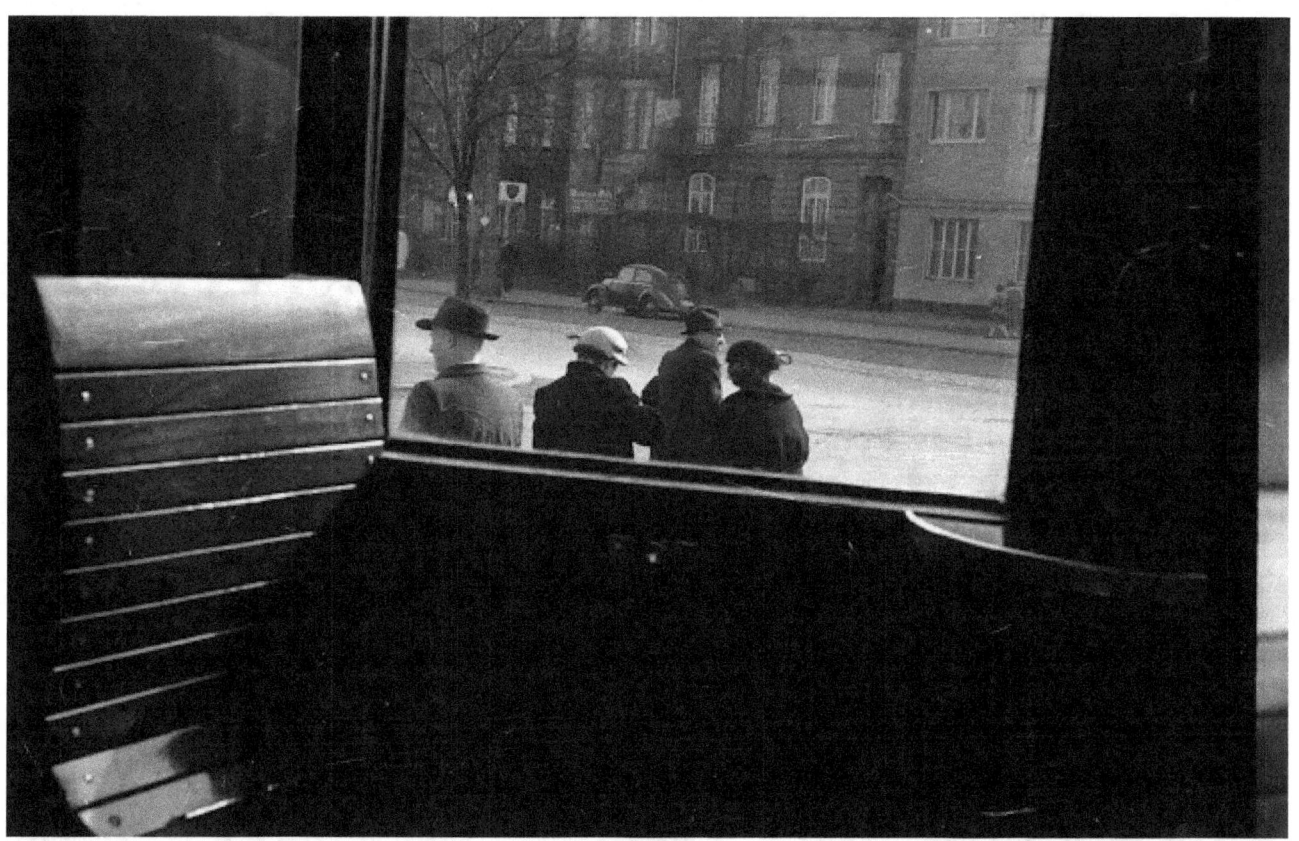
Germany

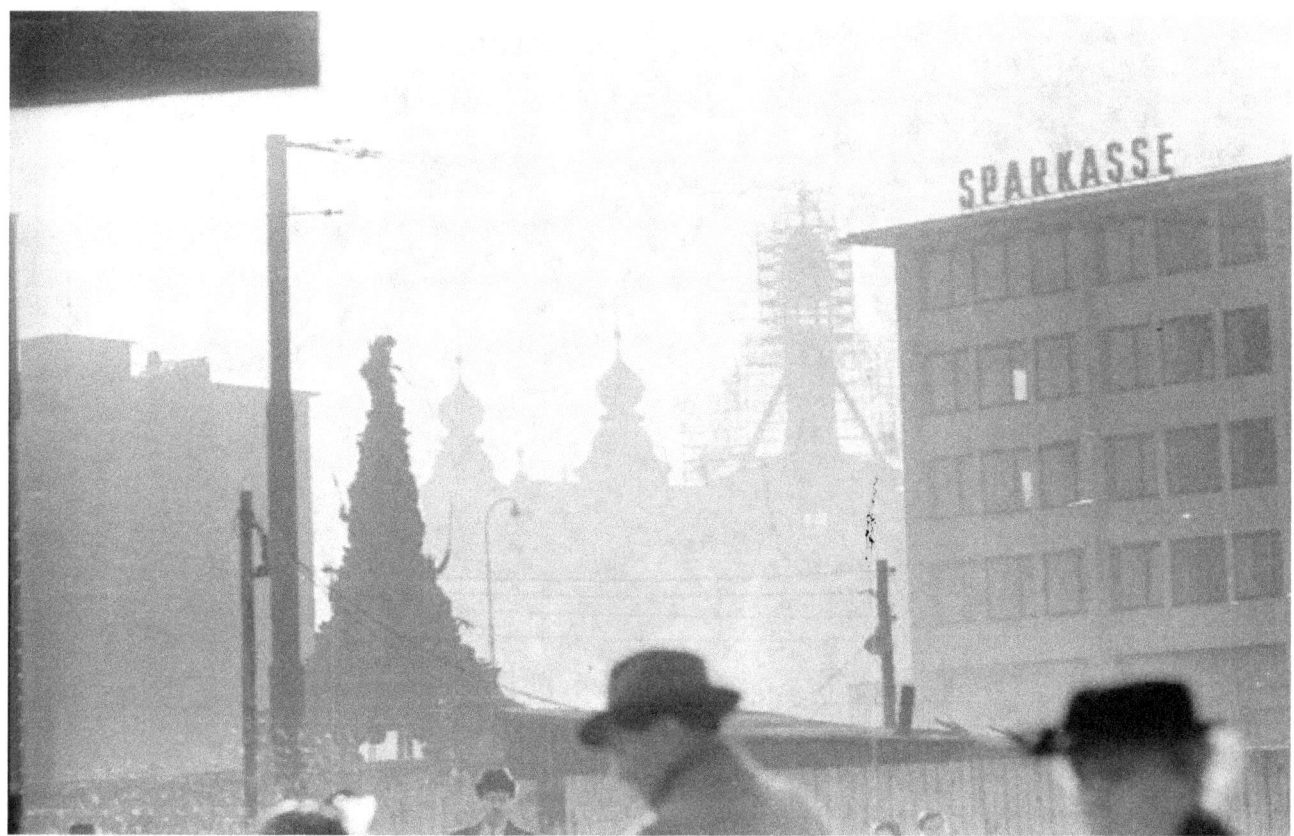
Mannheim

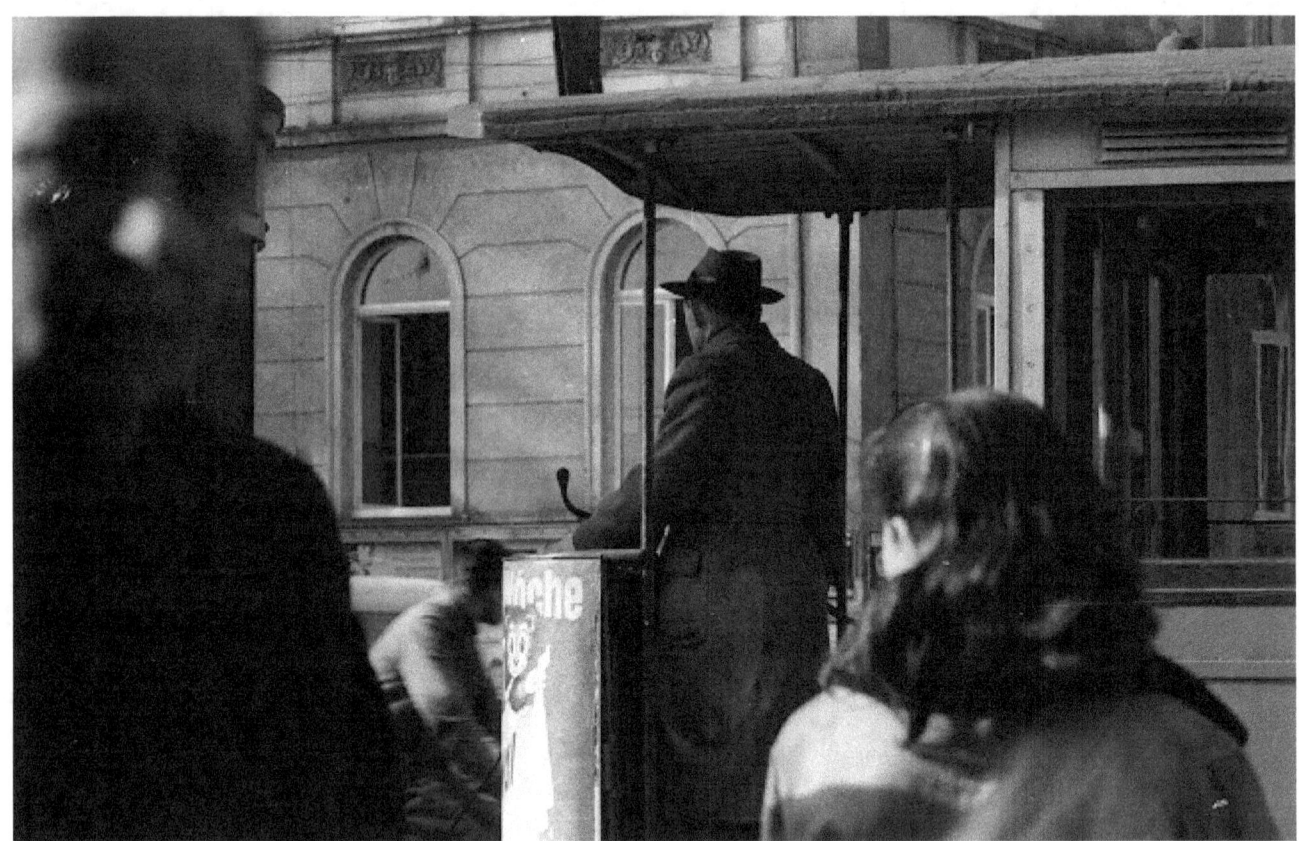
Germany

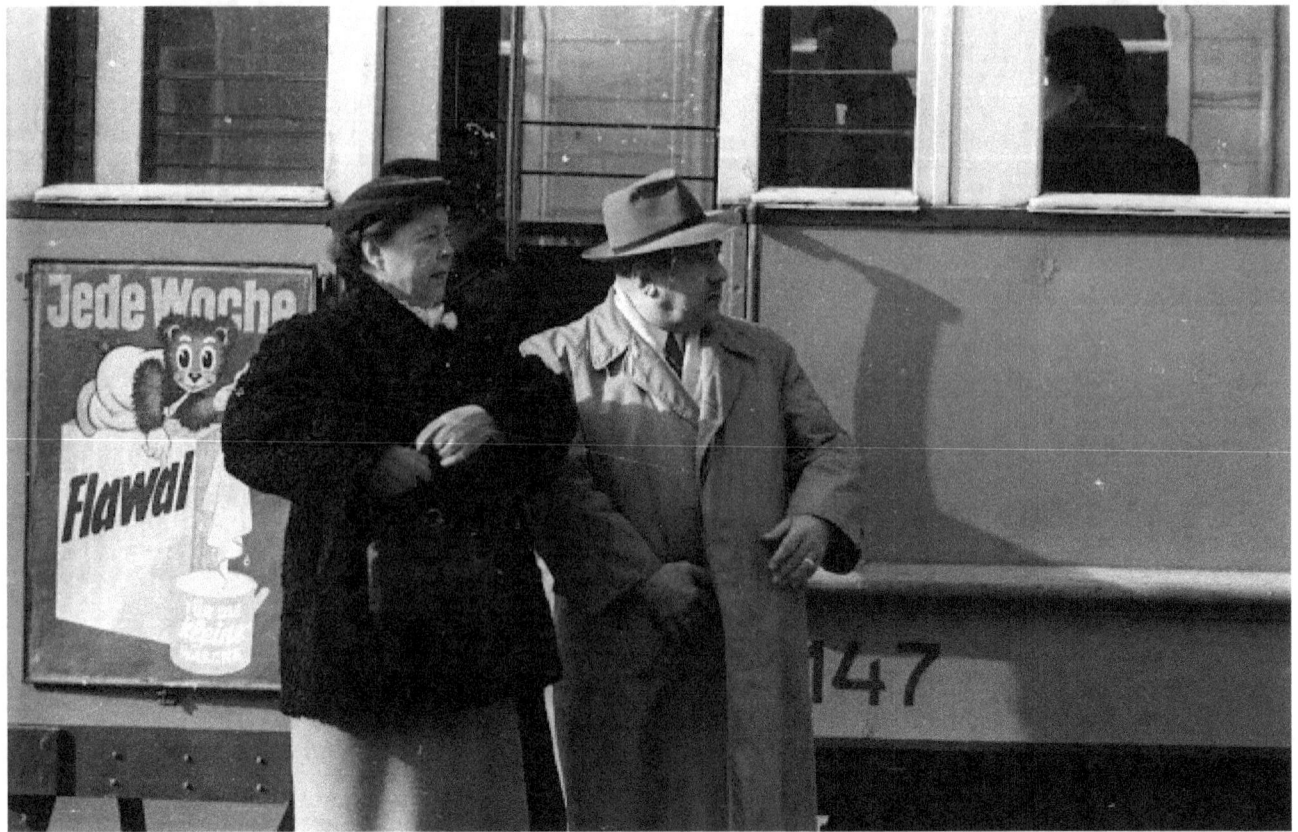
Older couple (Germany)

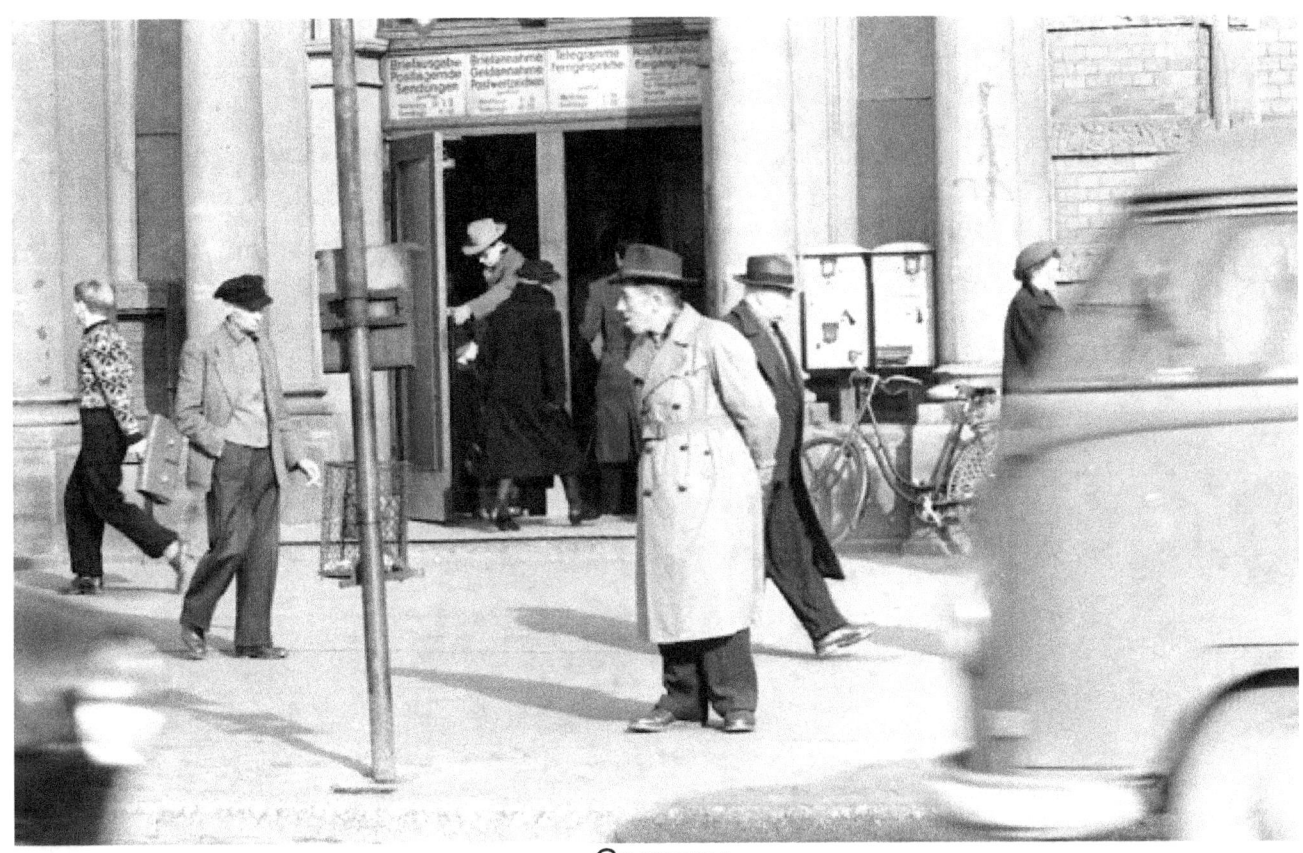
Germany

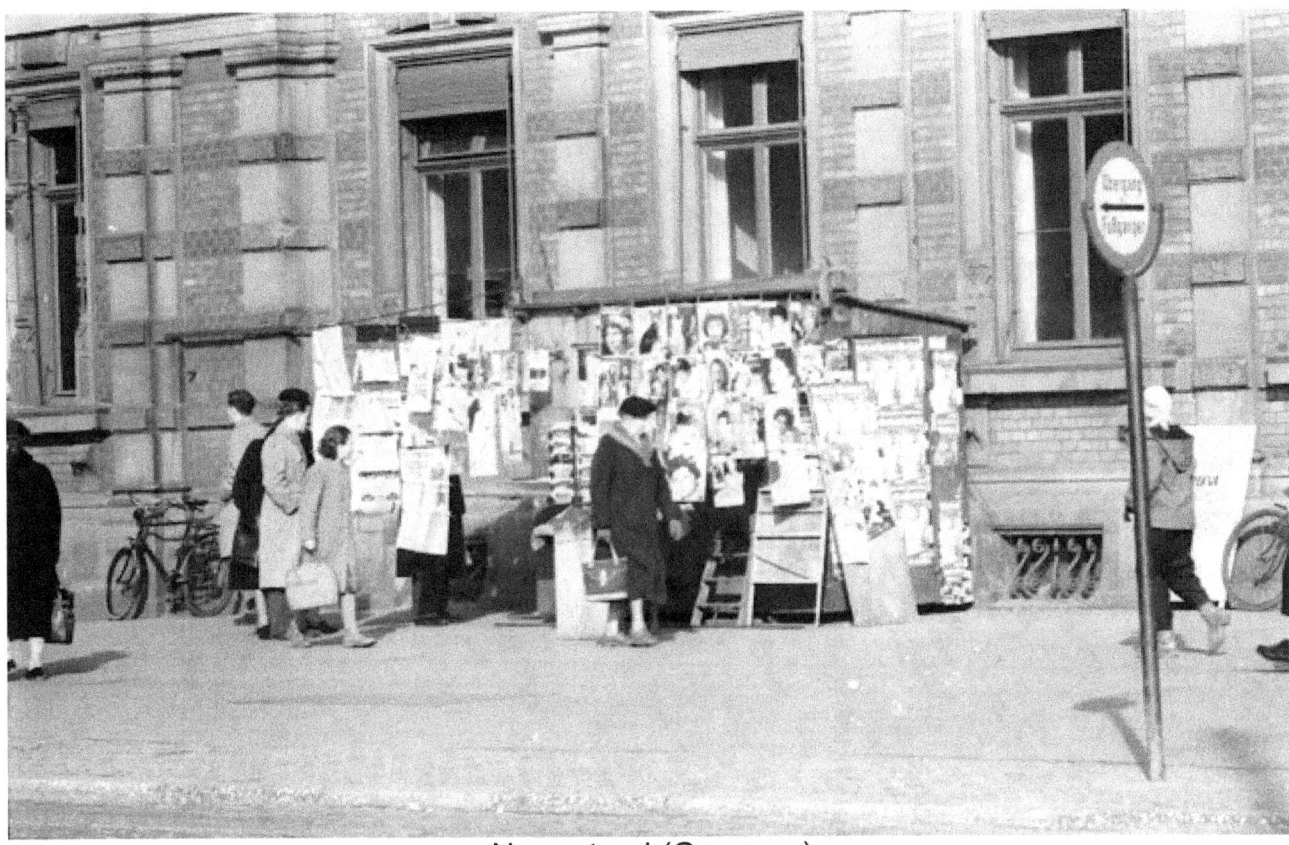
Newsstand (Germany)

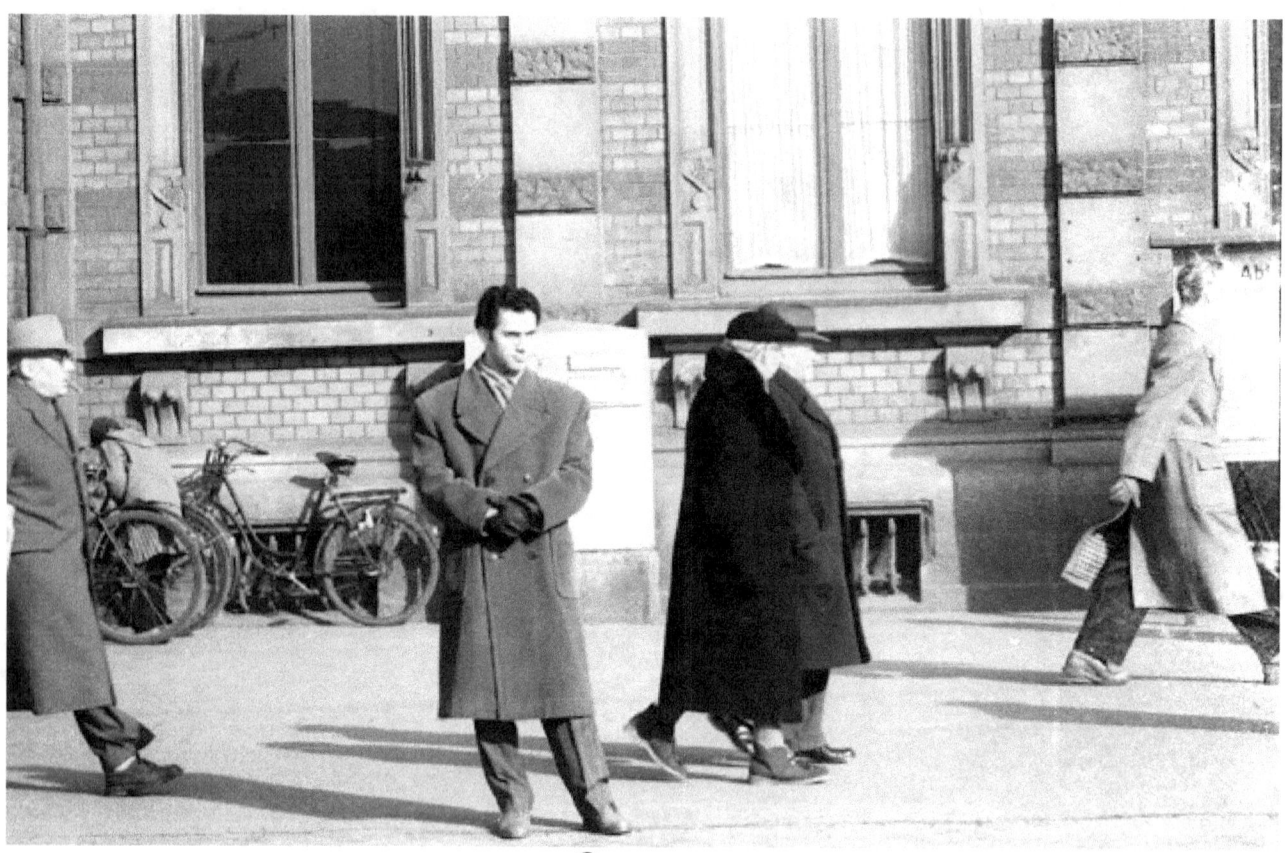
Germany

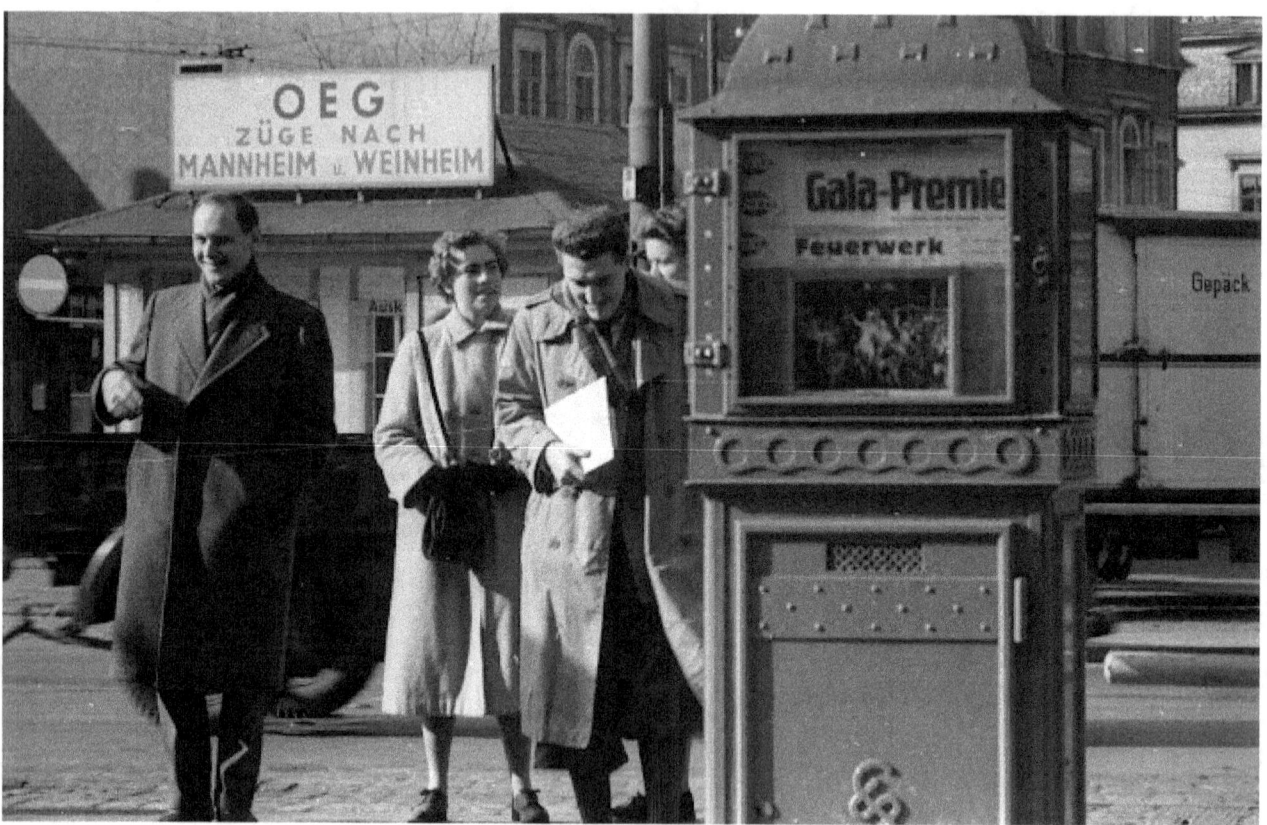
Tram stop, possibly Heidelberg

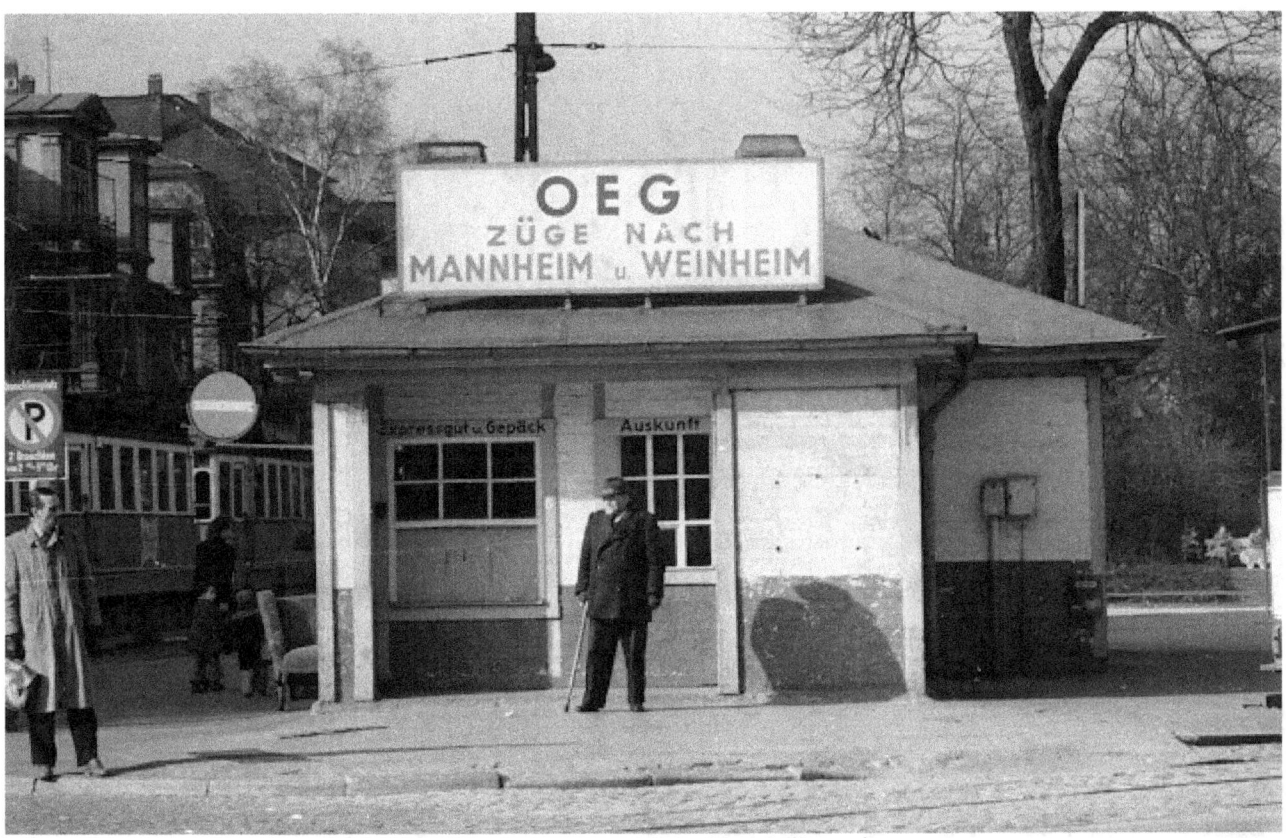
Tram stop (possibly Heidelberg)

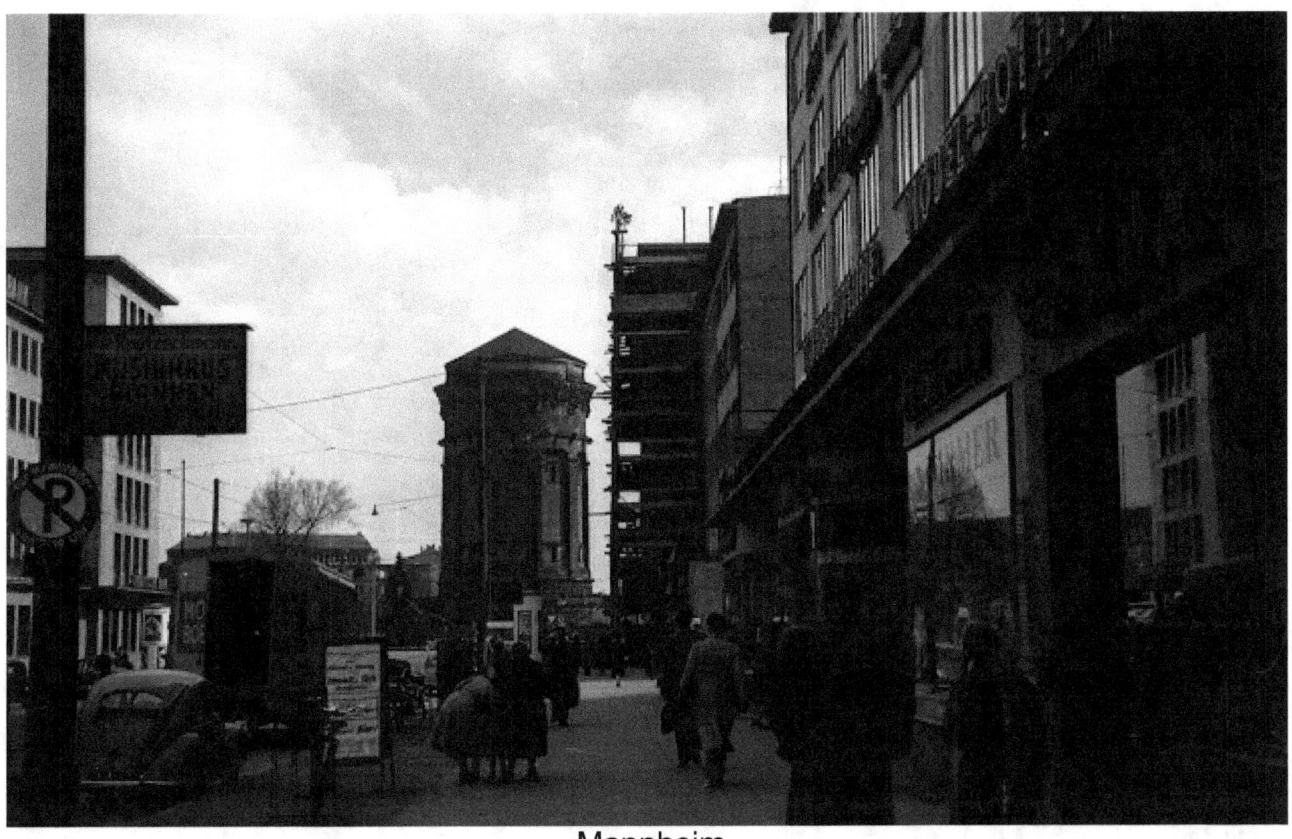
Mannheim

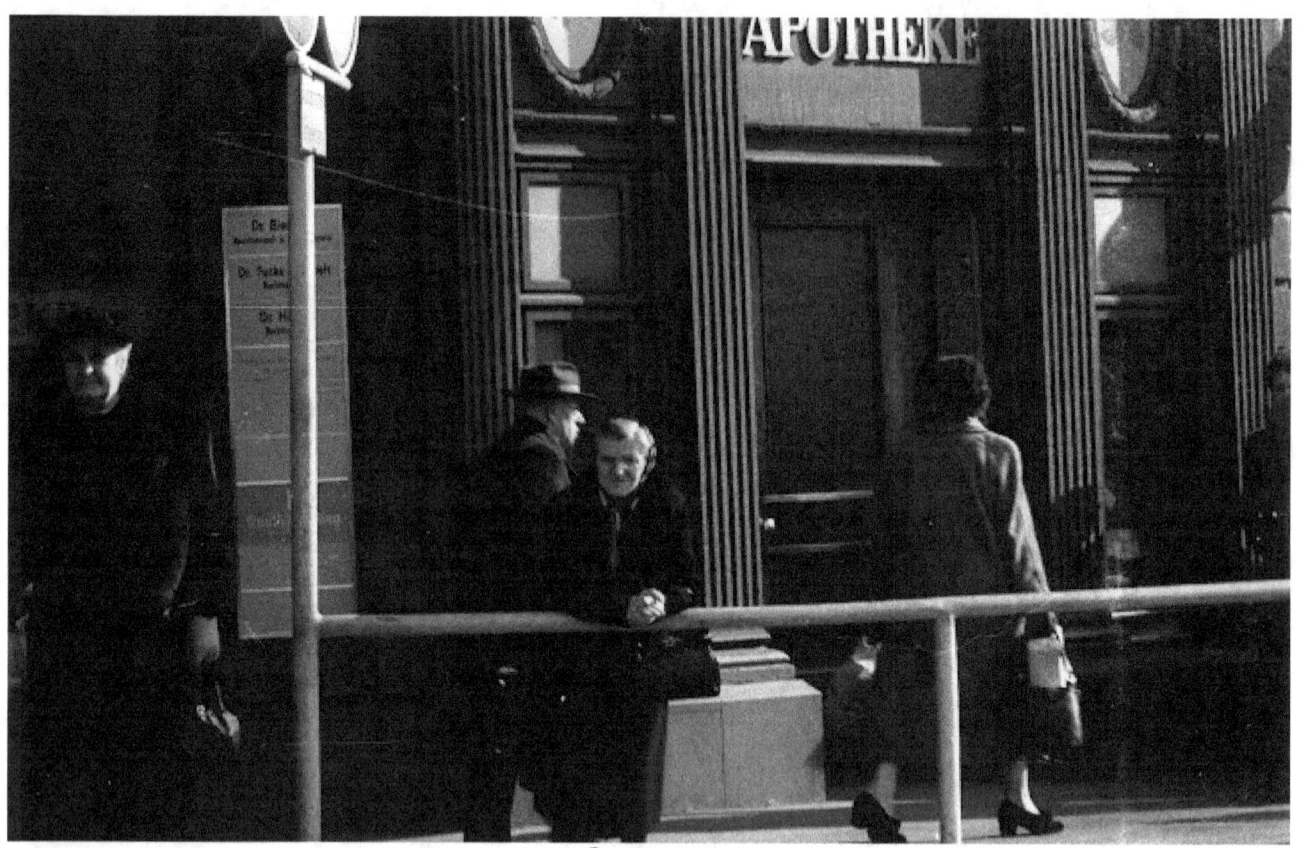
Germany

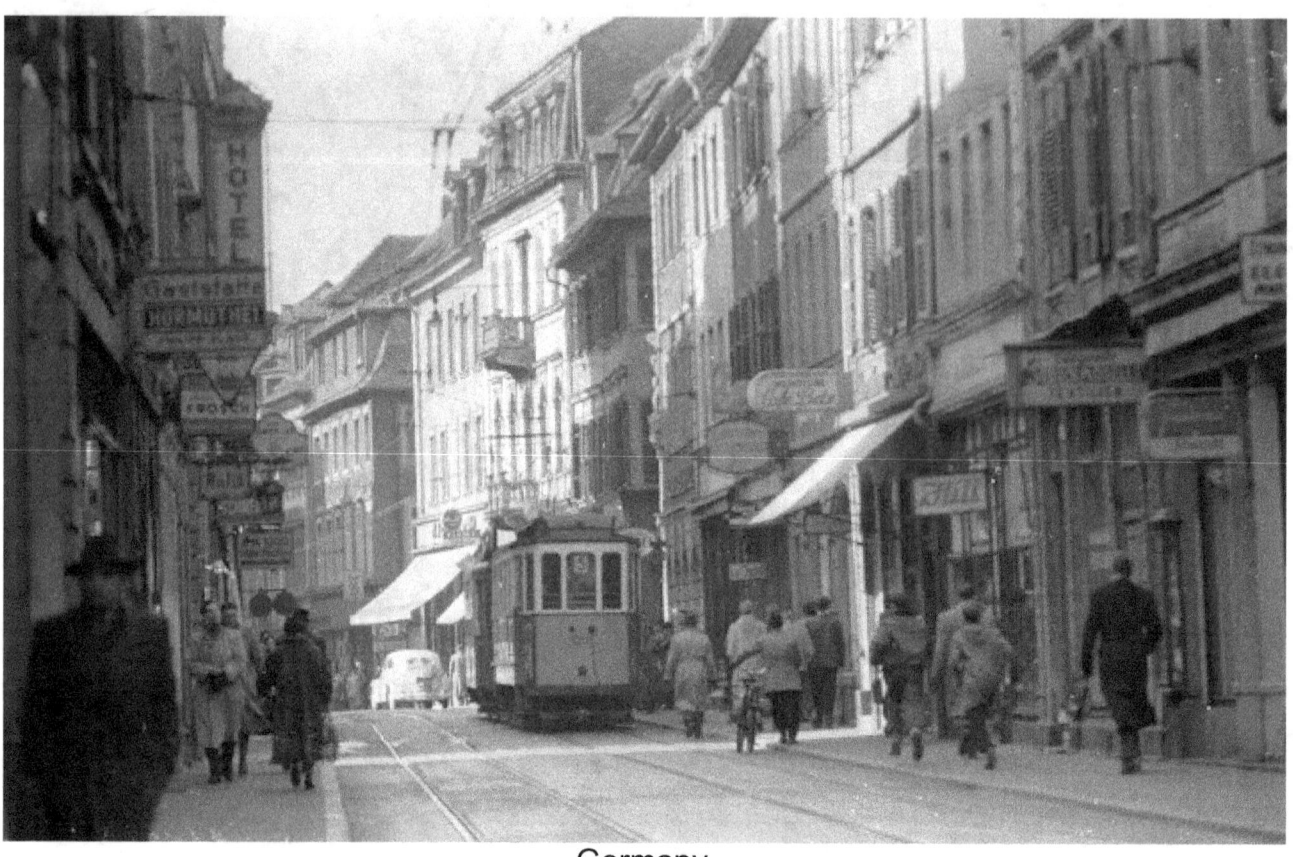
Germany

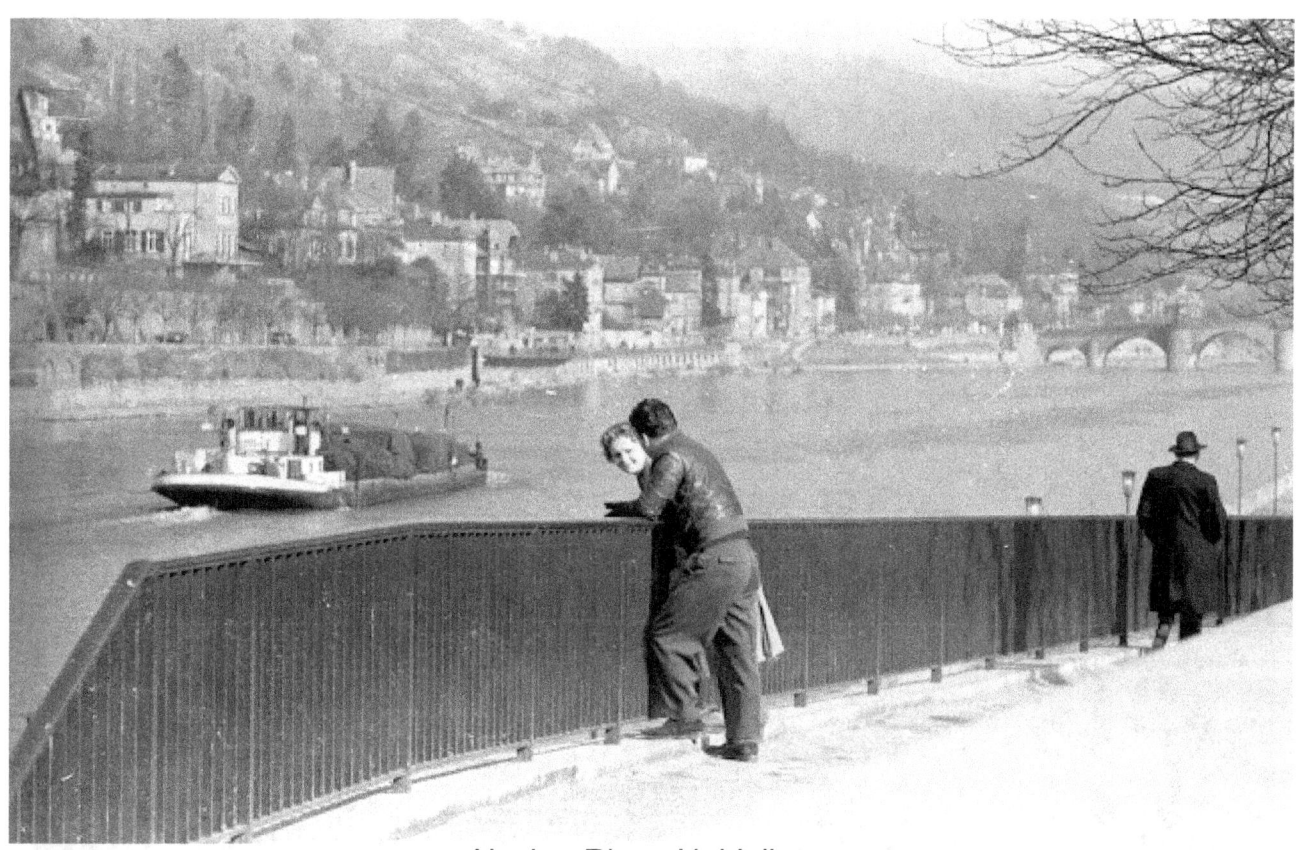
Neckar River, Heidelberg

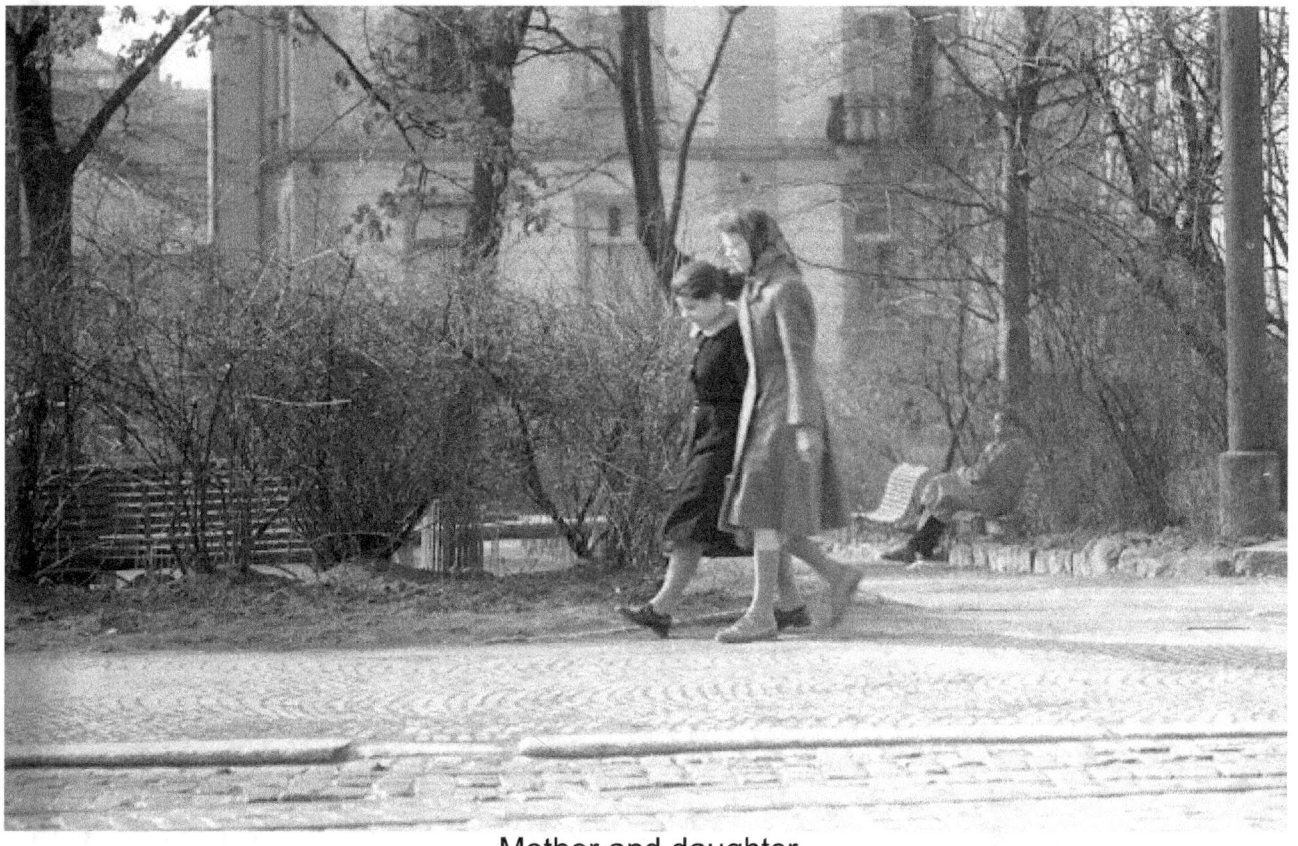
Mother and daughter

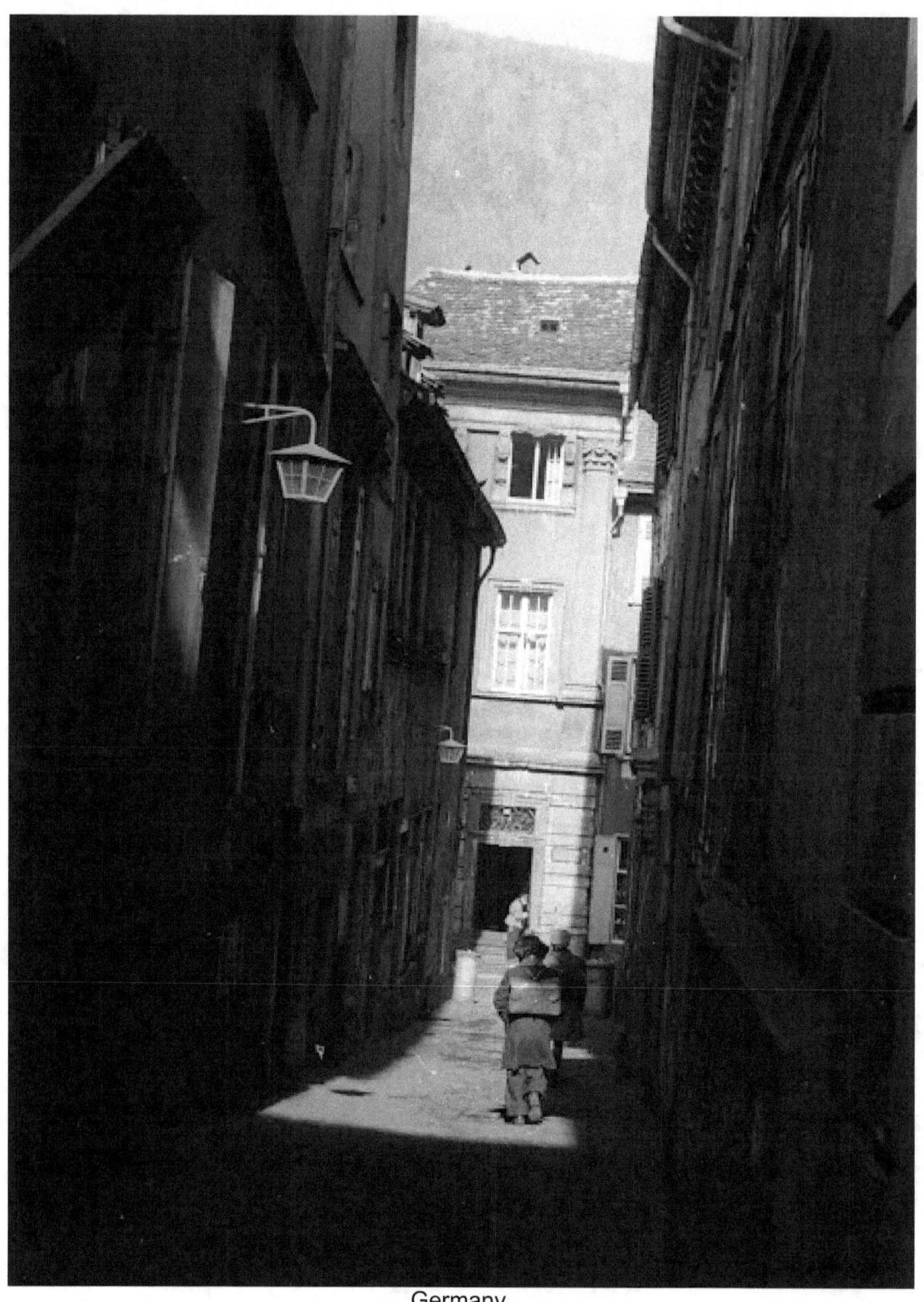
Germany

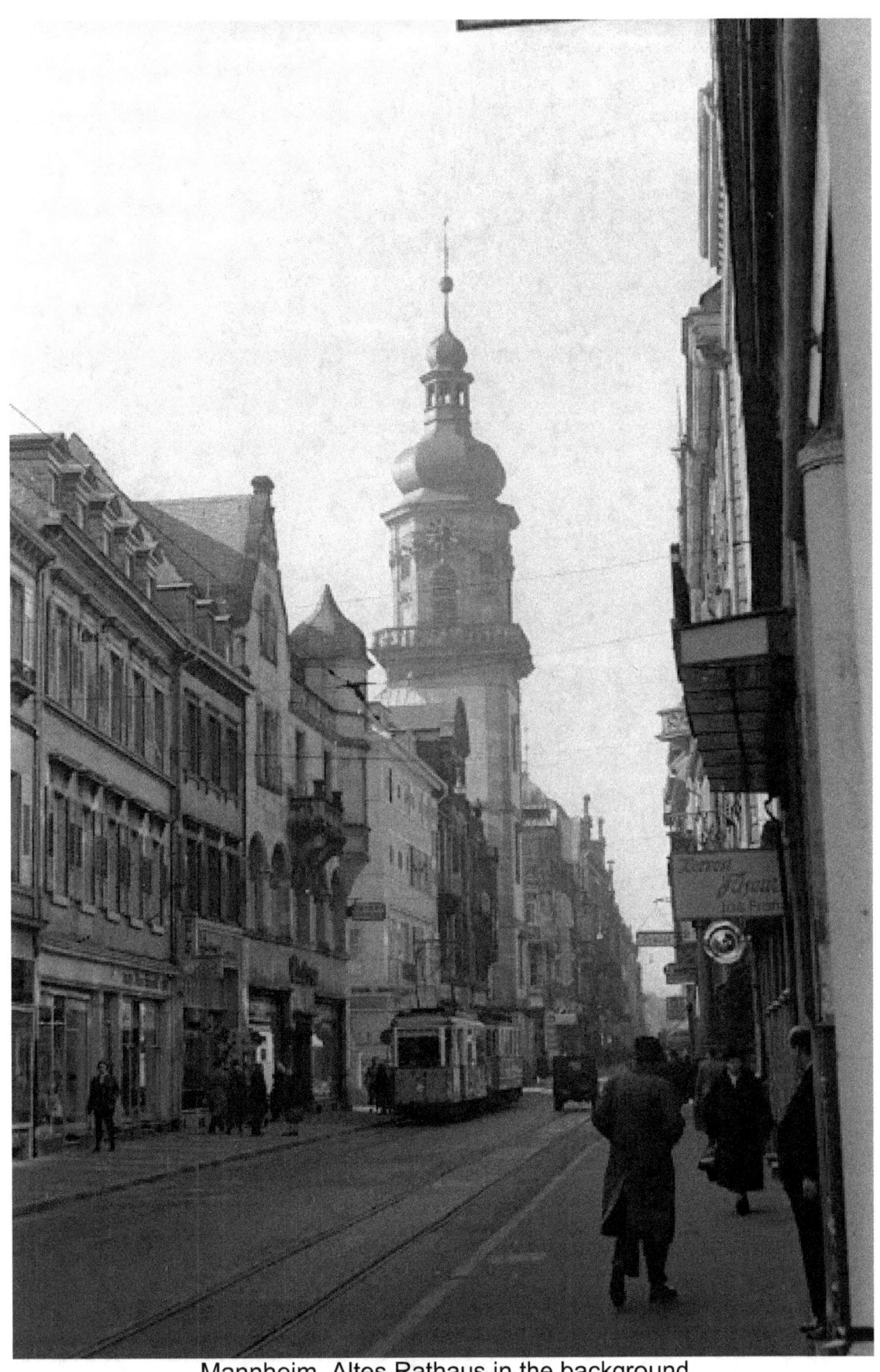

Mannheim, Altes Rathaus in the background

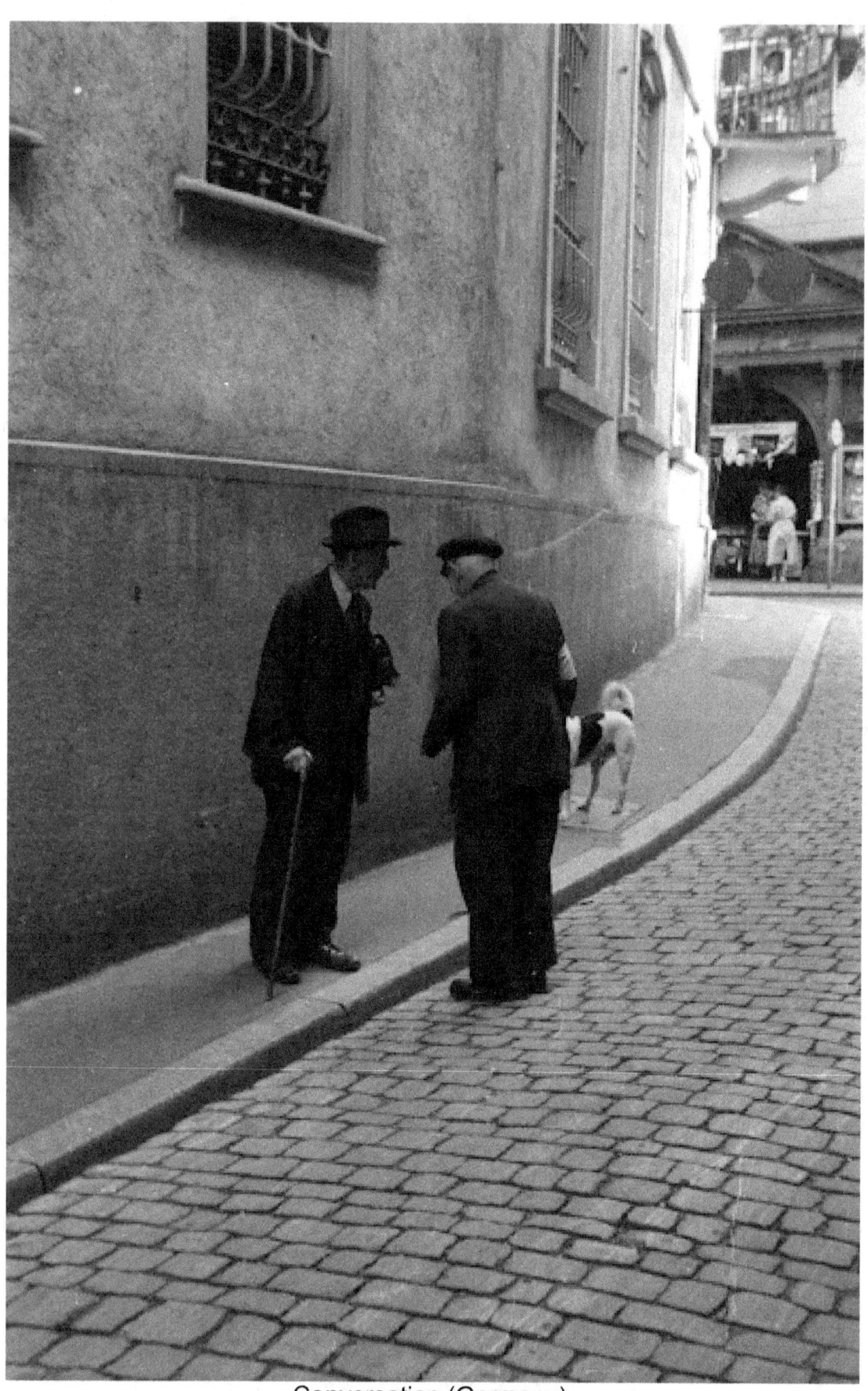
Conversation (Germany)

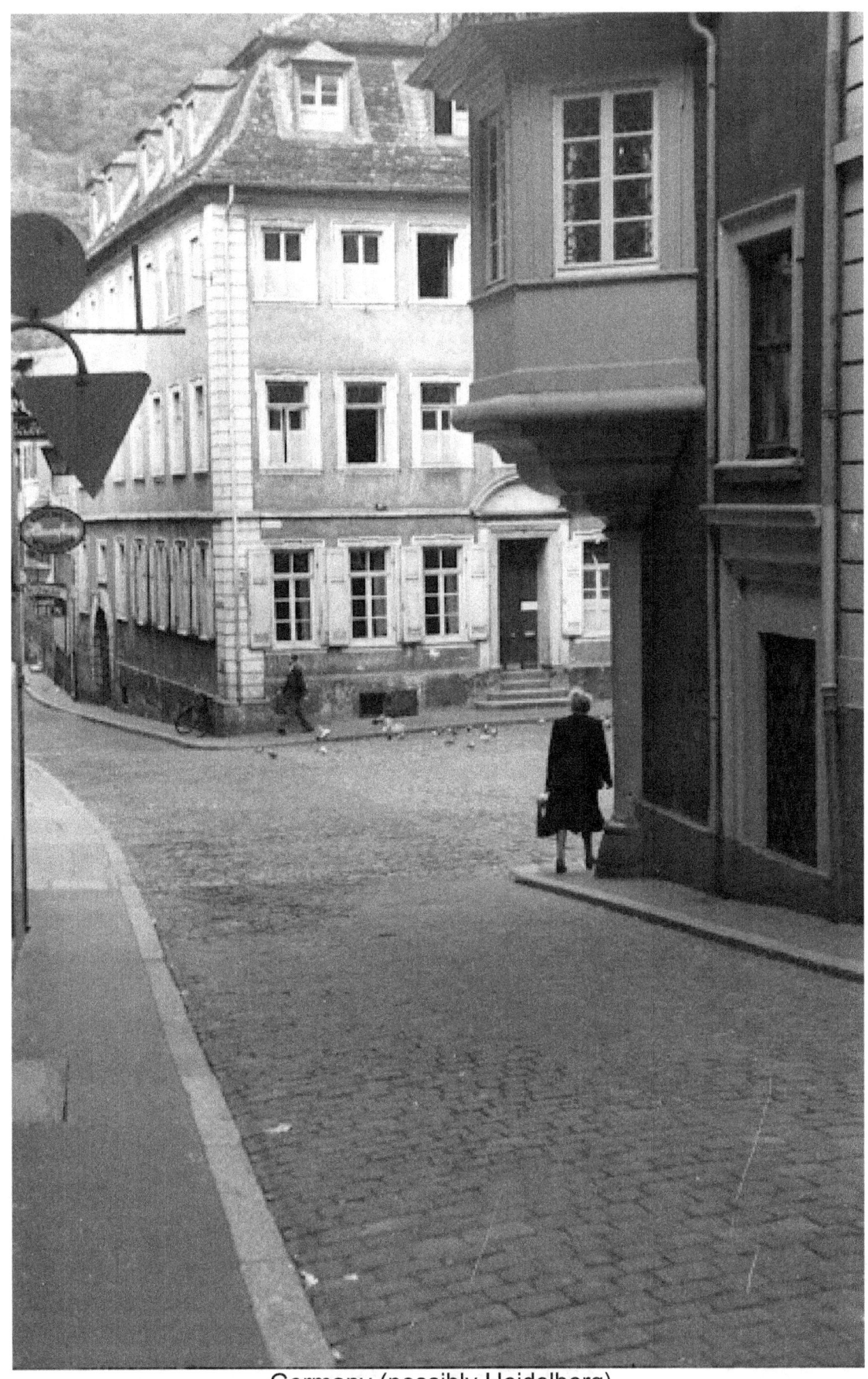
Germany (possibly Heidelberg)

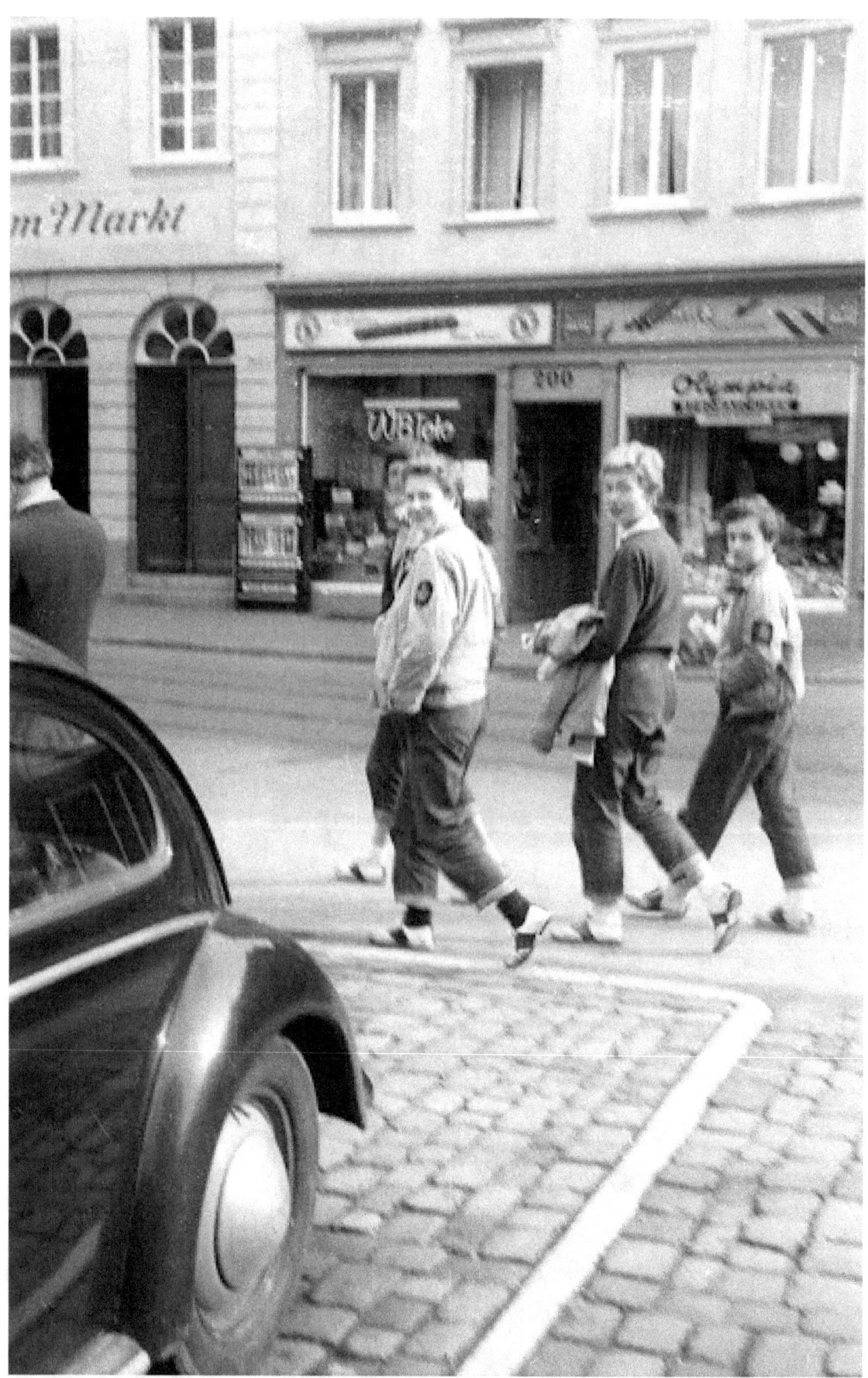
Bobby Soxers (Germany)

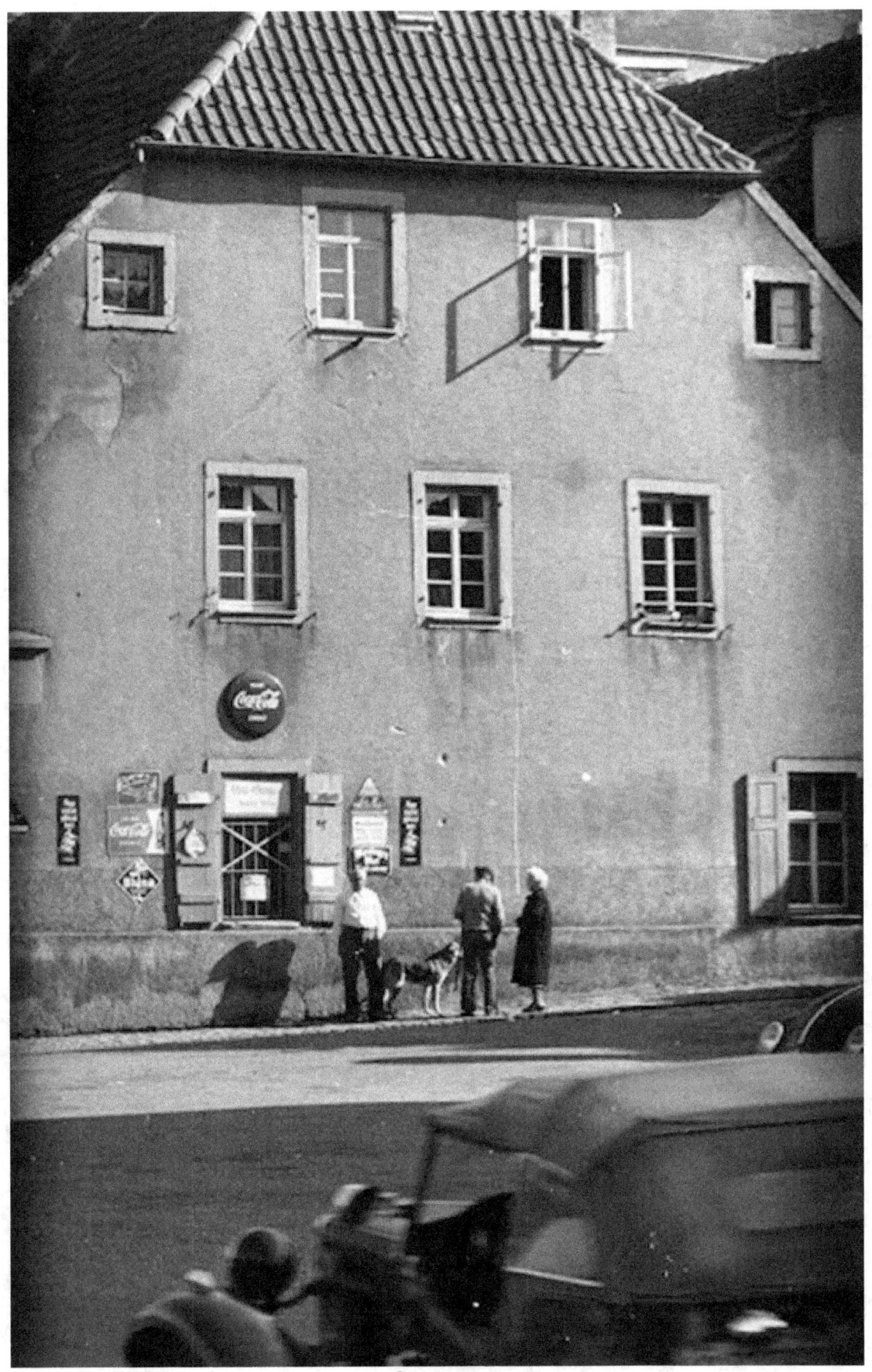

Germany

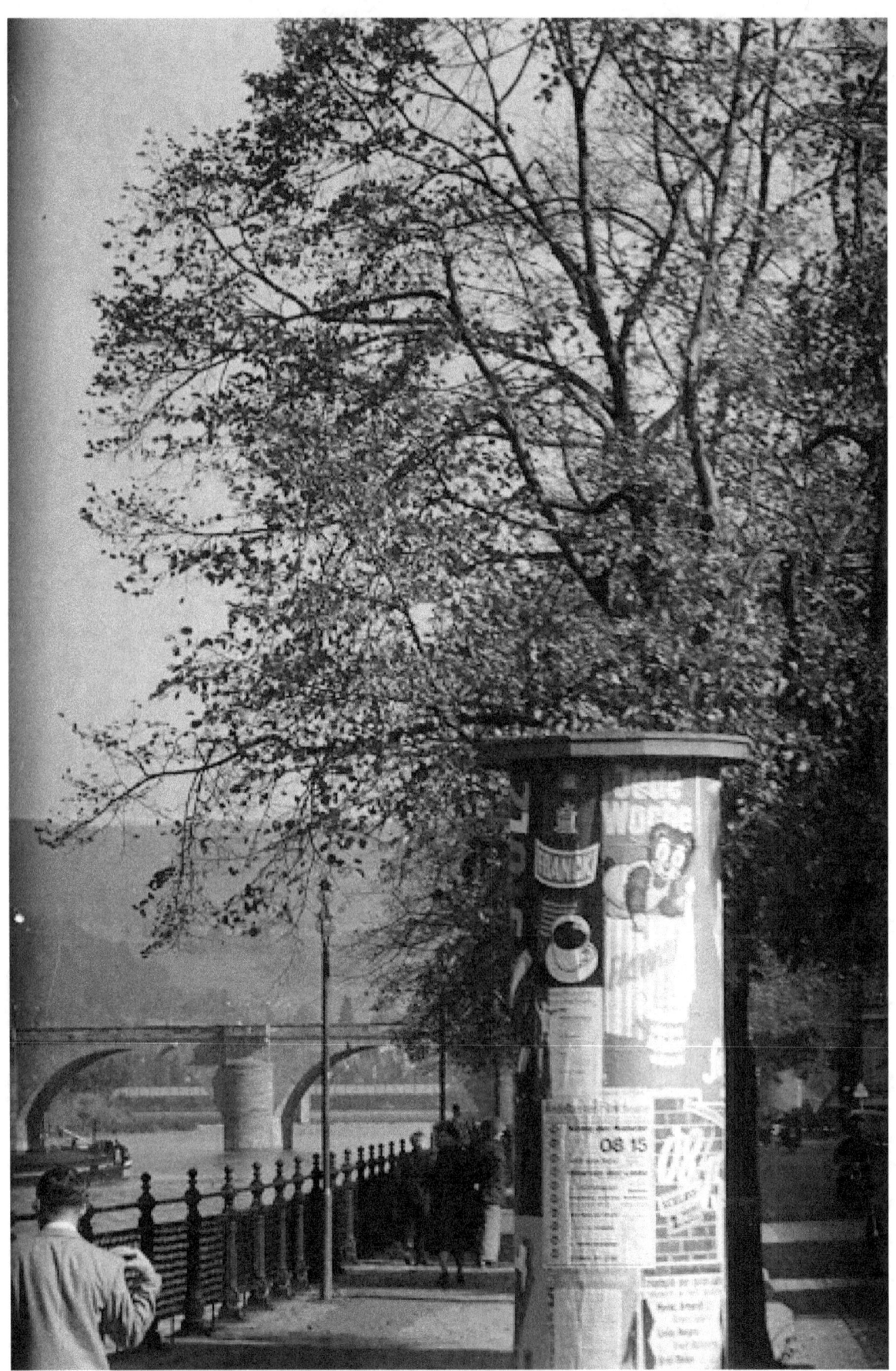
Heidelberg

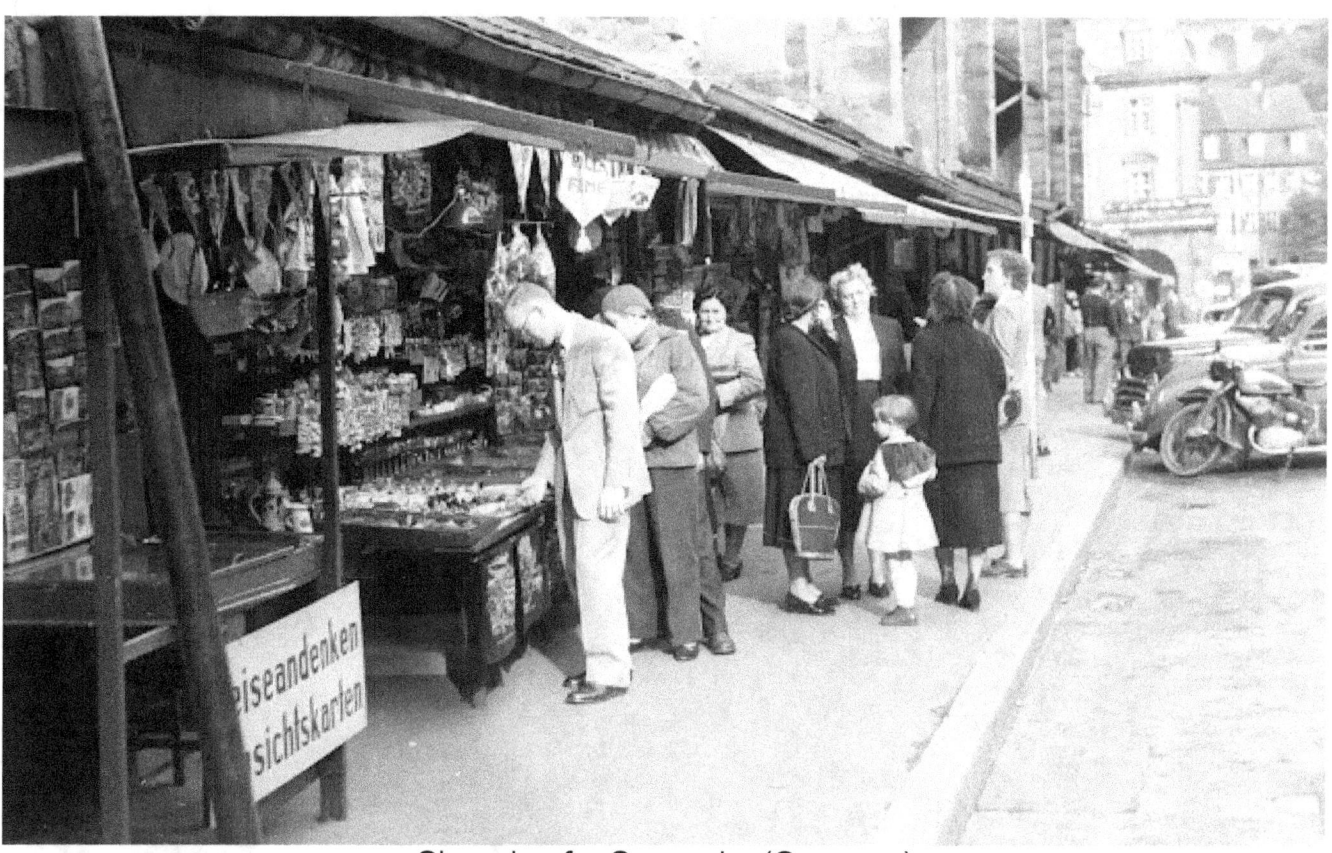
Shopping for Souvenirs (Germany)

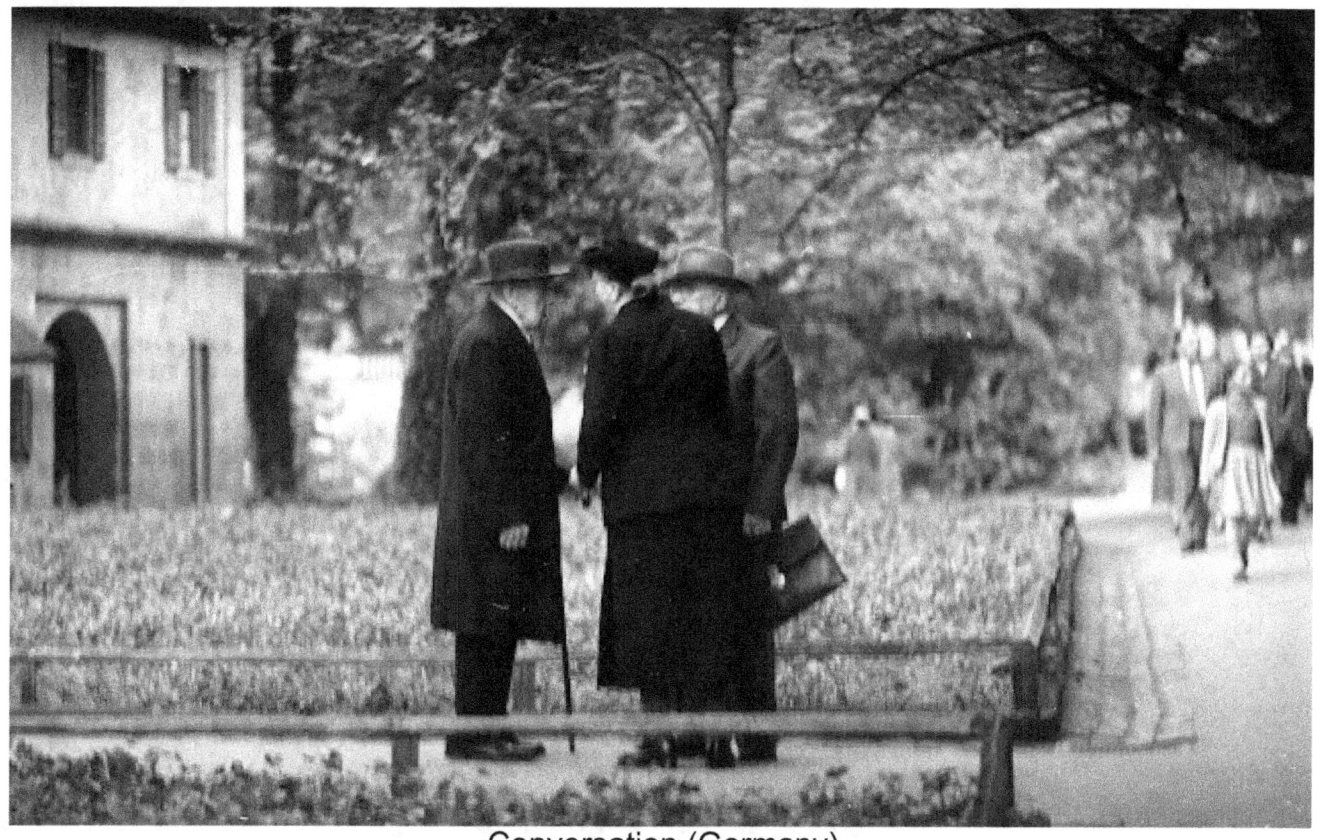
Conversation (Germany)

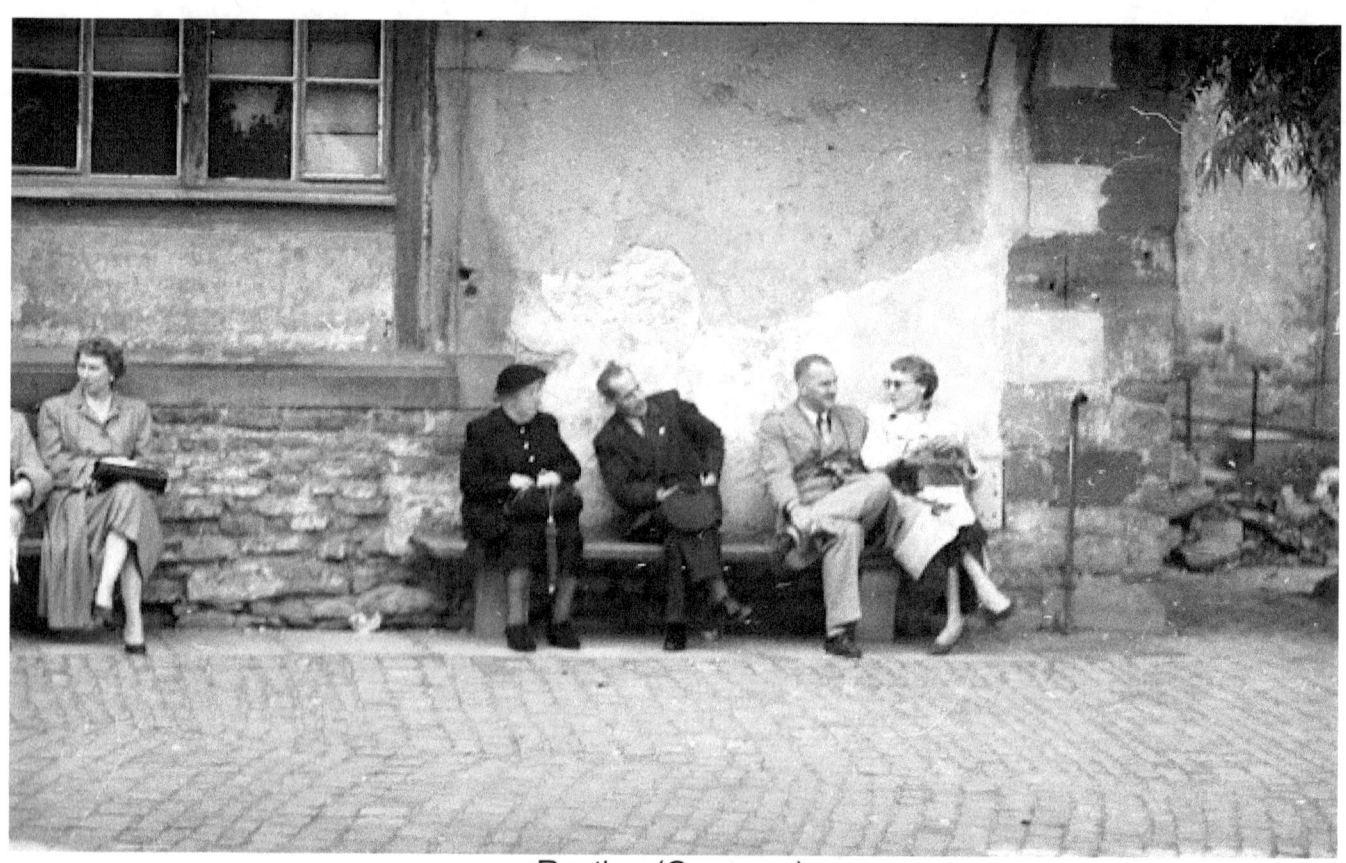
Resting (Germany)

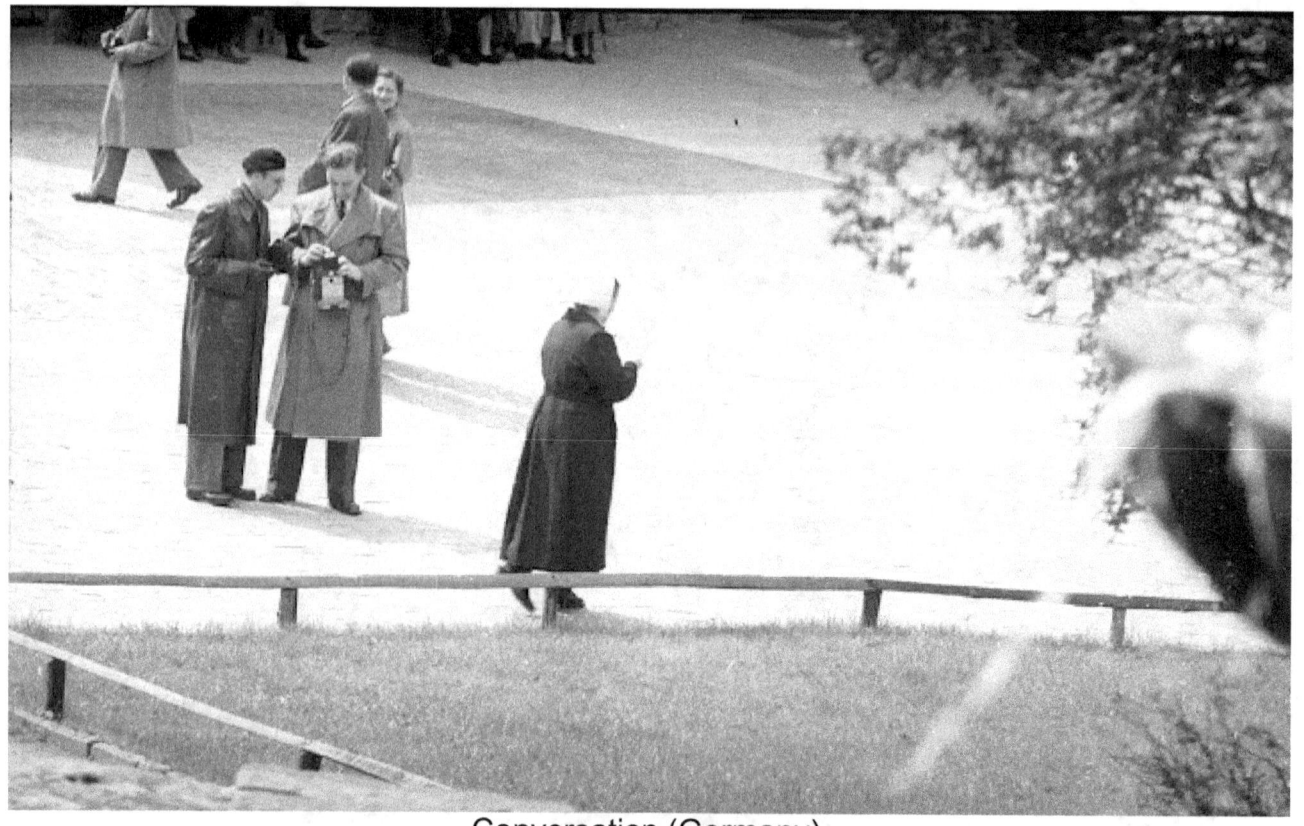
Conversation (Germany)

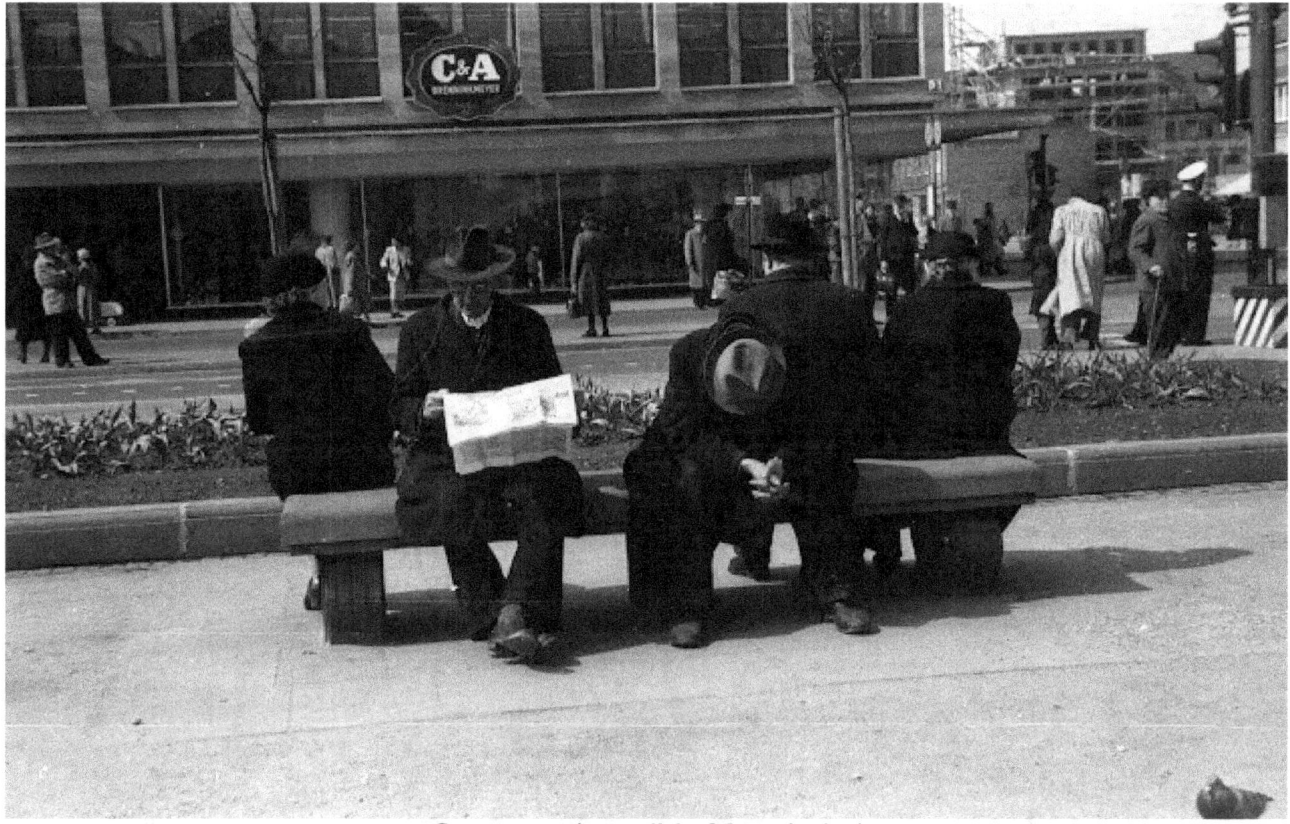
Germany (possibly Mannheim)

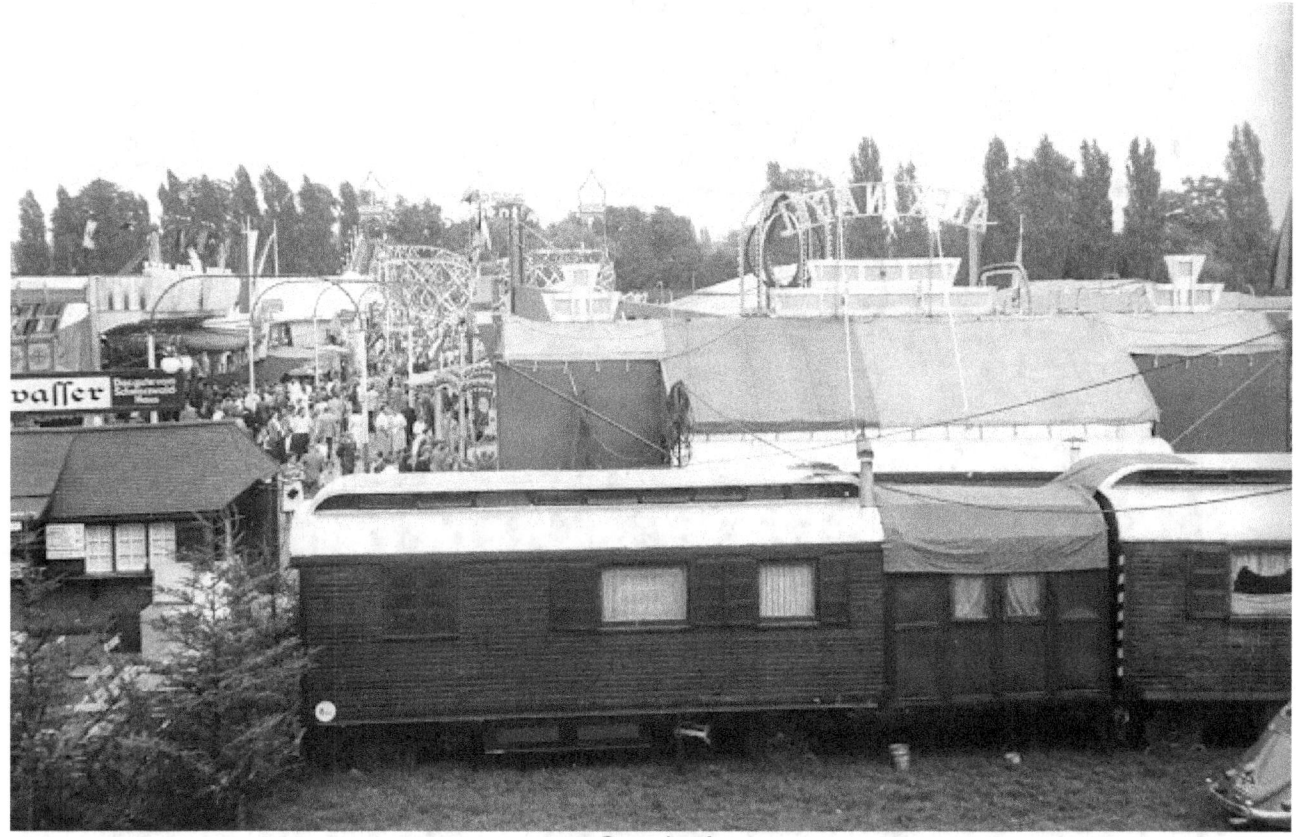
Carnival

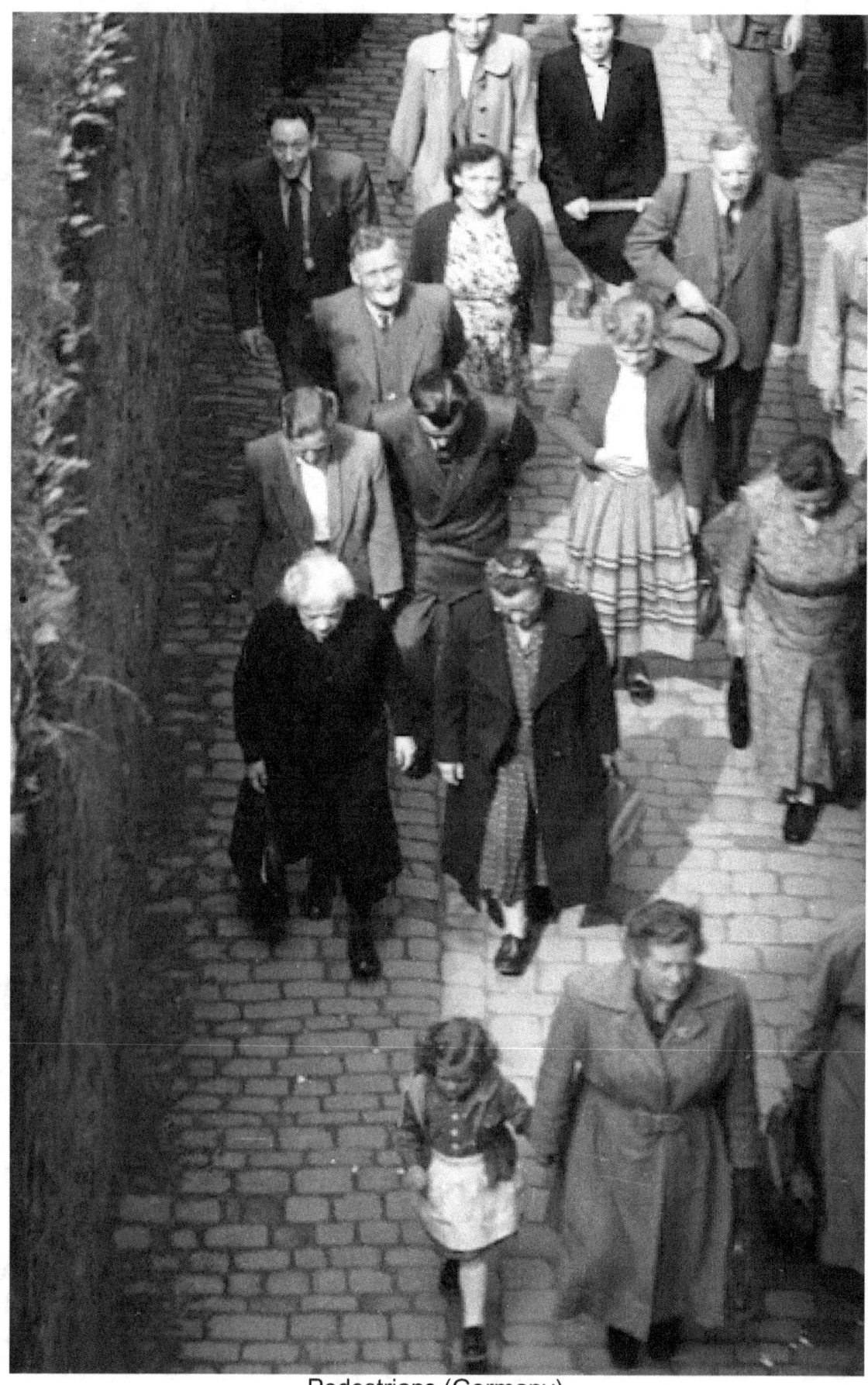
Pedestrians (Germany)

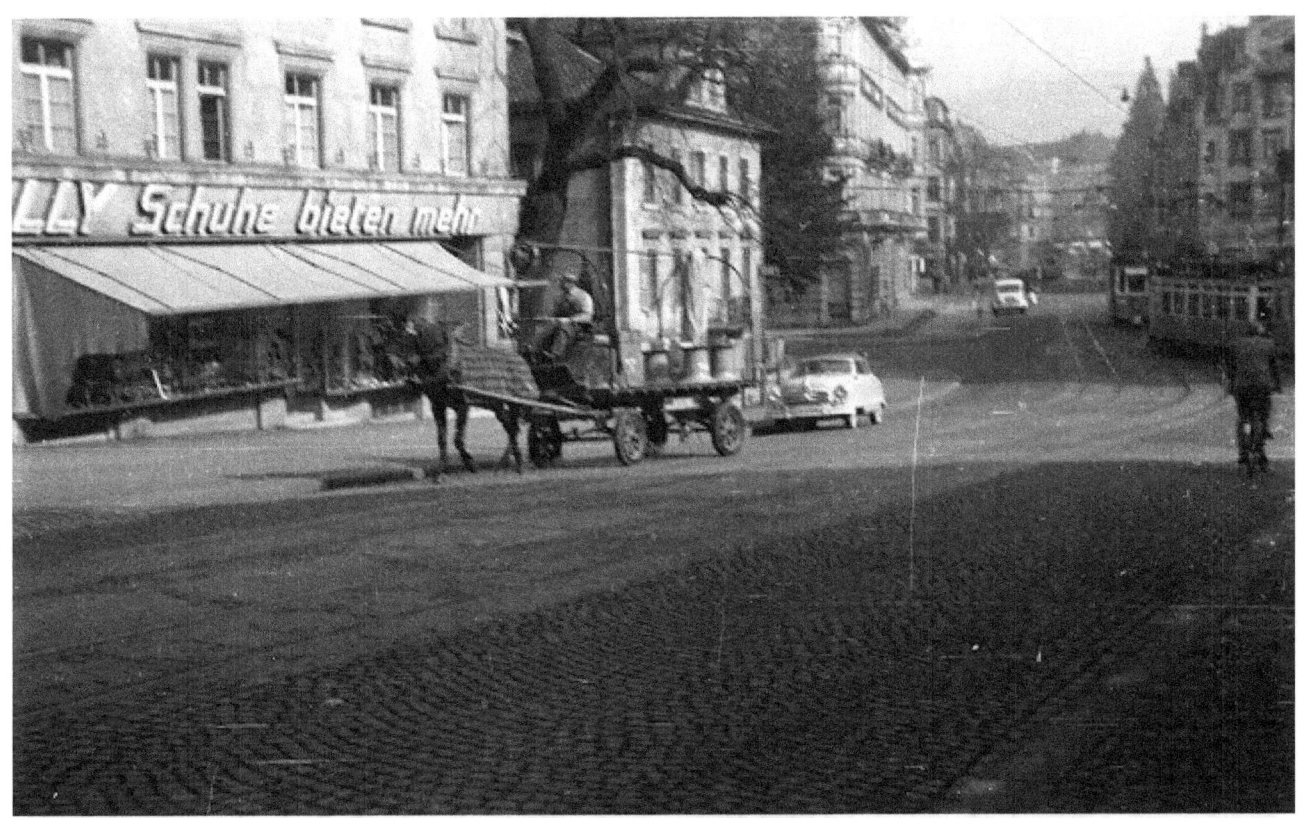
Horse Cart (Germany)

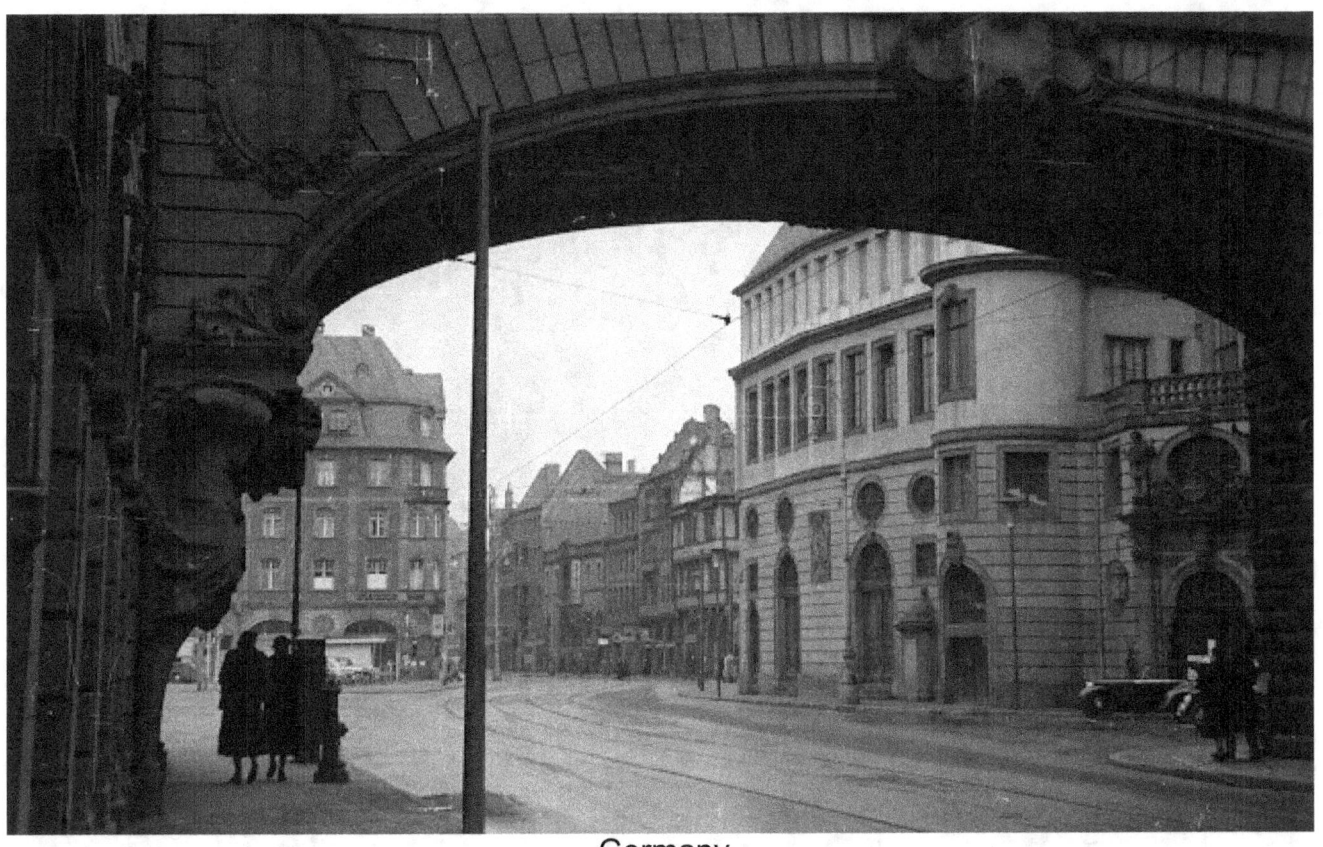
Germany

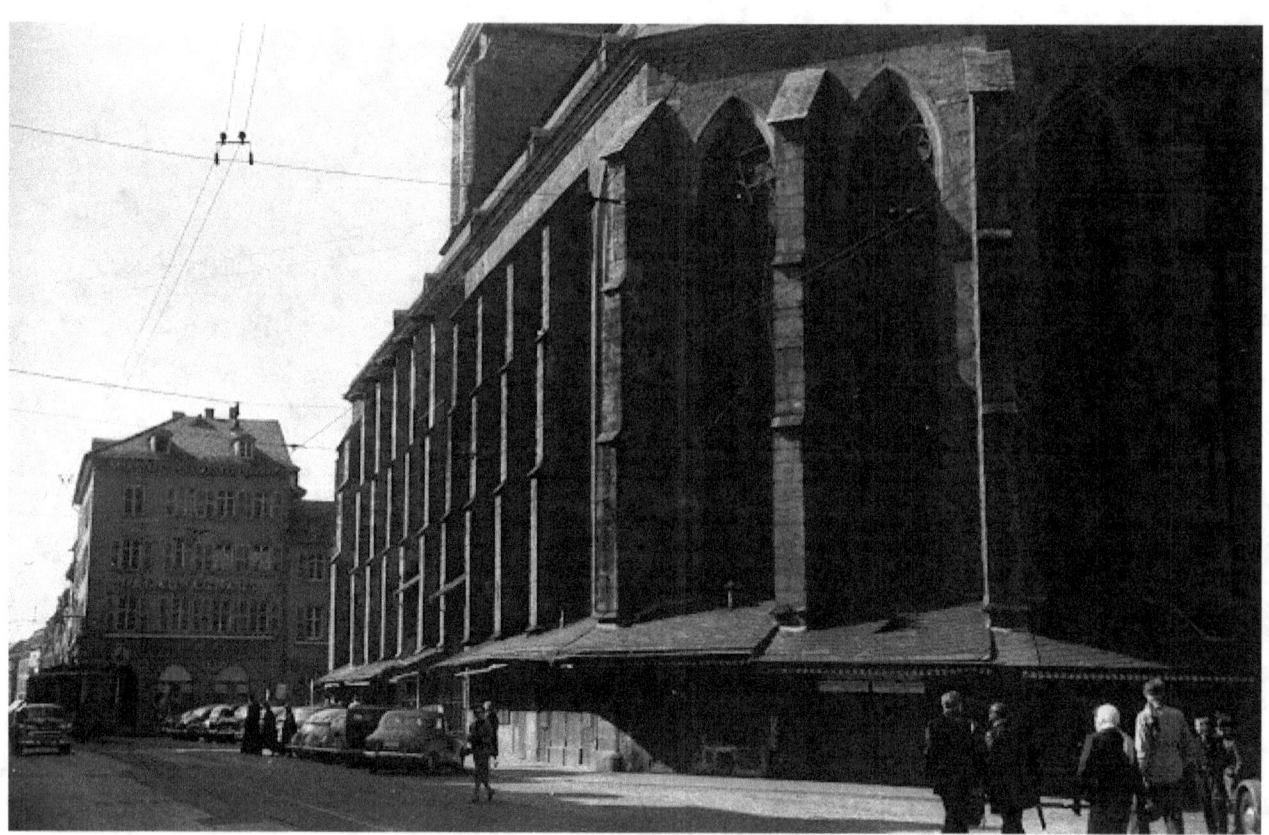
Germany

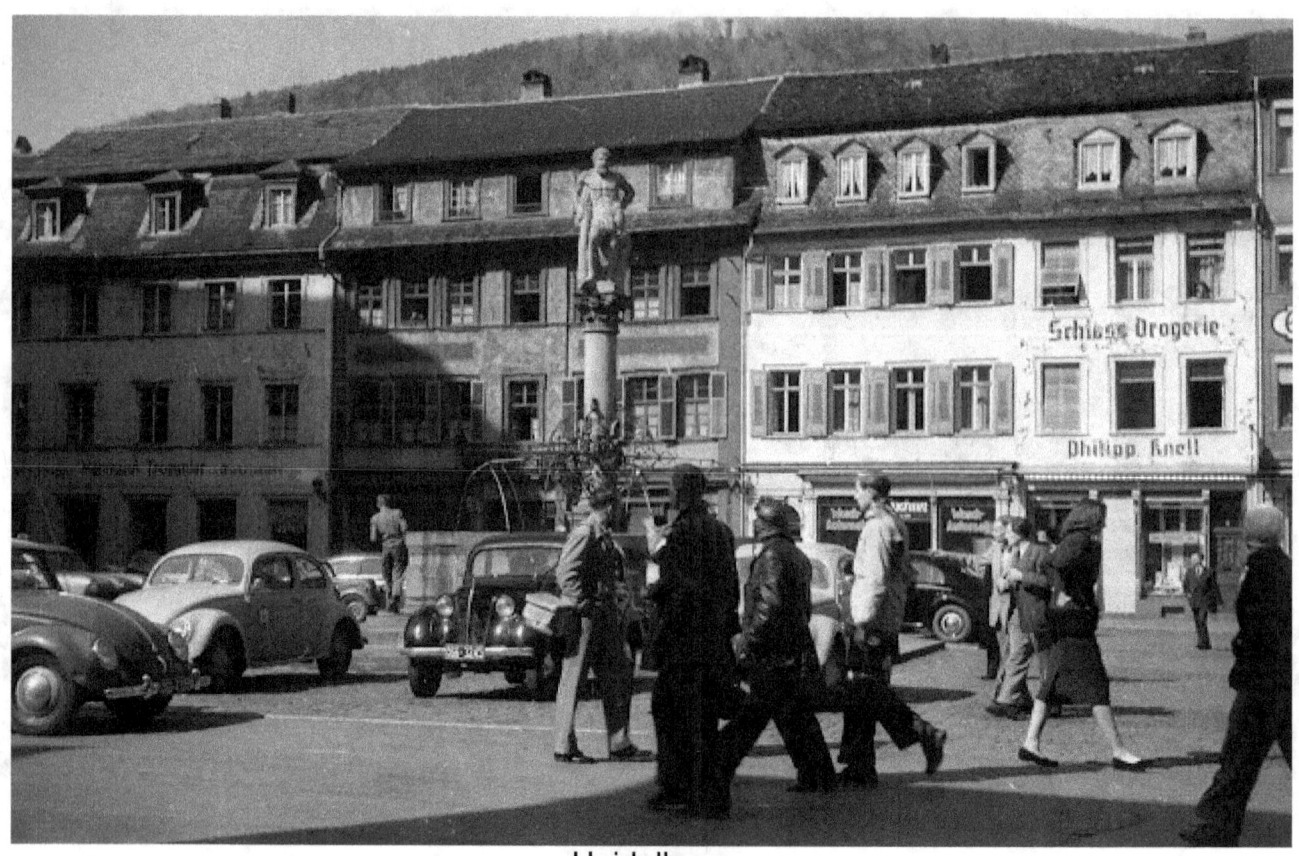
Heidelberg

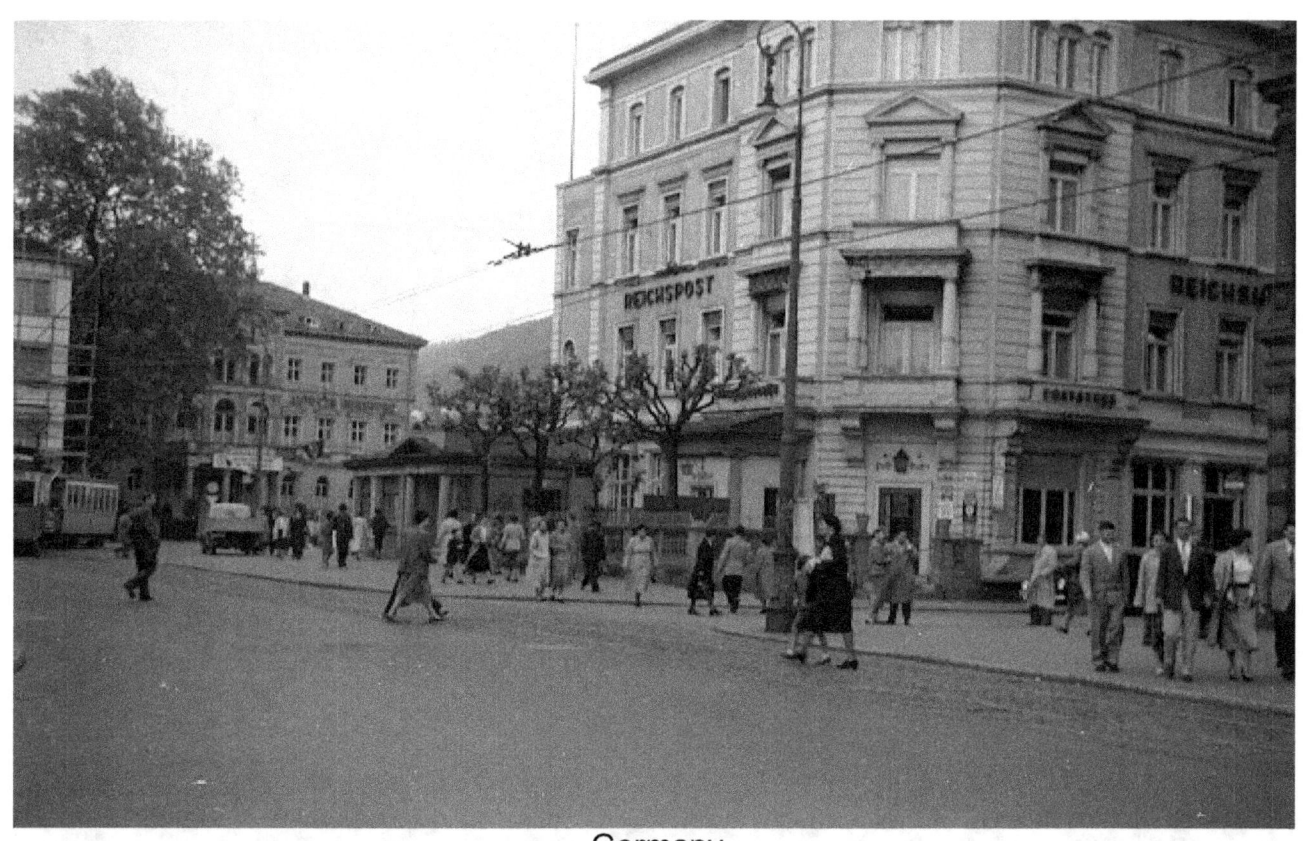
Germany

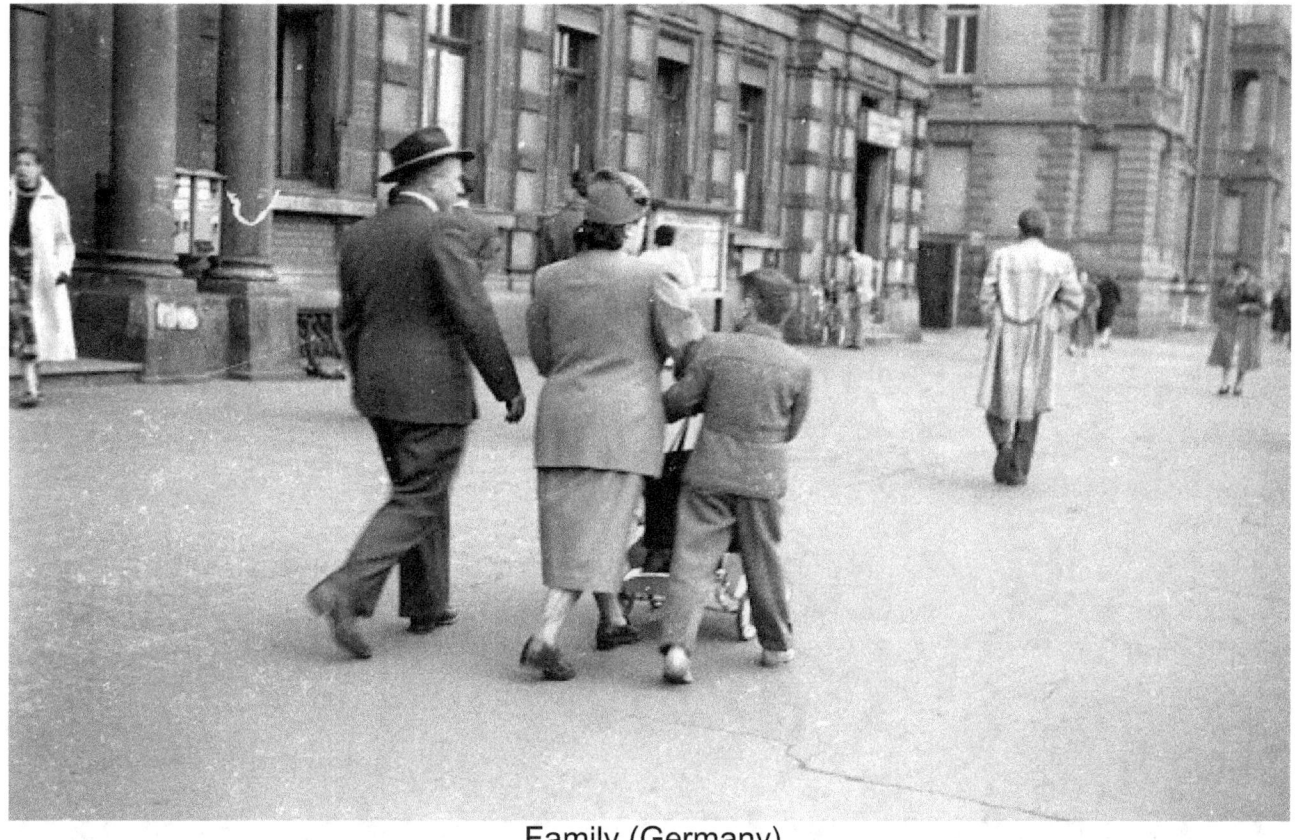
Family (Germany)

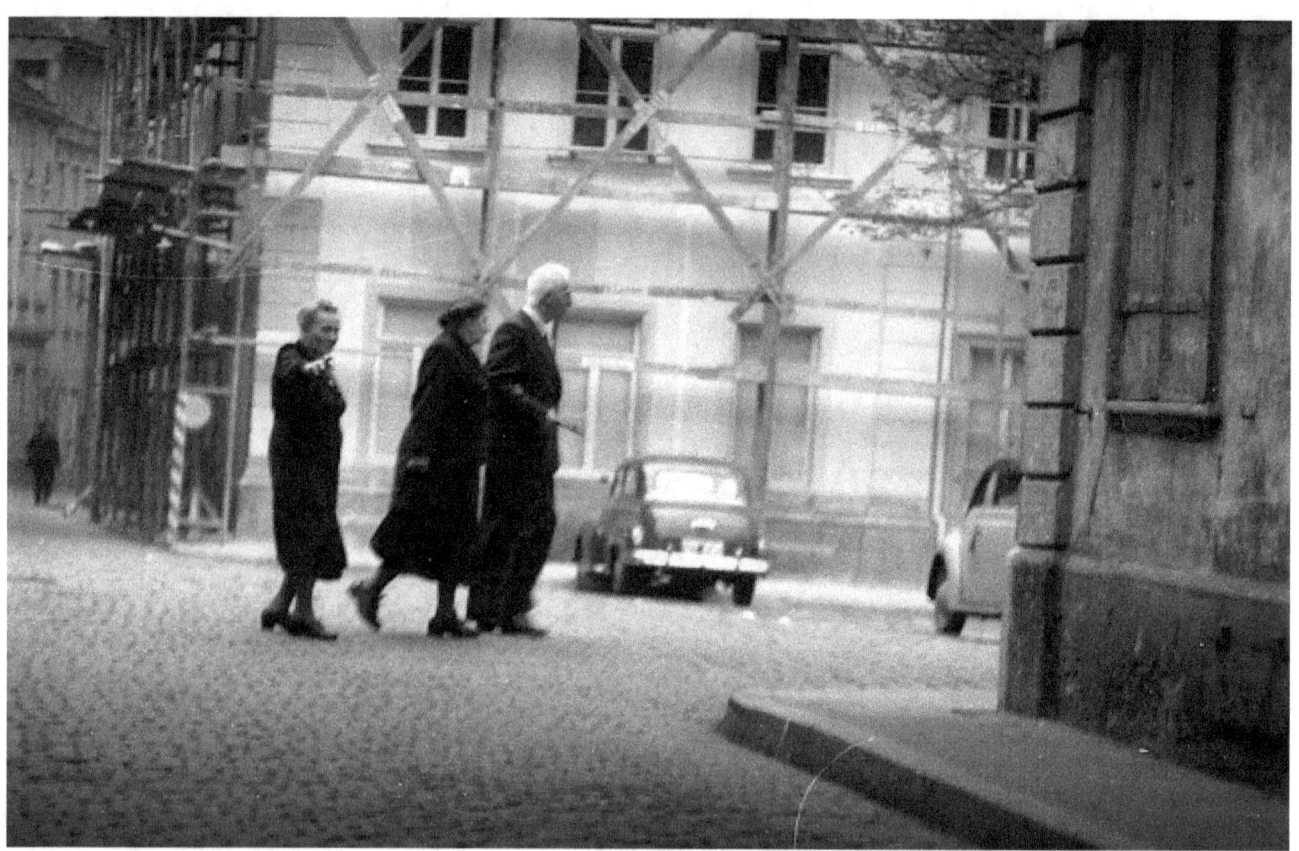
Germany

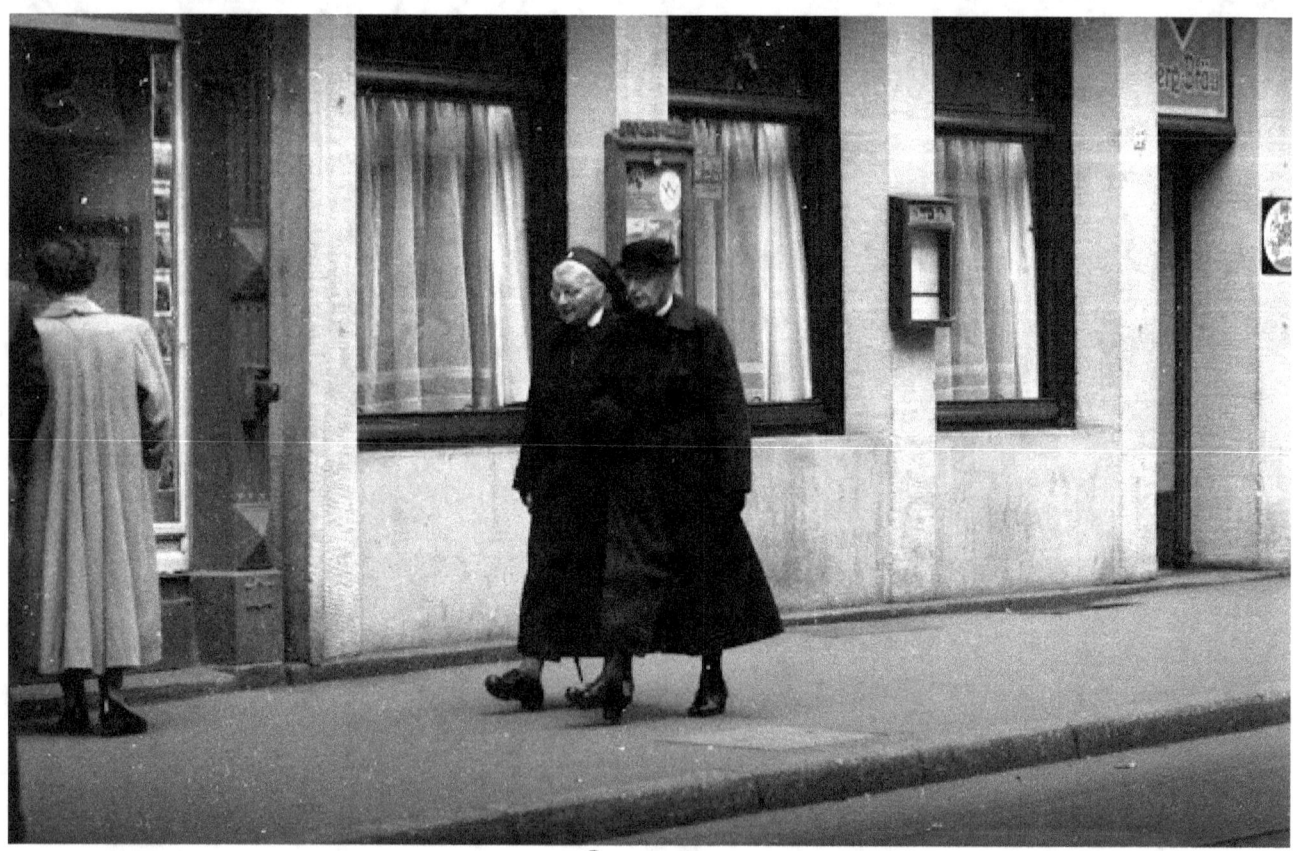
Germany

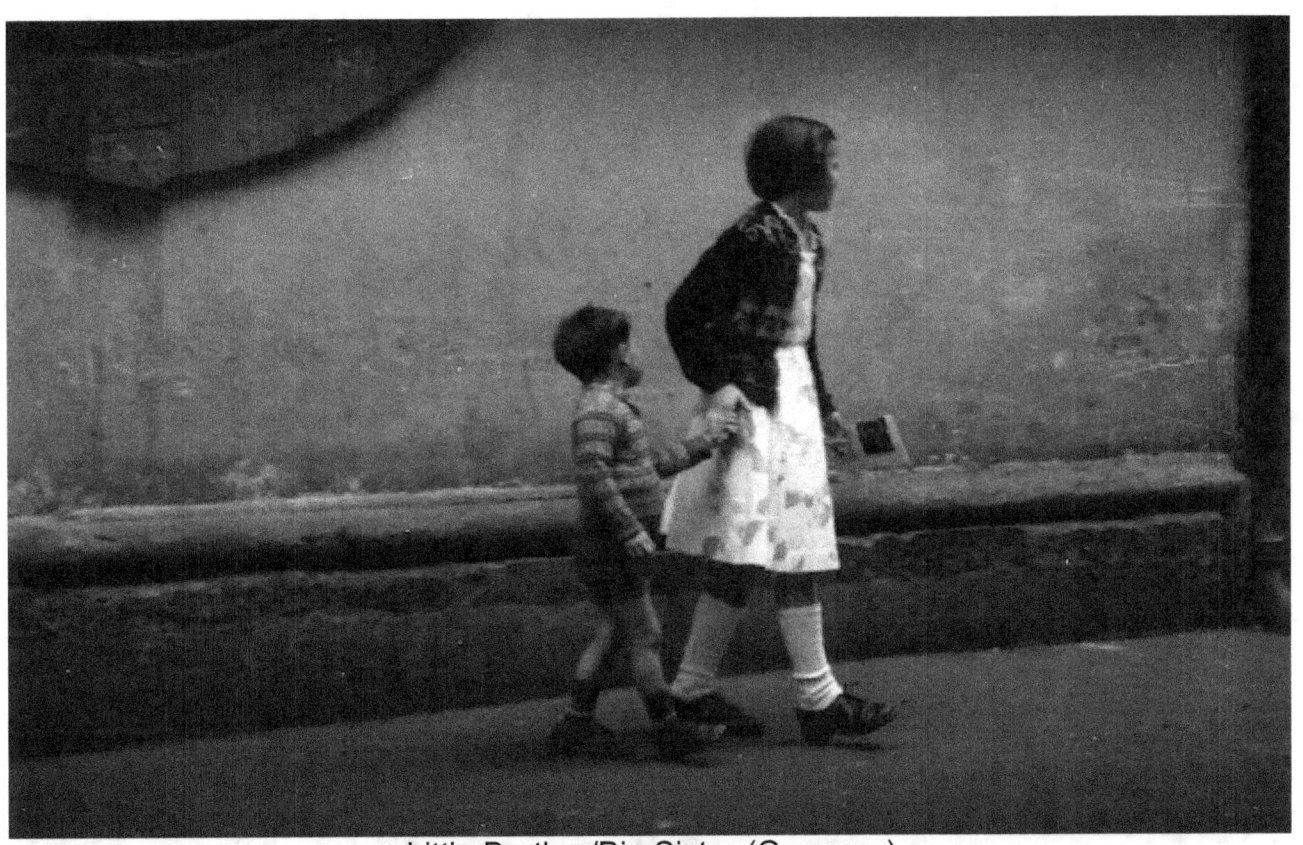
Little Brother/Big Sister (Germany)

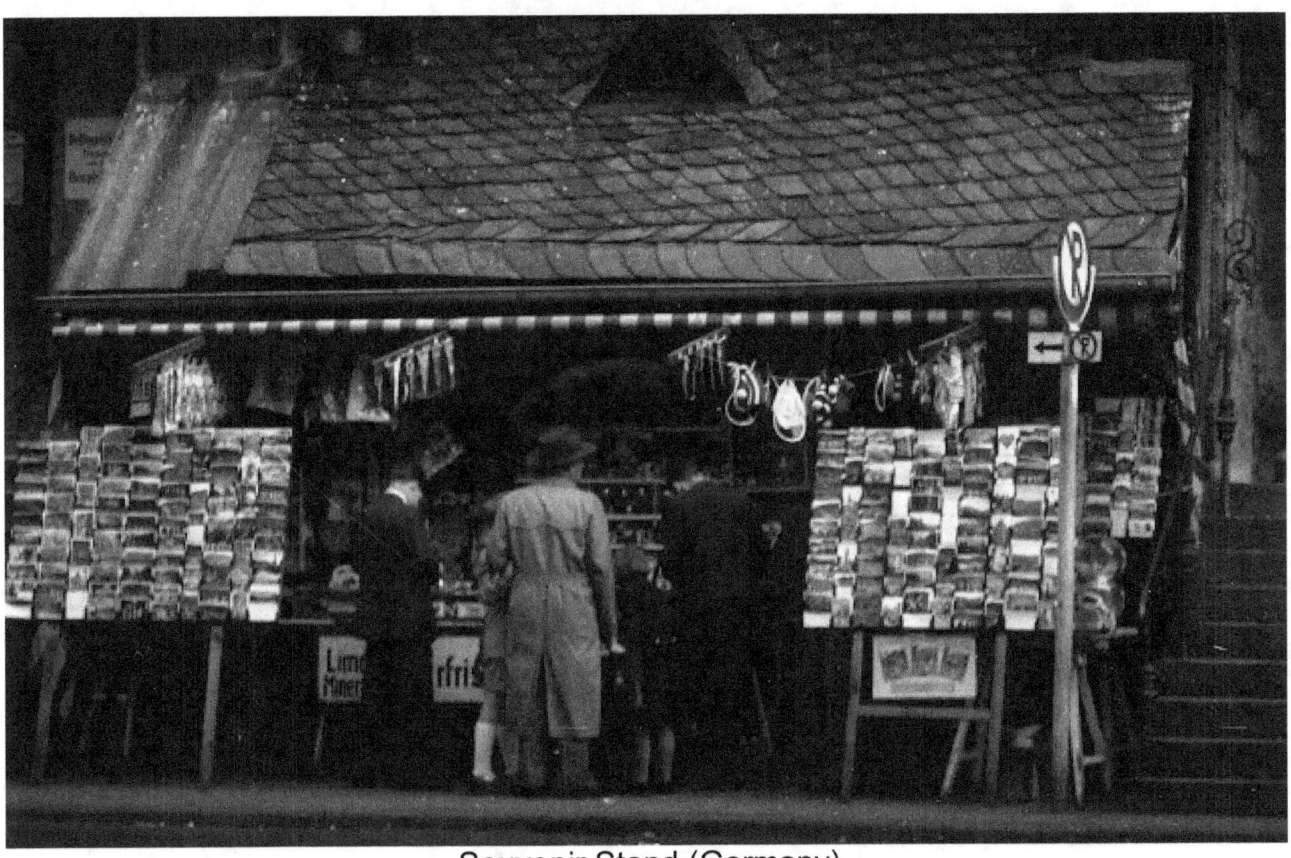
Souvenir Stand (Germany)

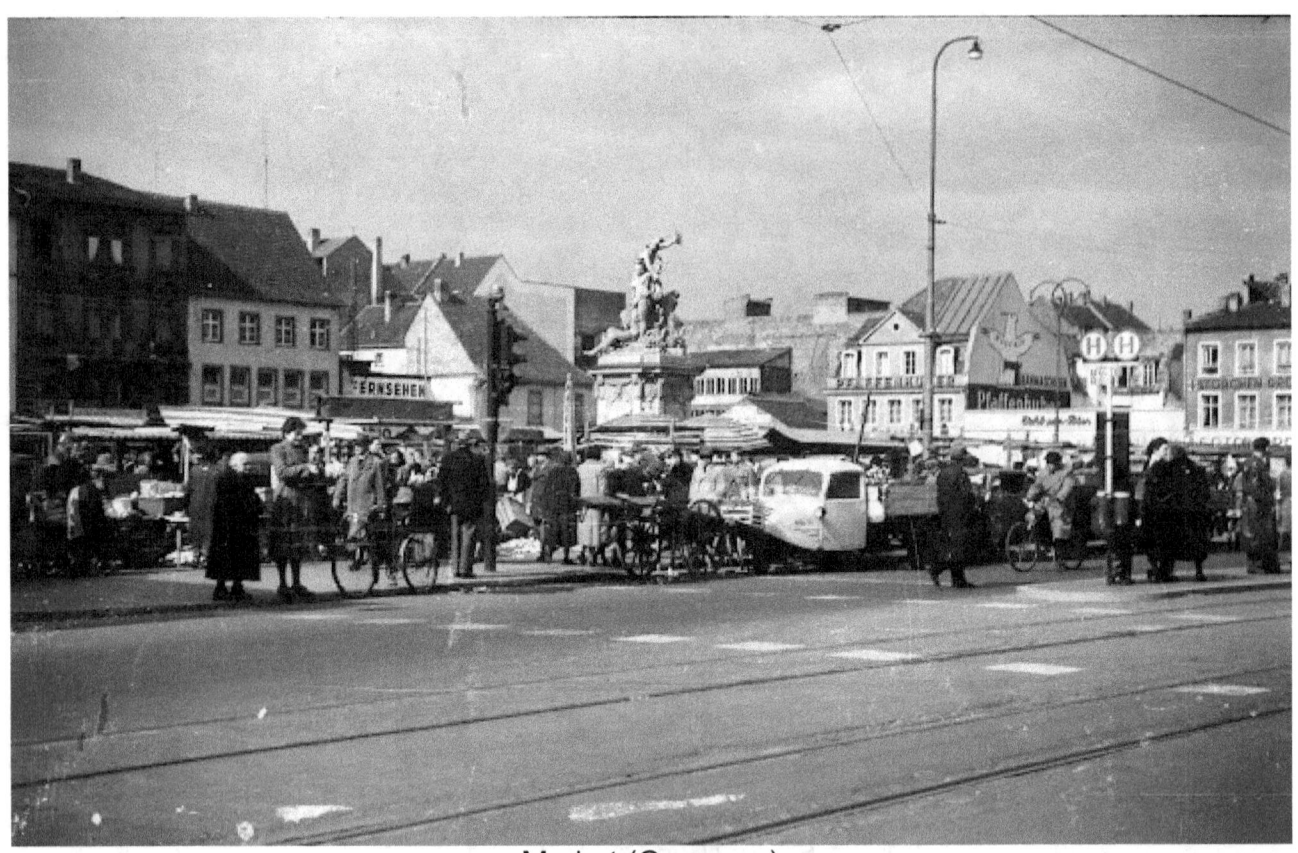
Market (Germany)

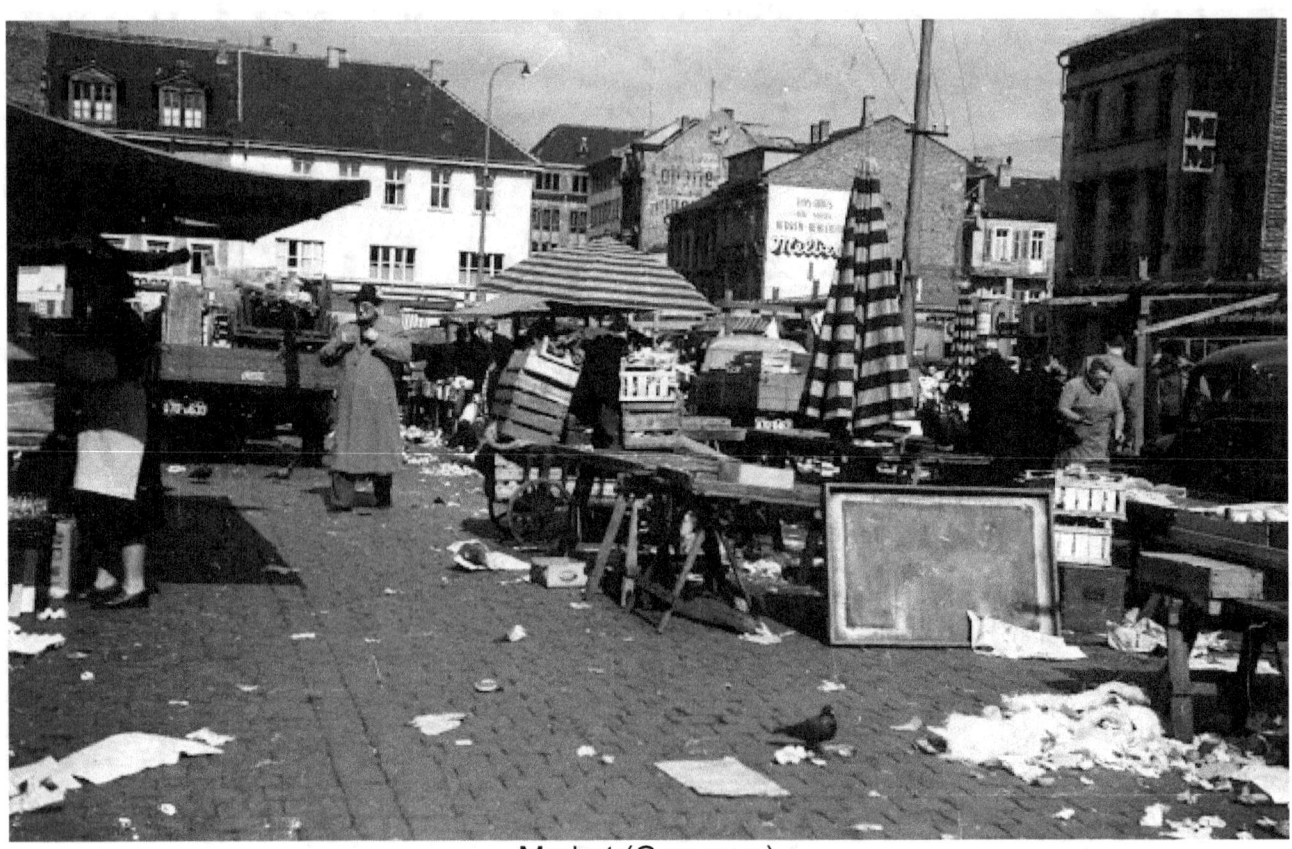
Market (Germany)

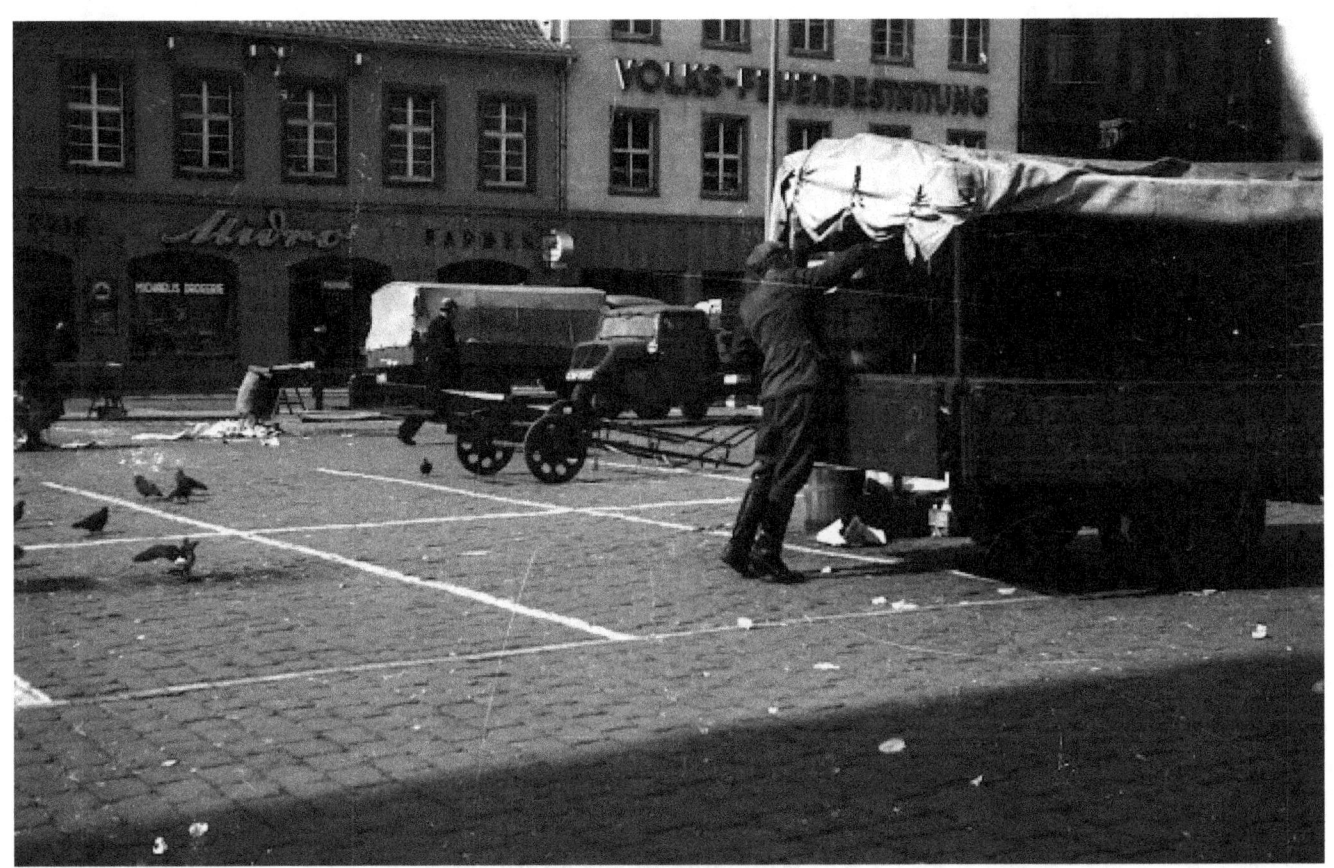
Market (Germany)

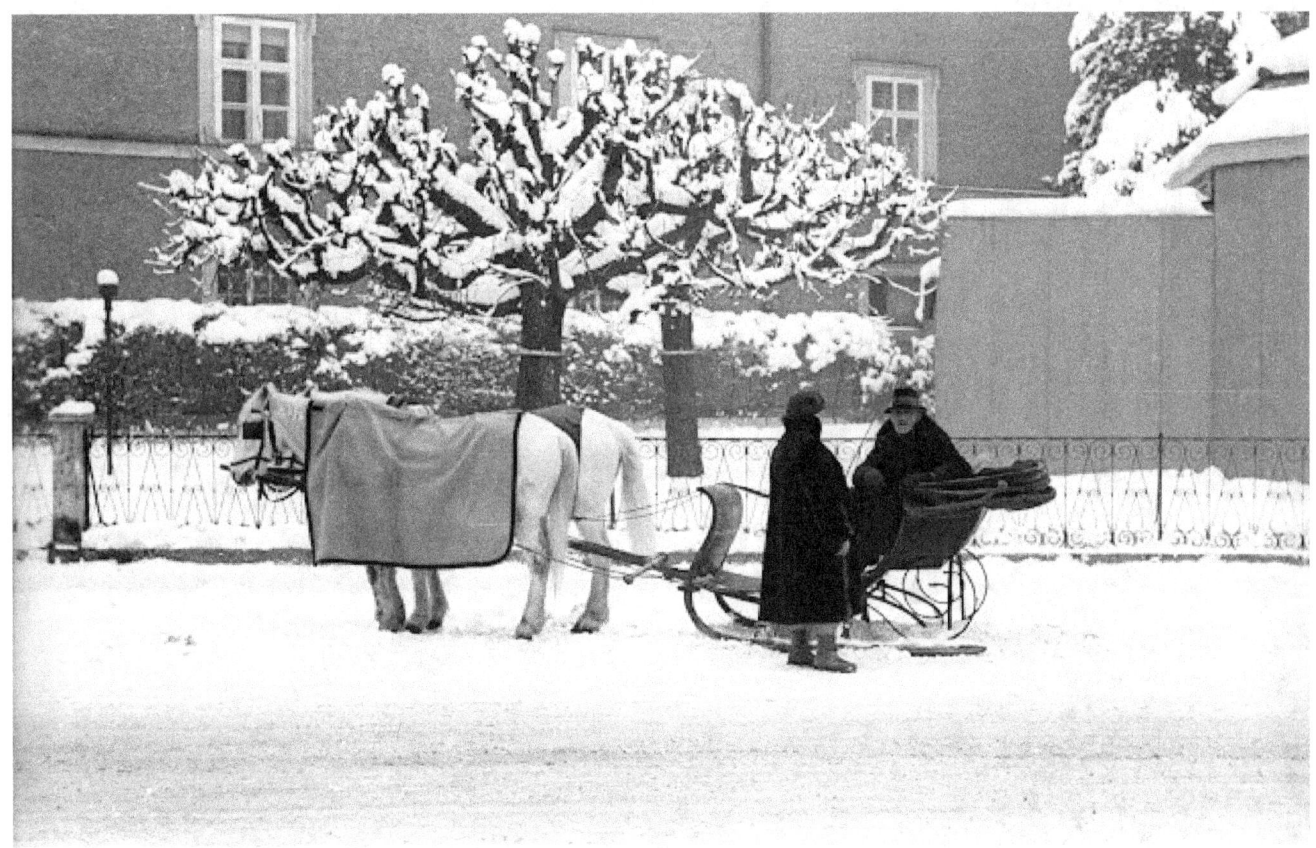
Sleigh, Salzburg, Austria

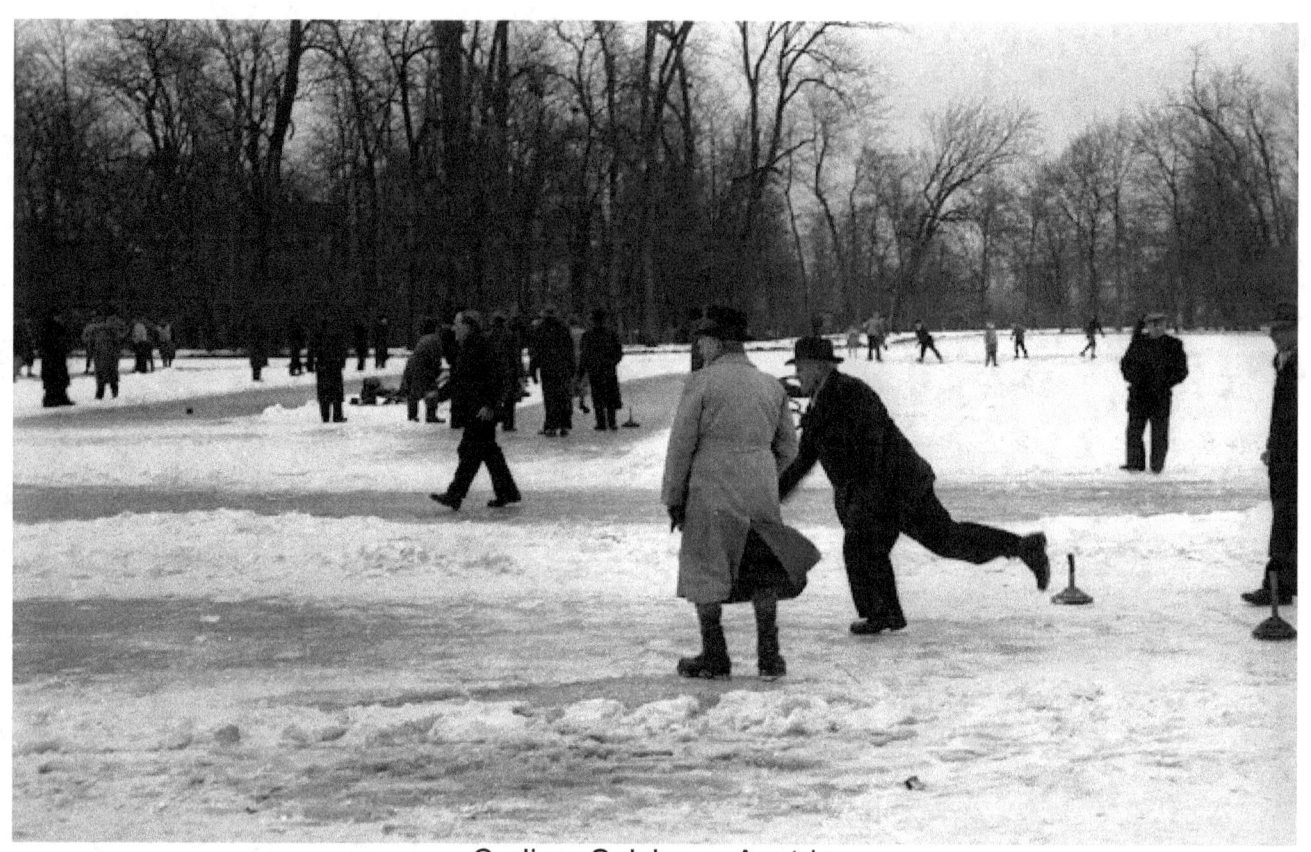
Curling, Salzburg, Austria

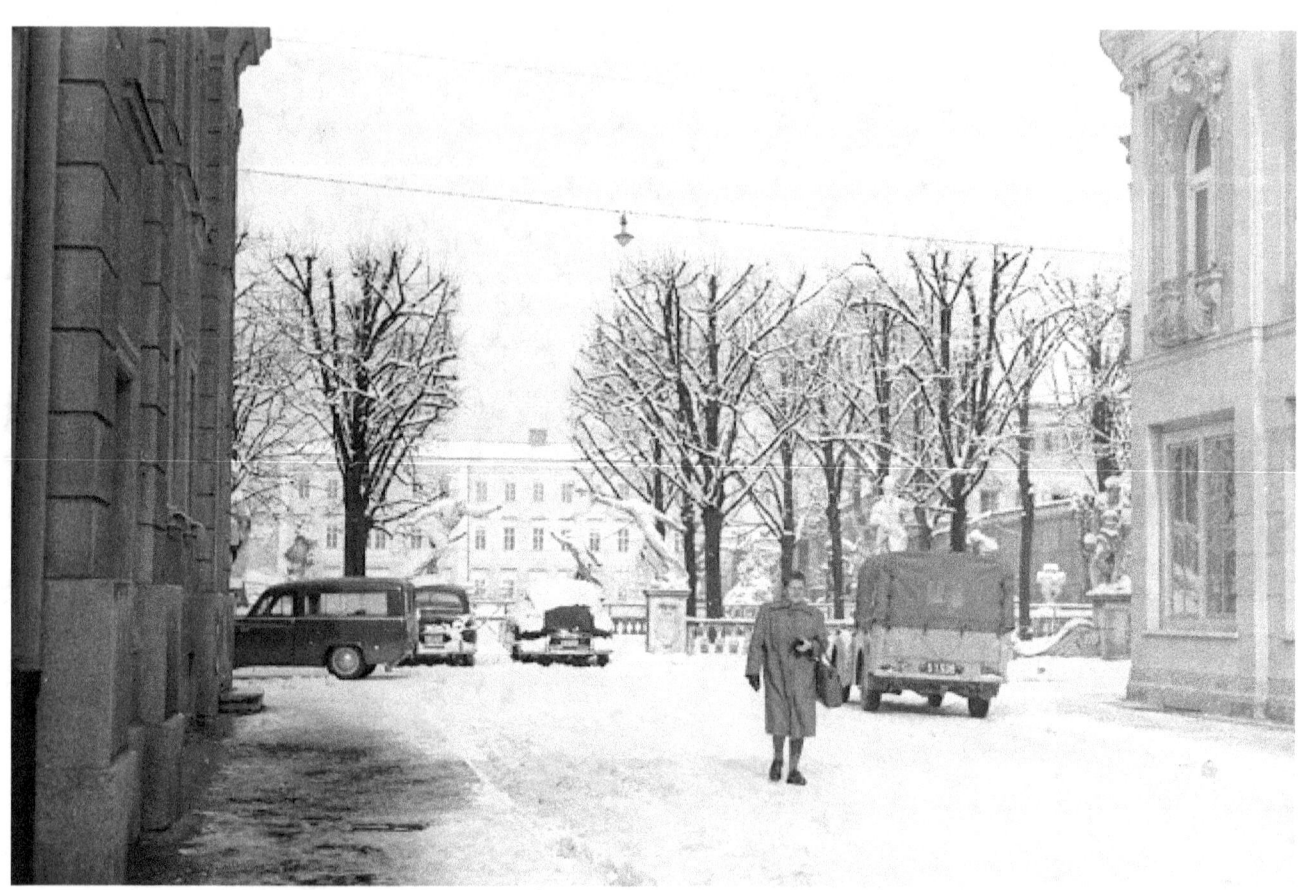
Salzburg, Austria

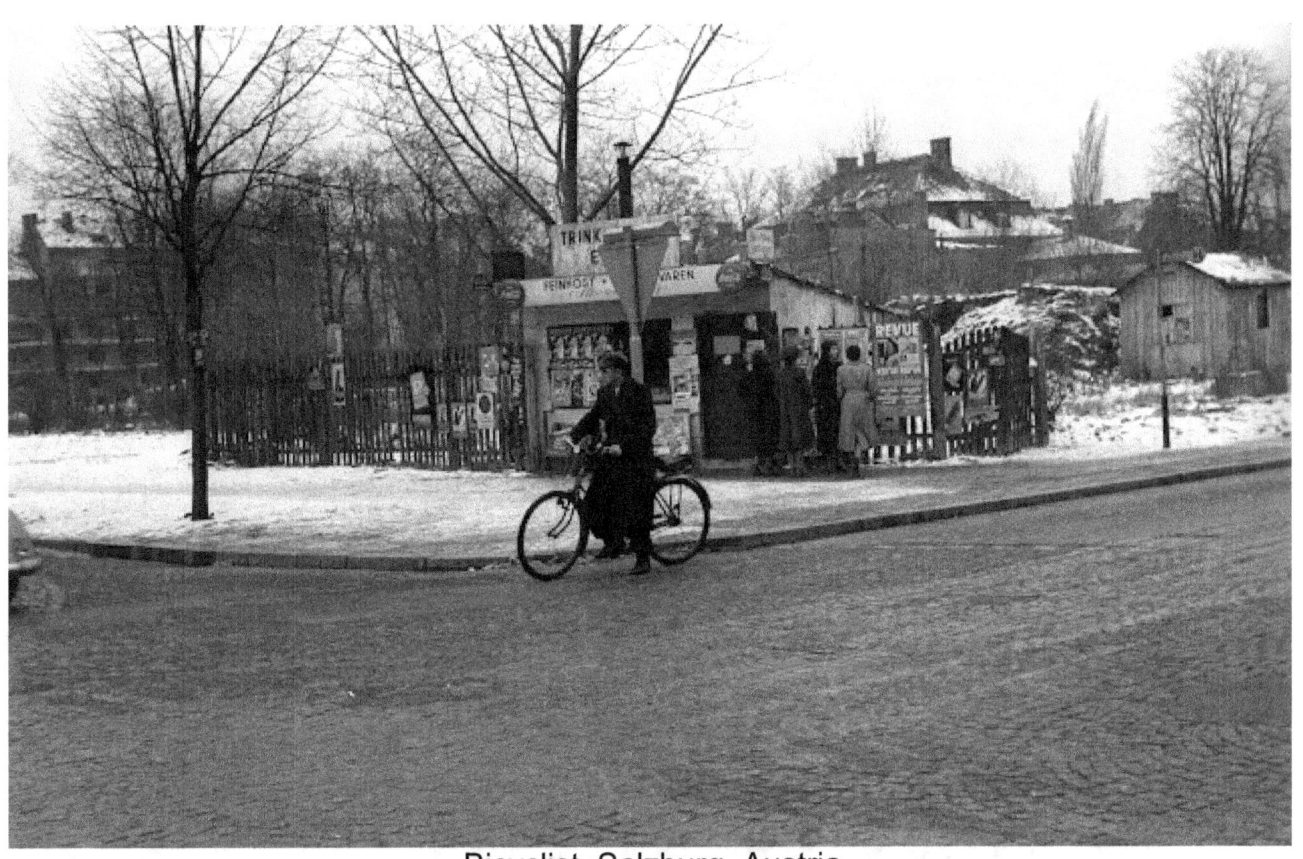

Bicyclist, Salzburg, Austria

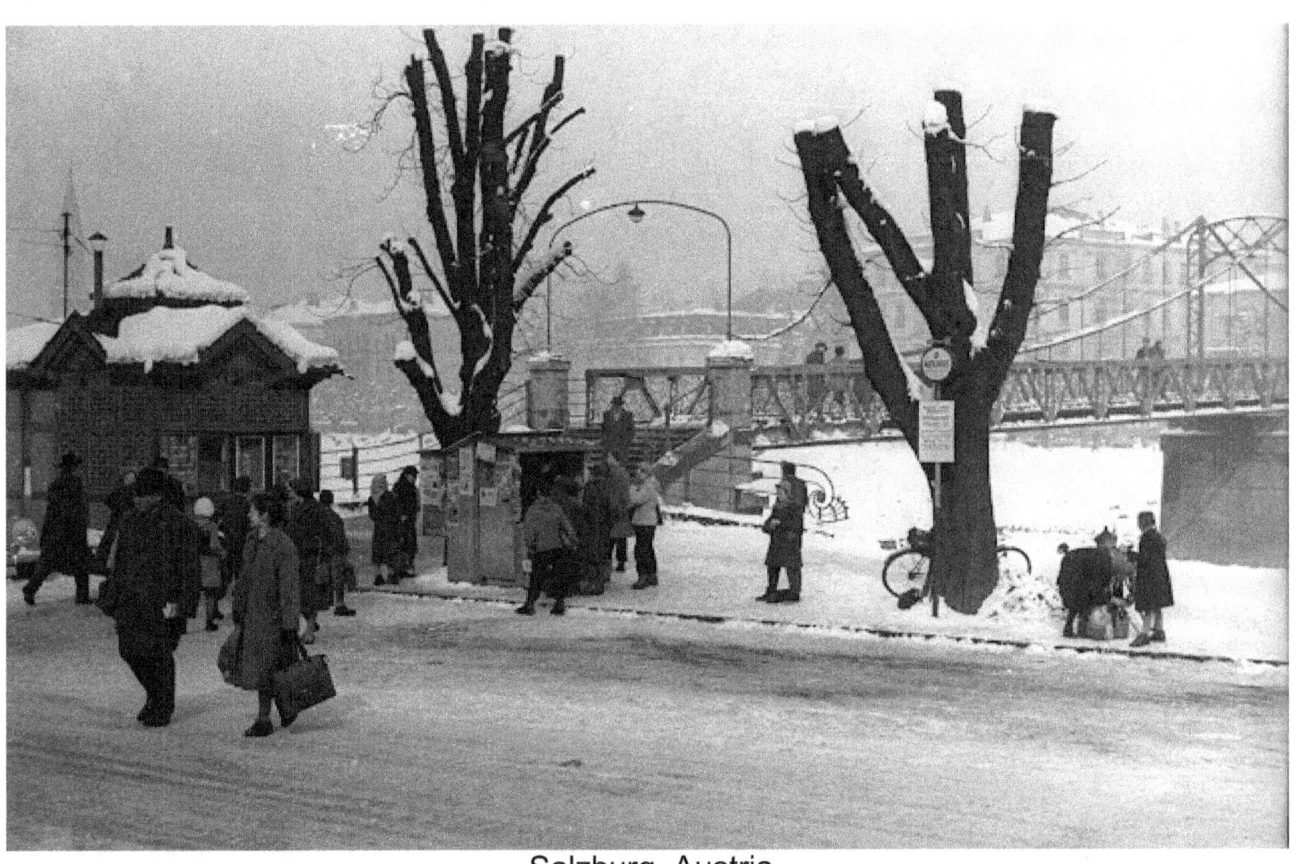

Salzburg, Austria

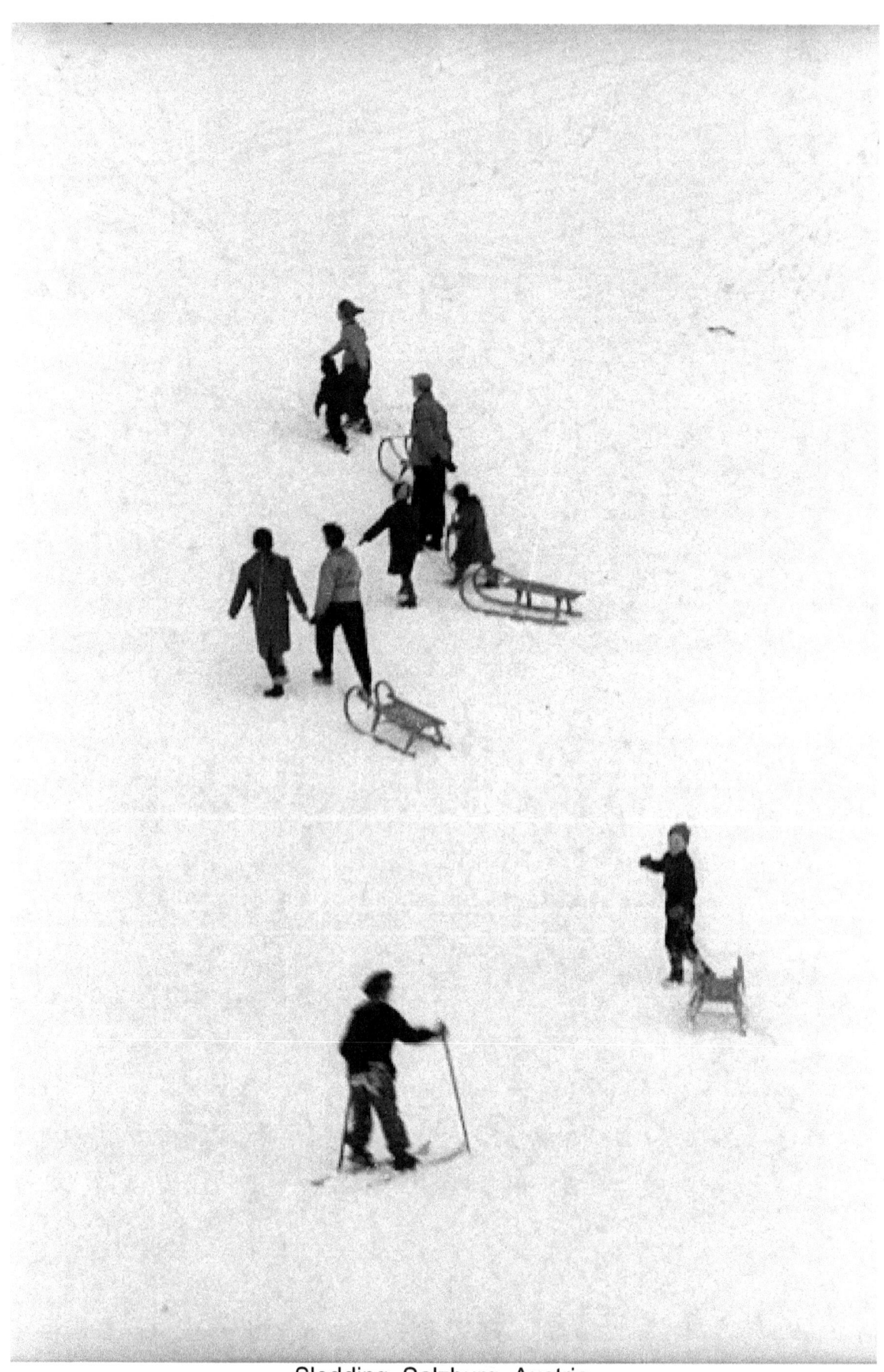
Sledding, Salzburg, Austria

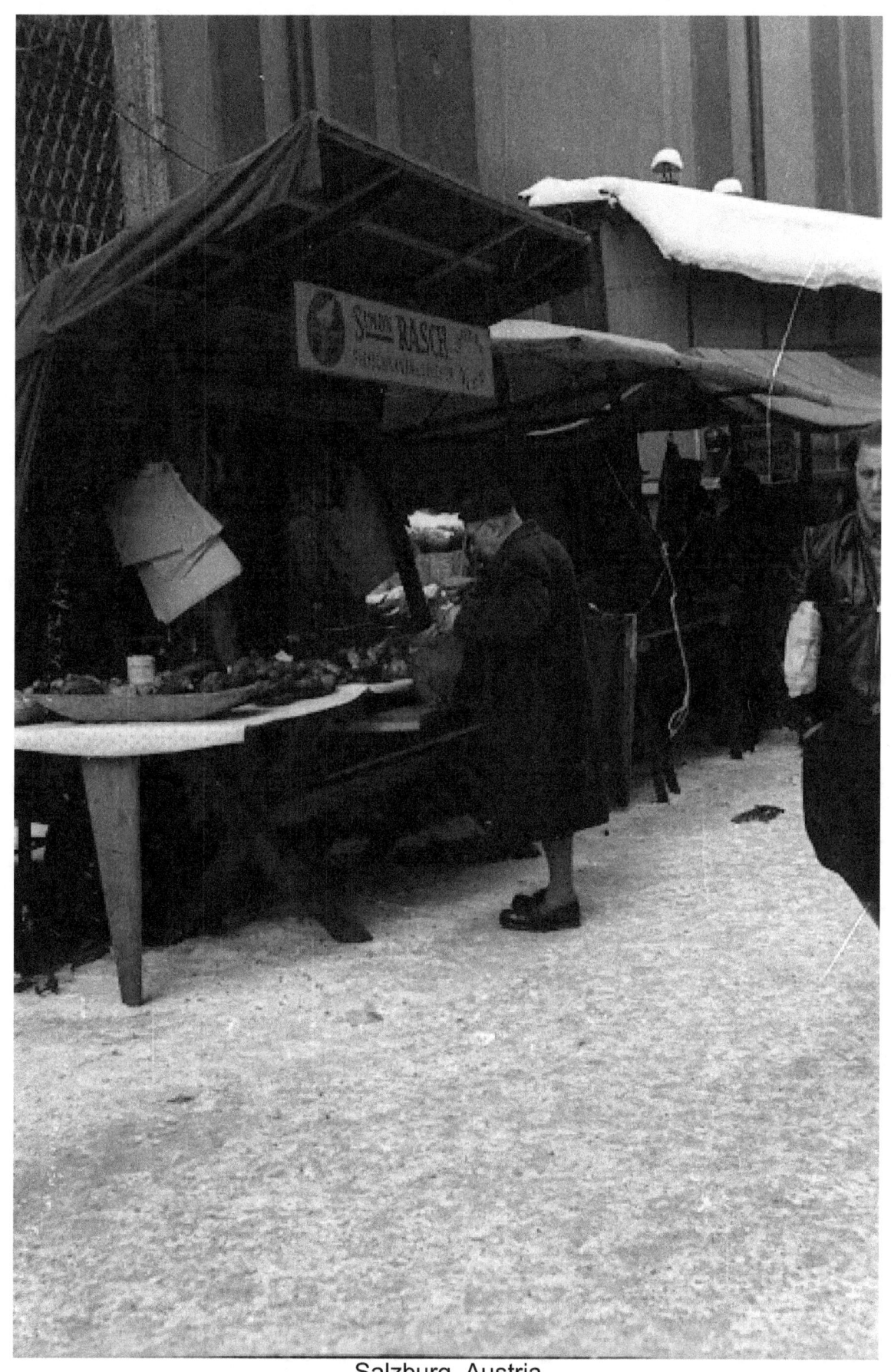
Salzburg, Austria

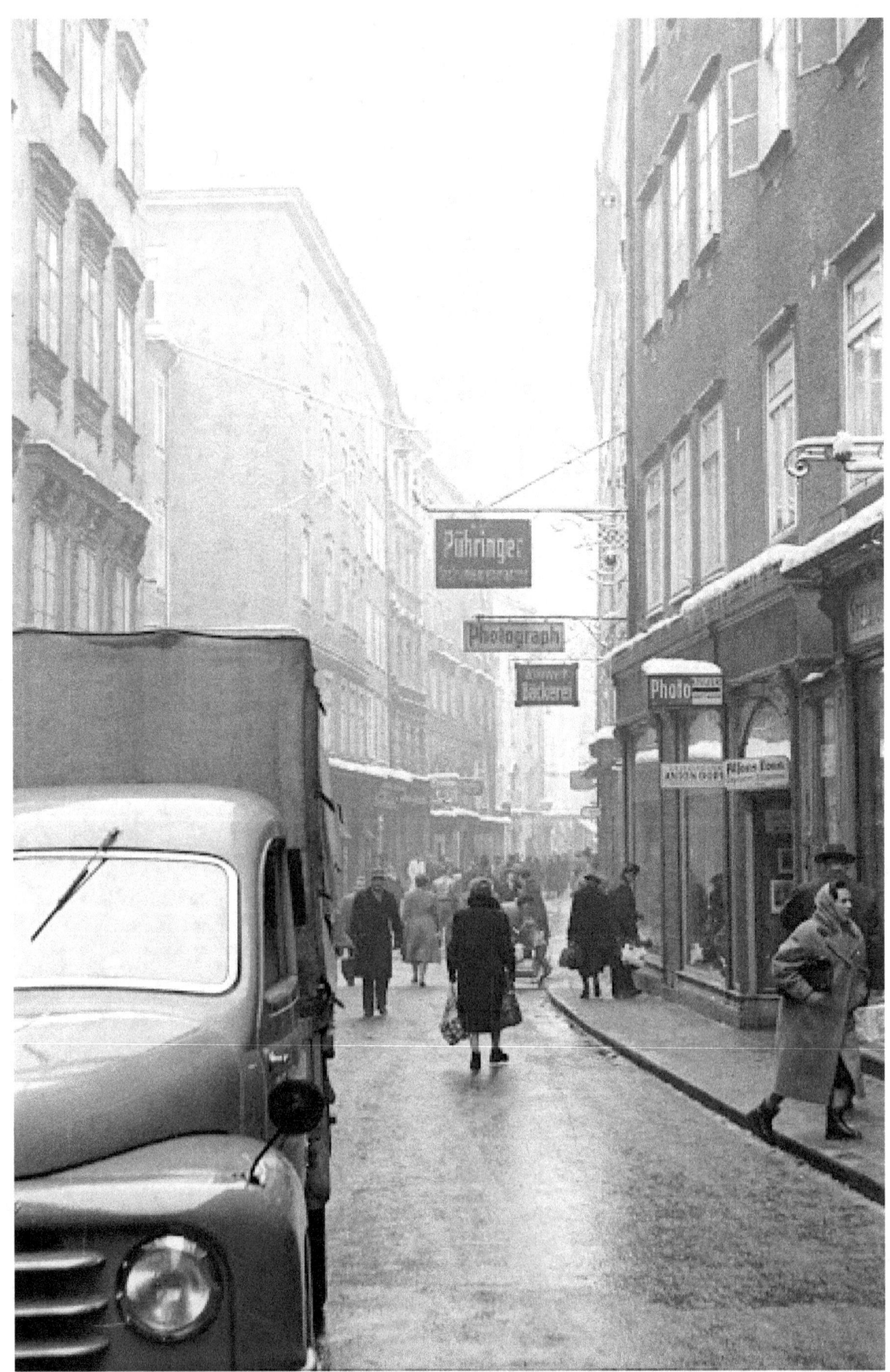
Salzburg, Austria

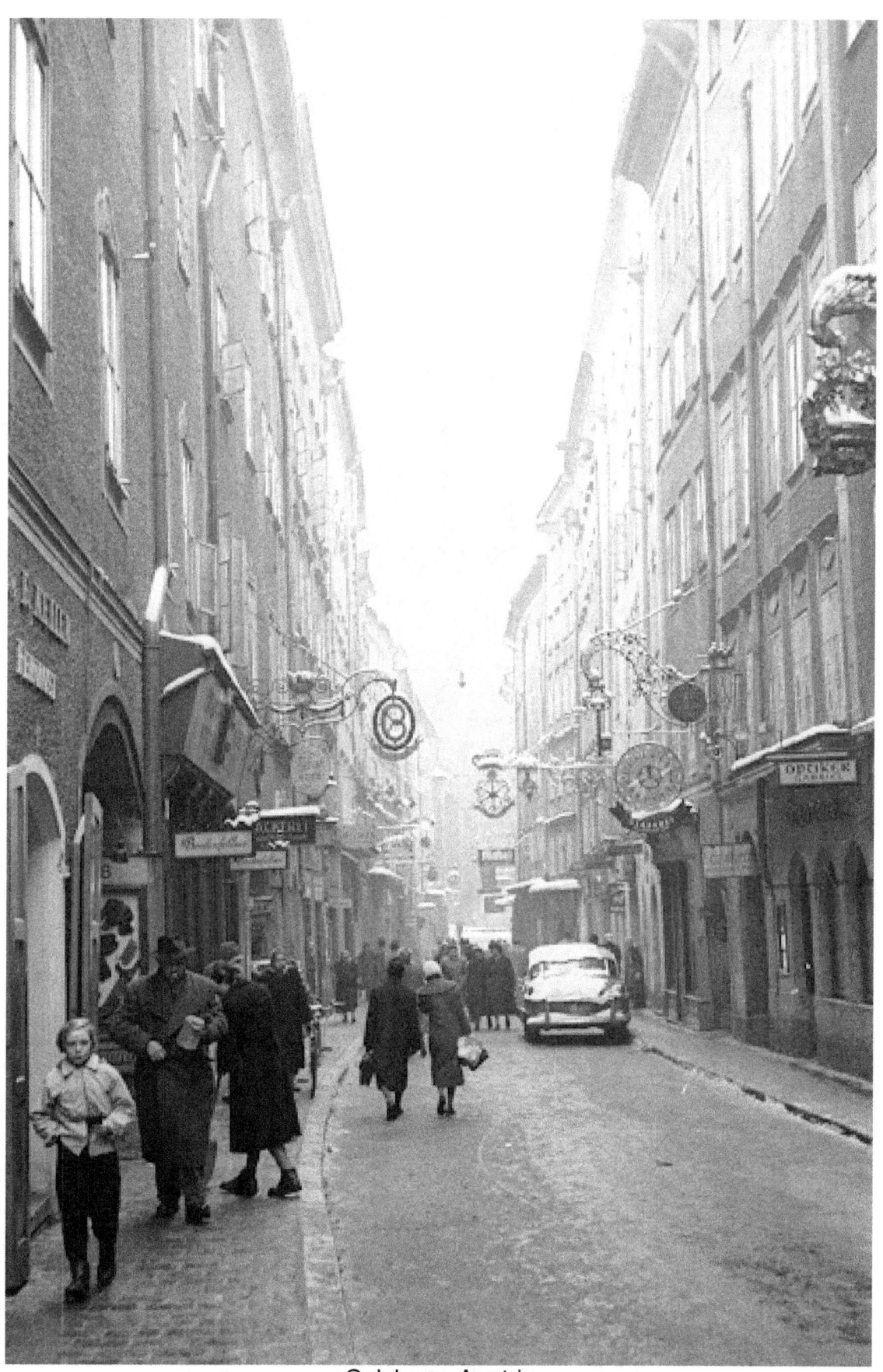
Salzburg, Austria

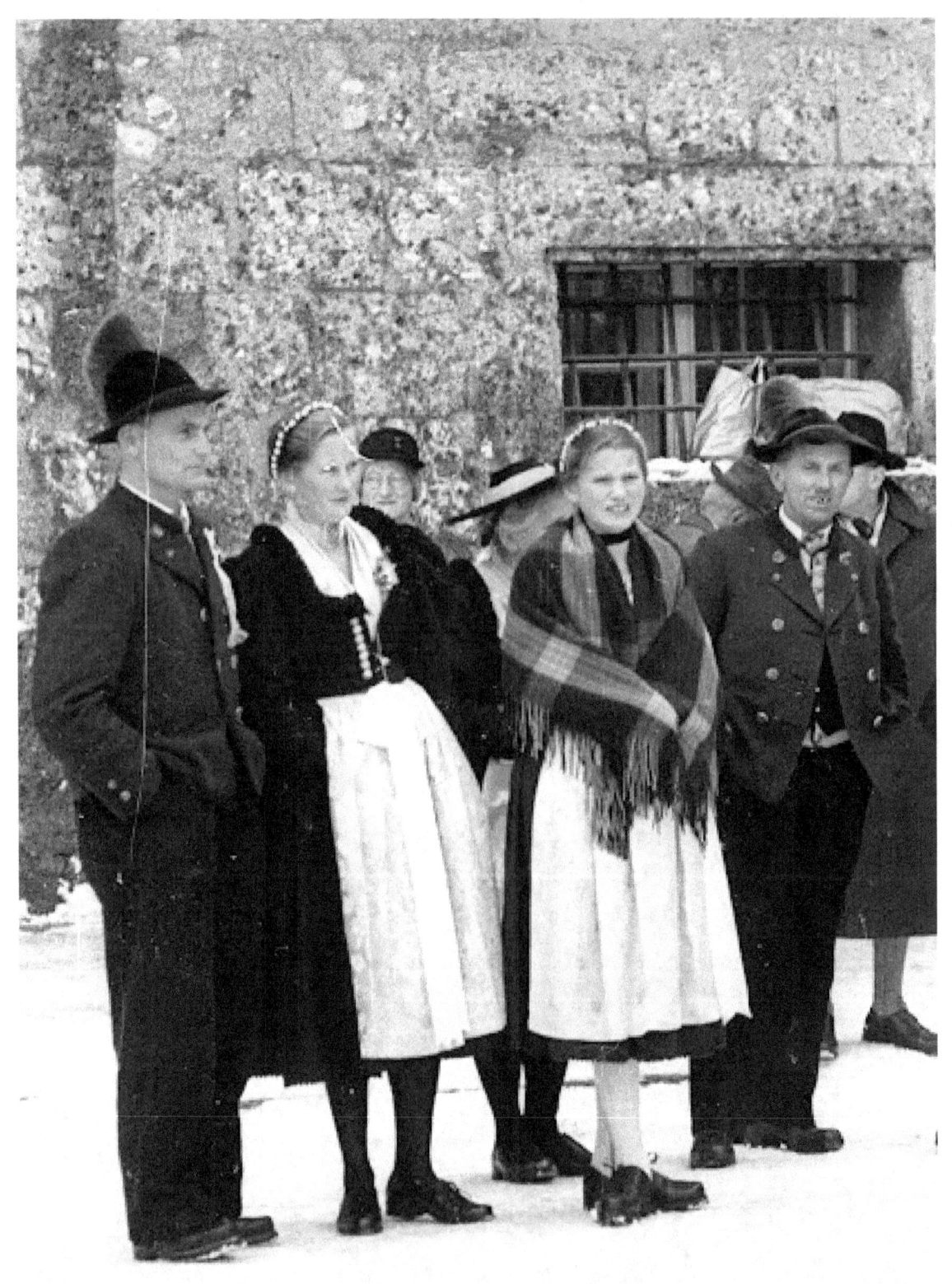
Trachten (folk clothing), Salzburg, Austria

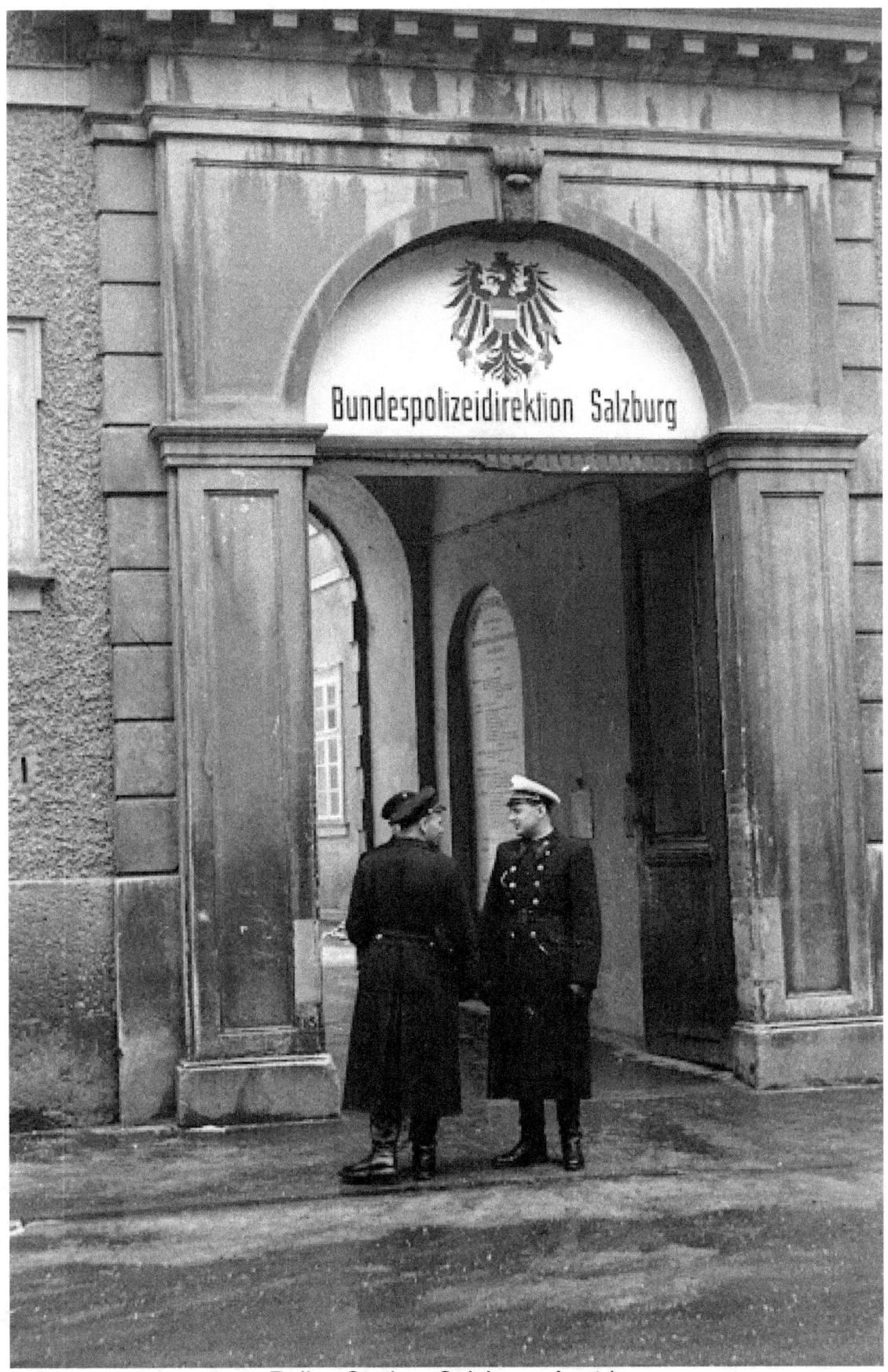

Police Station, Salzburg, Austria

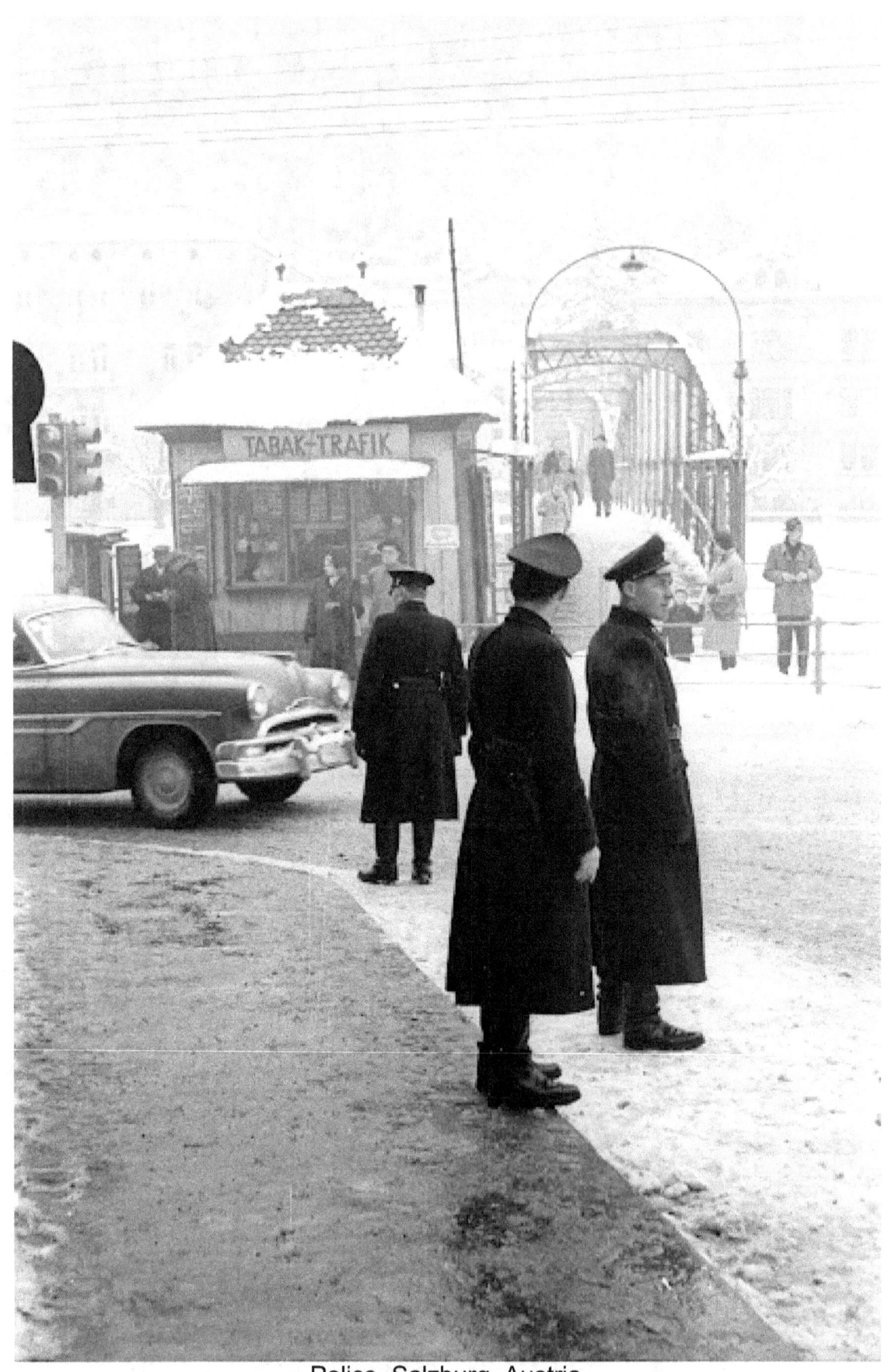

Police, Salzburg, Austria

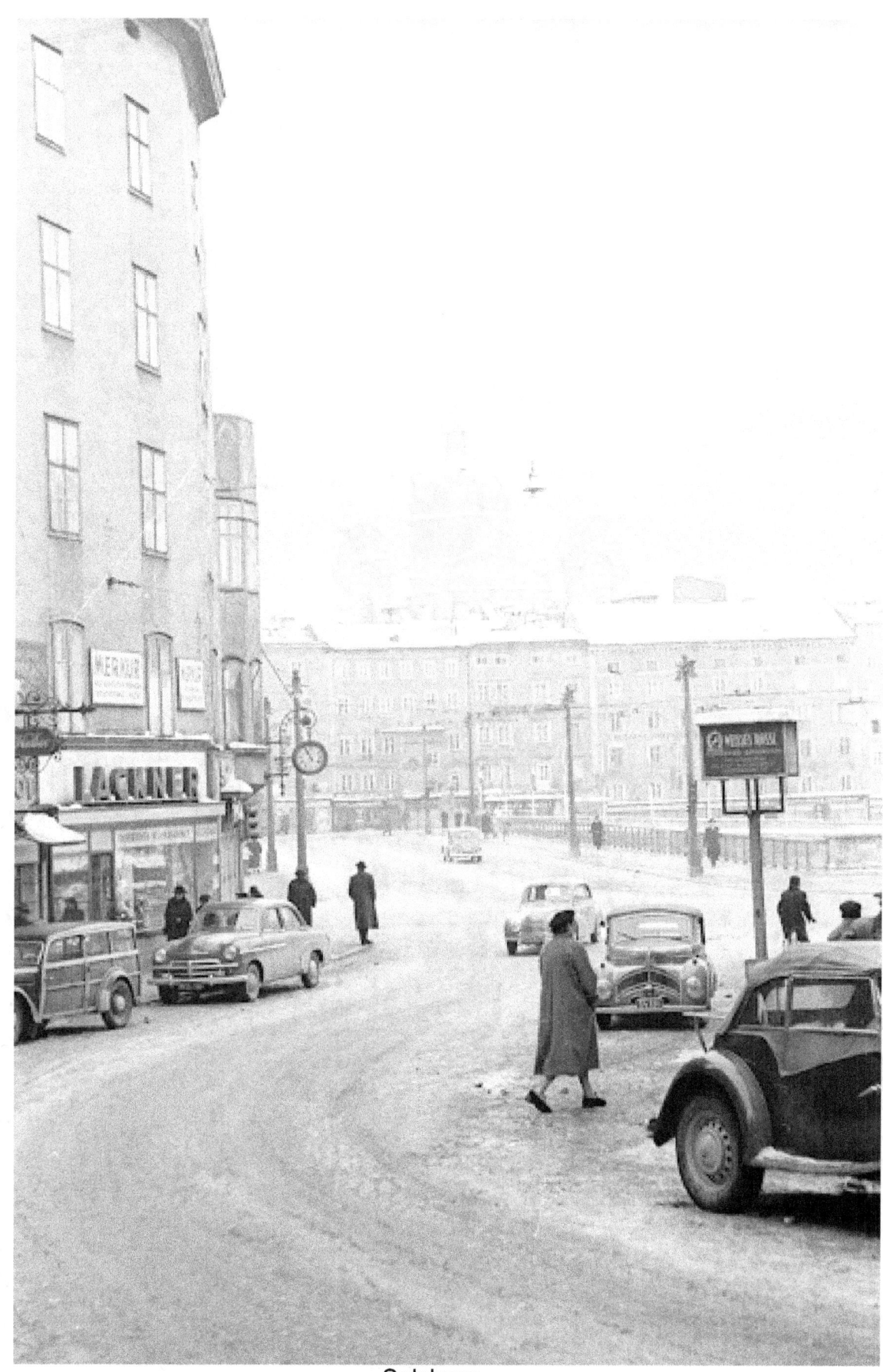

Salzburg

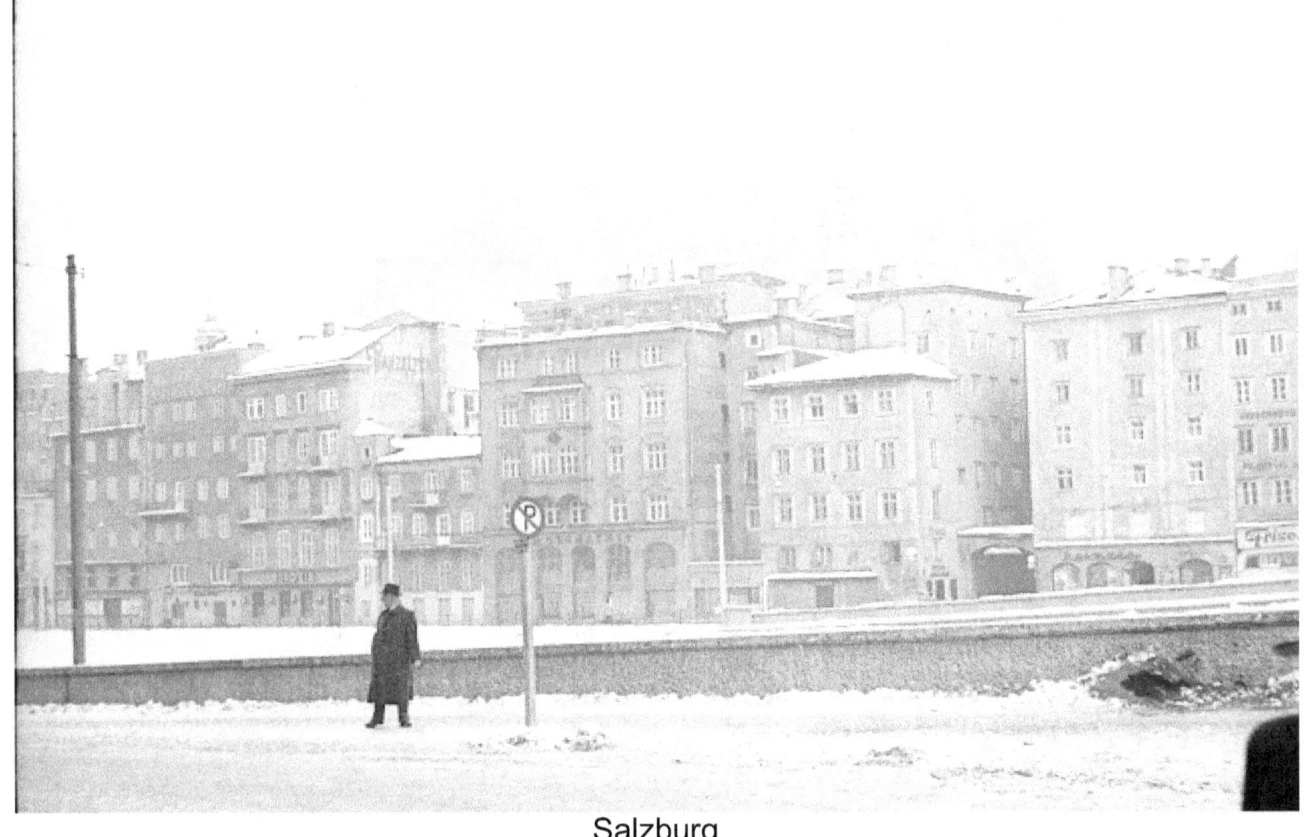
Salzburg

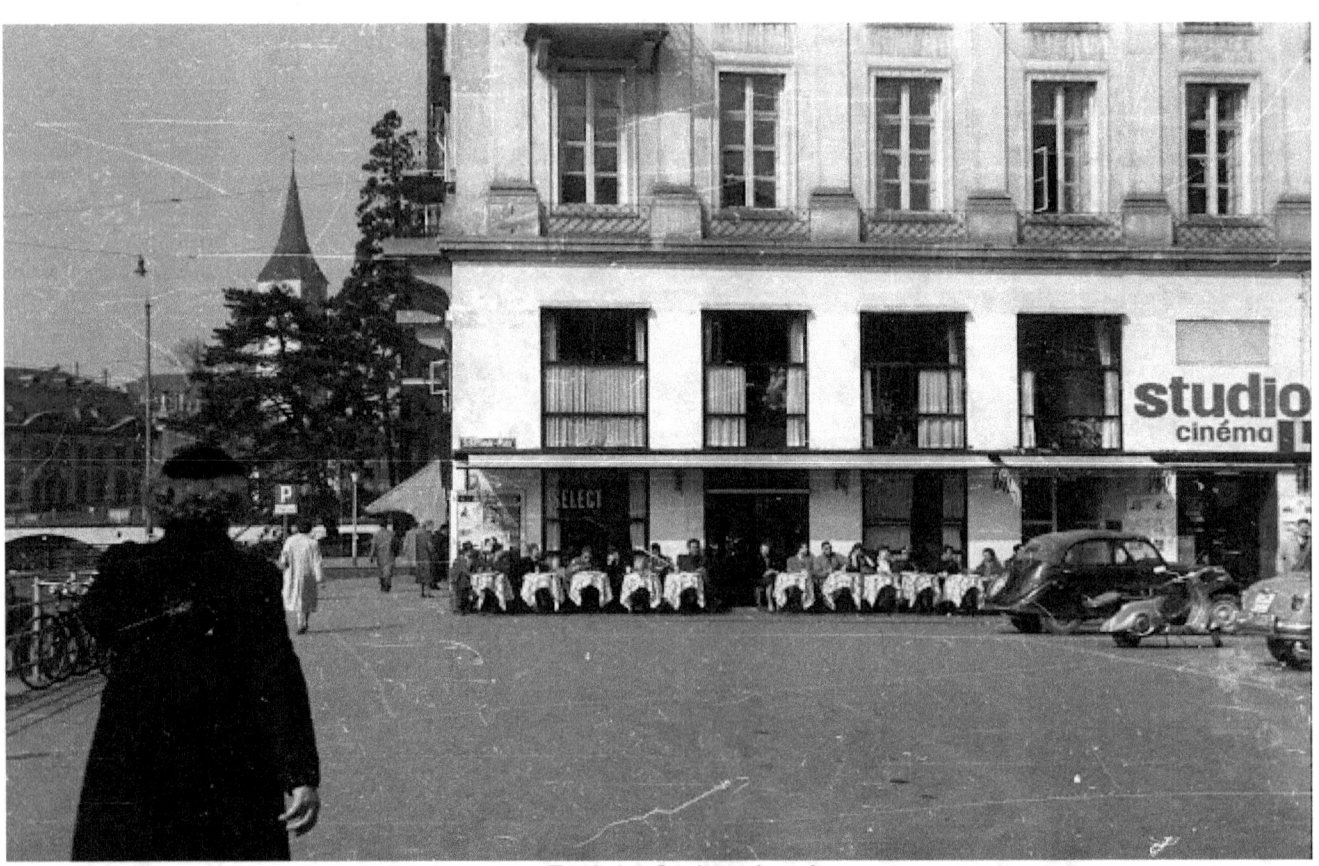
Zurich, Switzerland

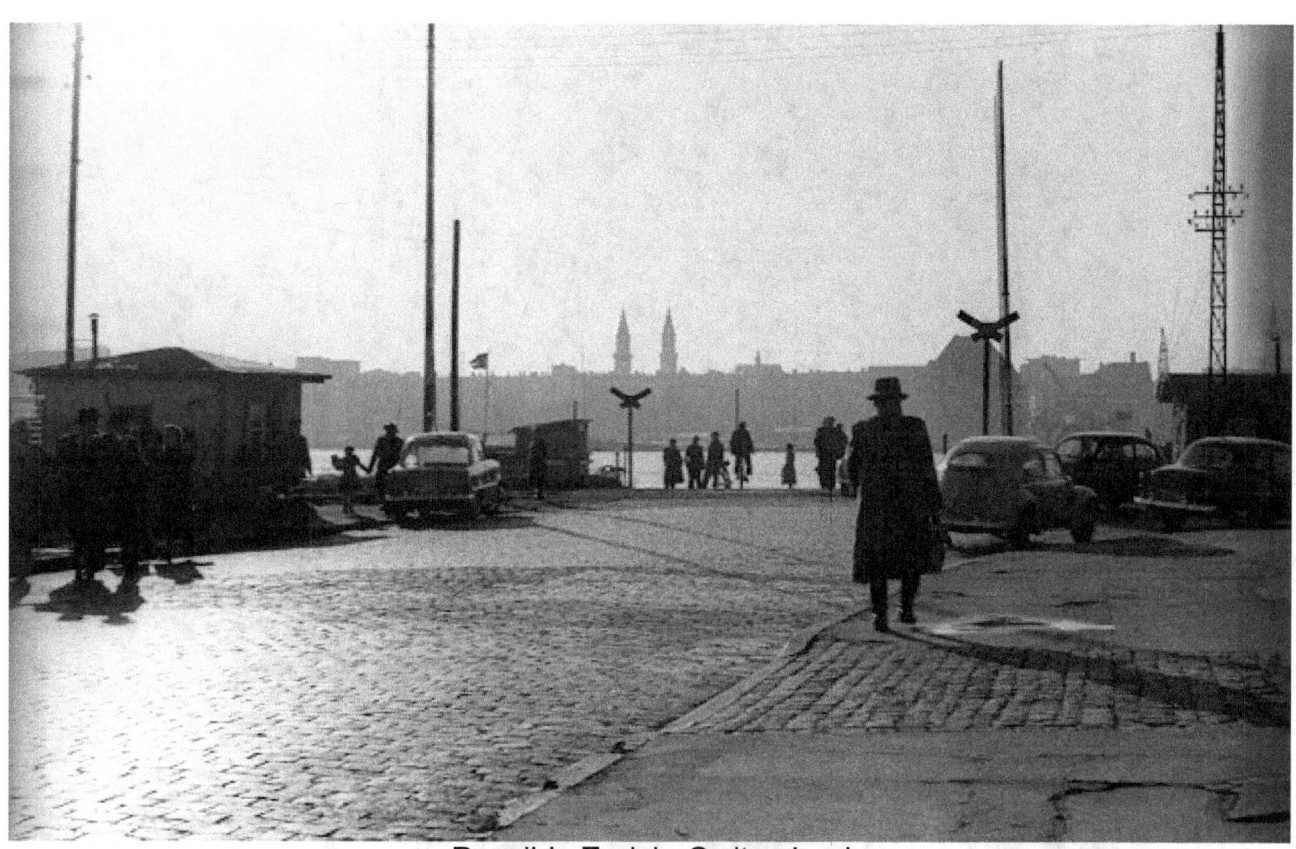
Possibly Zurich, Switzerland

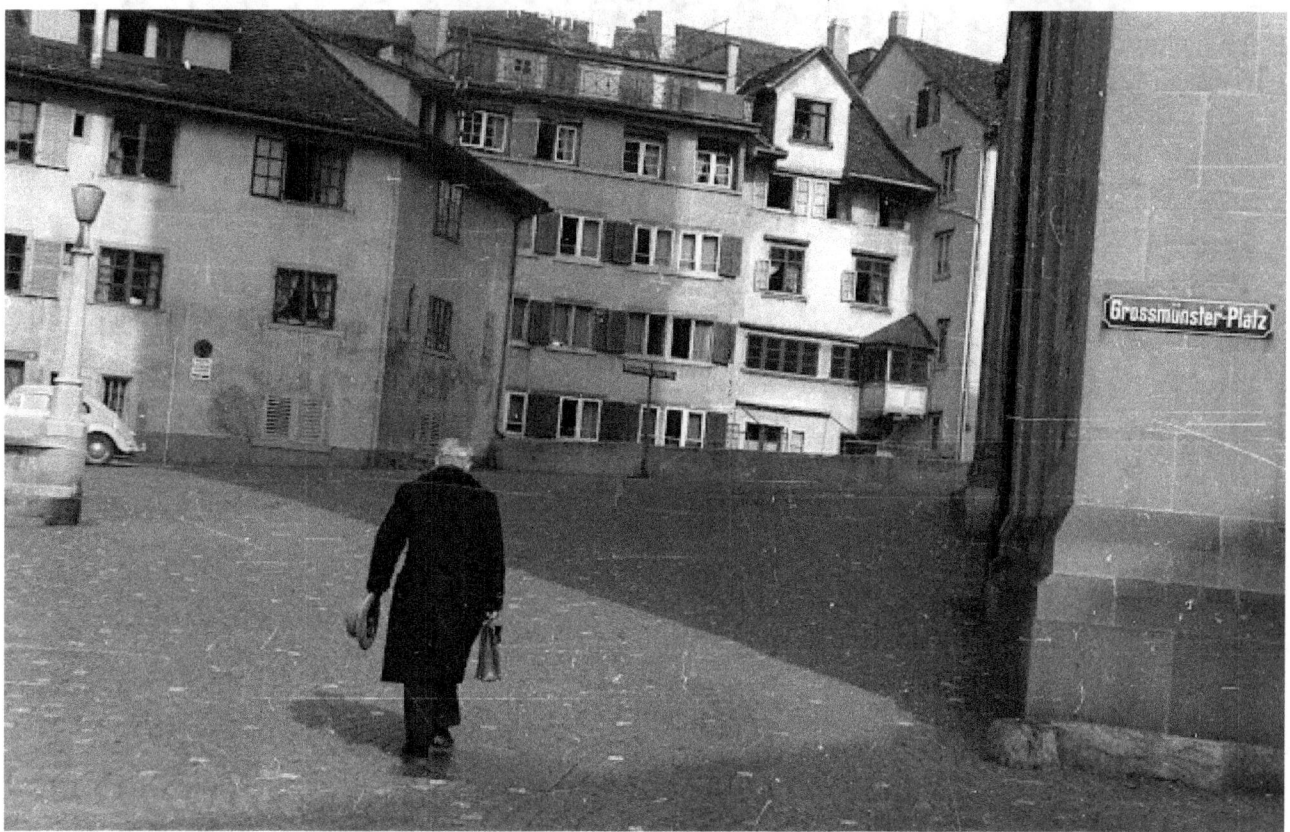
Grossmuenster-Platz Zurich, Switzerland

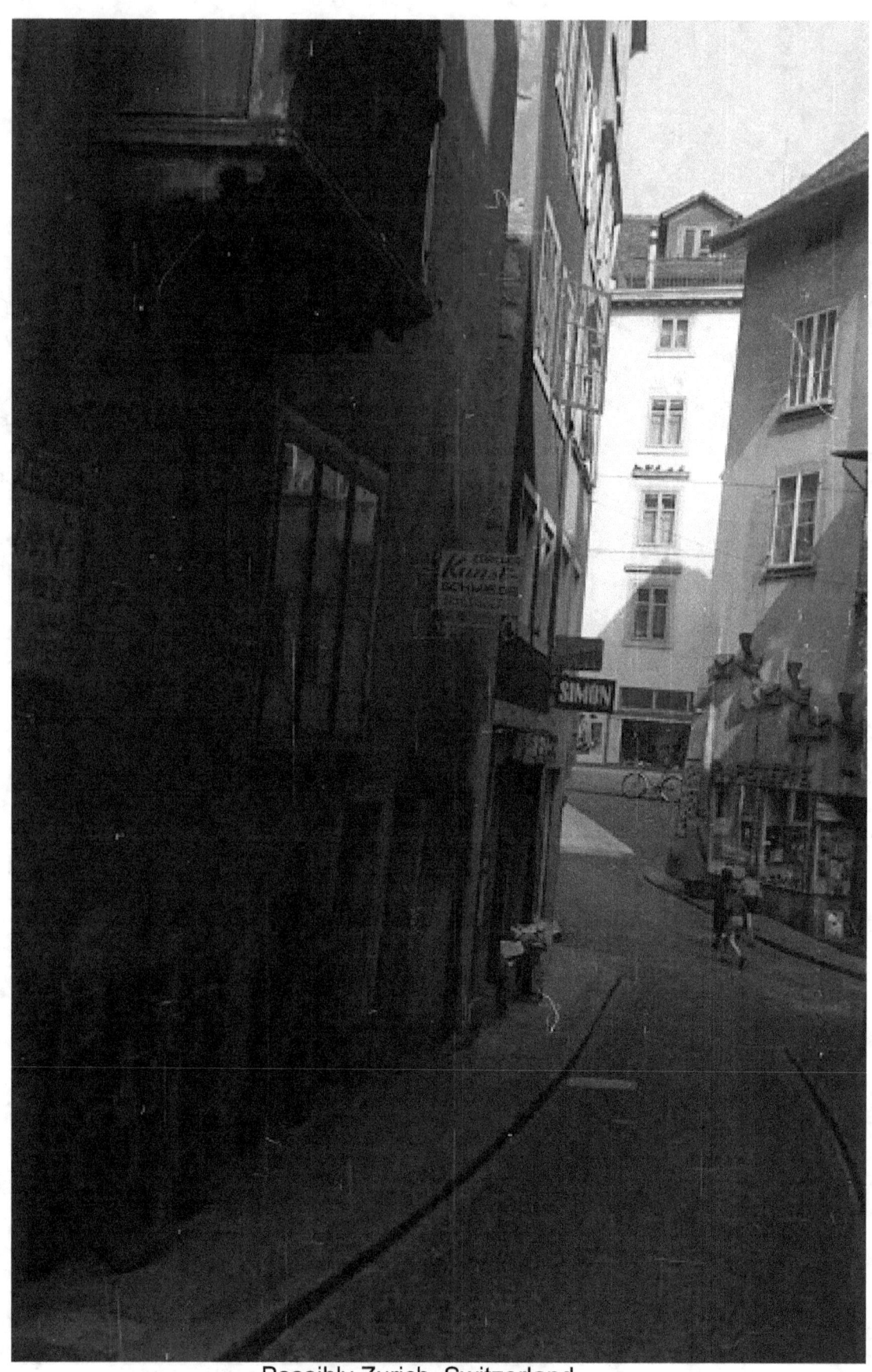
Possibly Zurich, Switzerland

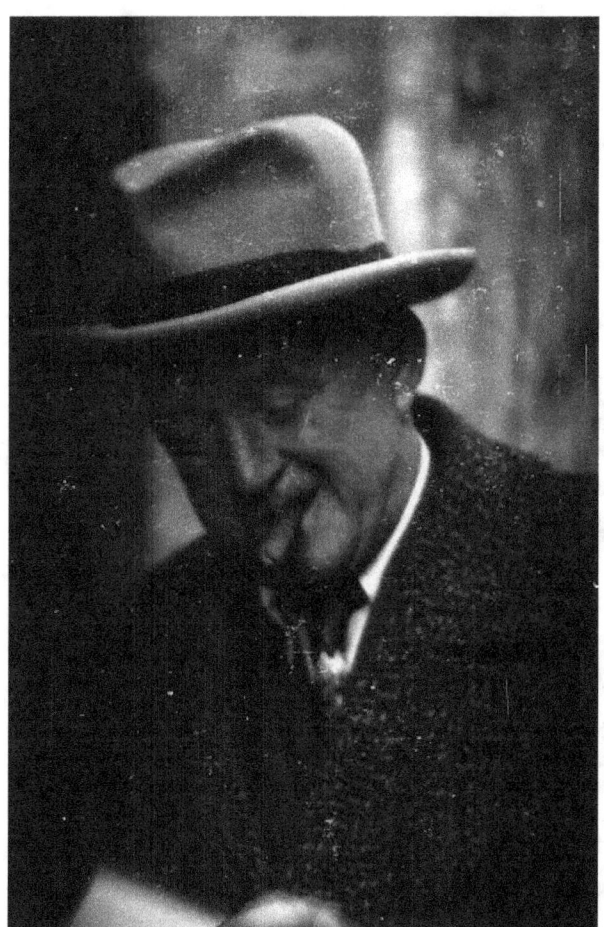
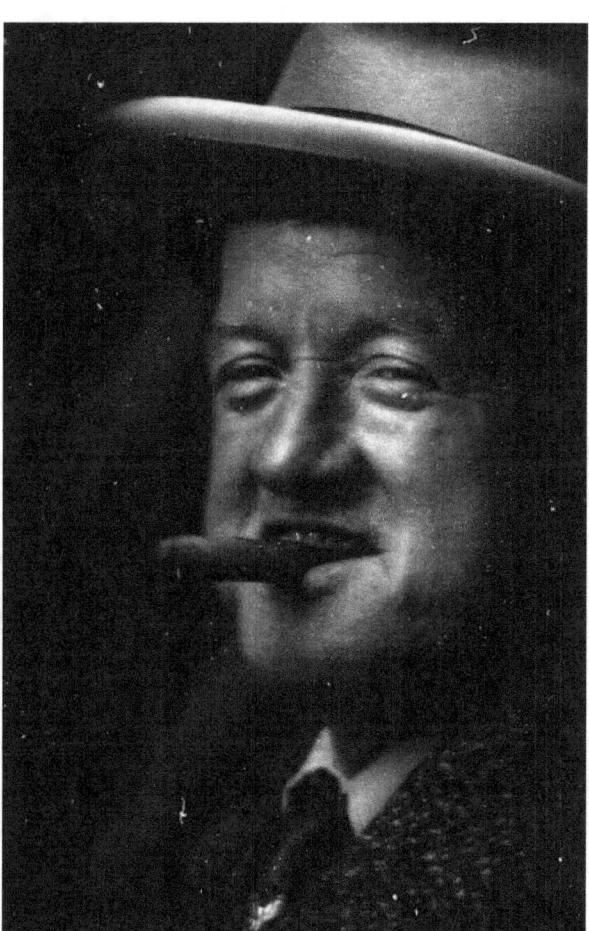

Man with cigar

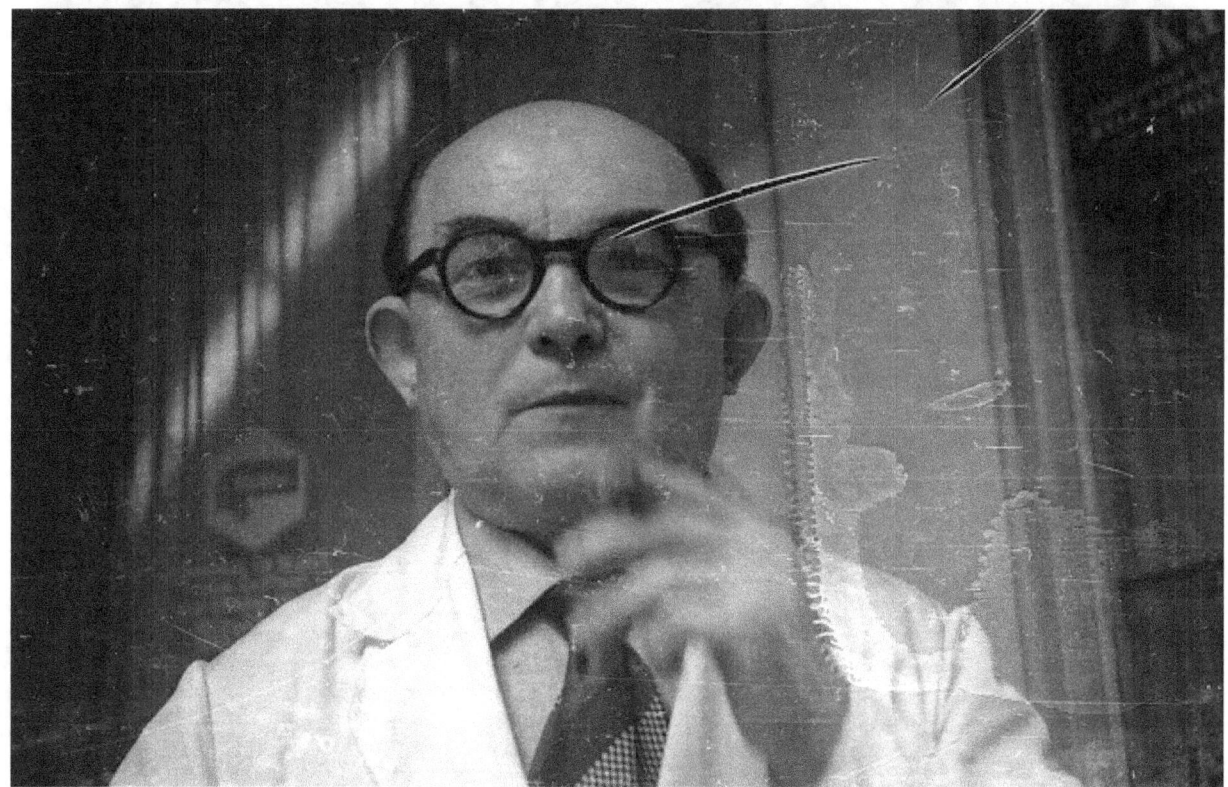

Man in lab coat with cigar

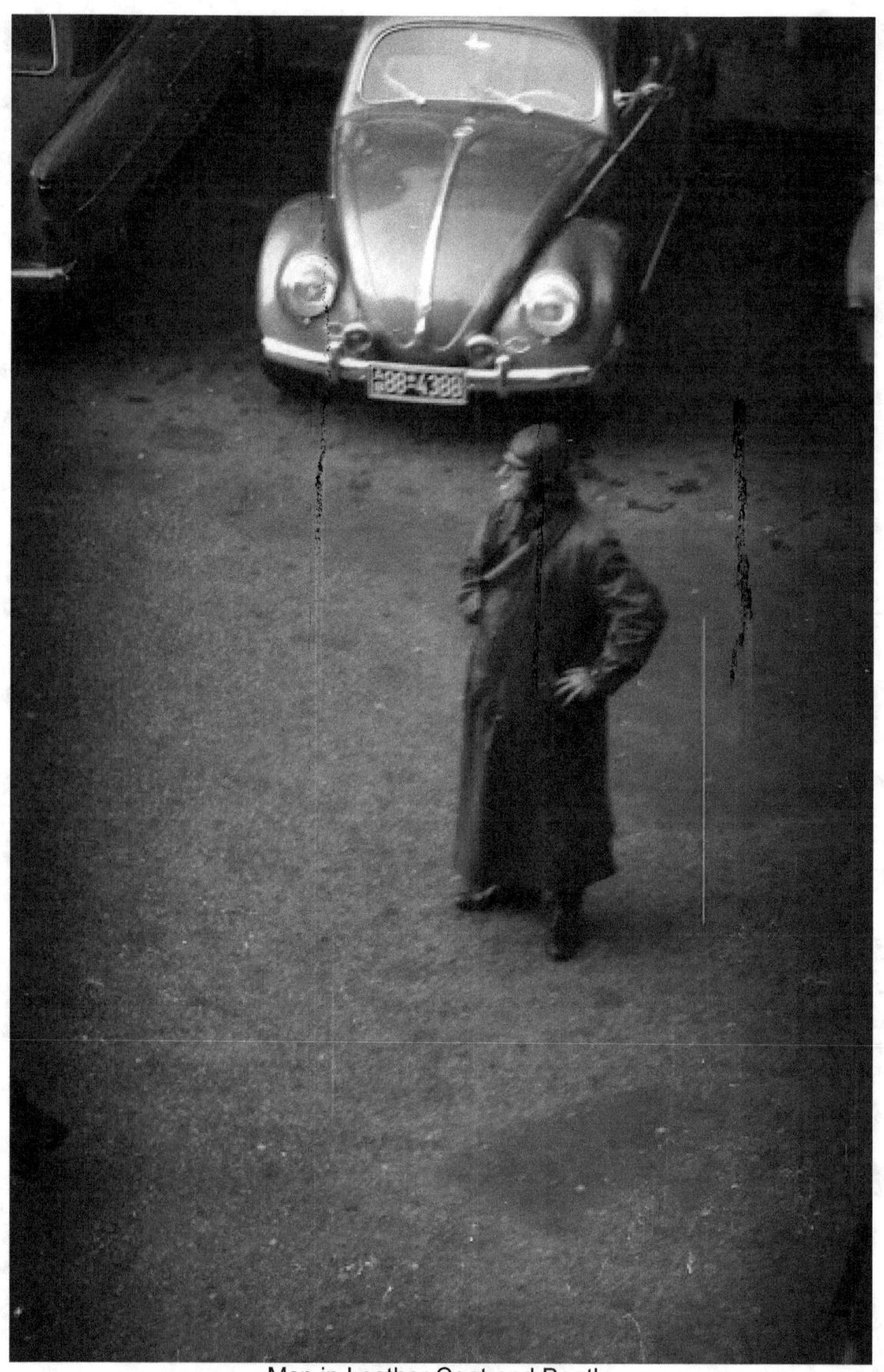

Man in Leather Coat and Beetle

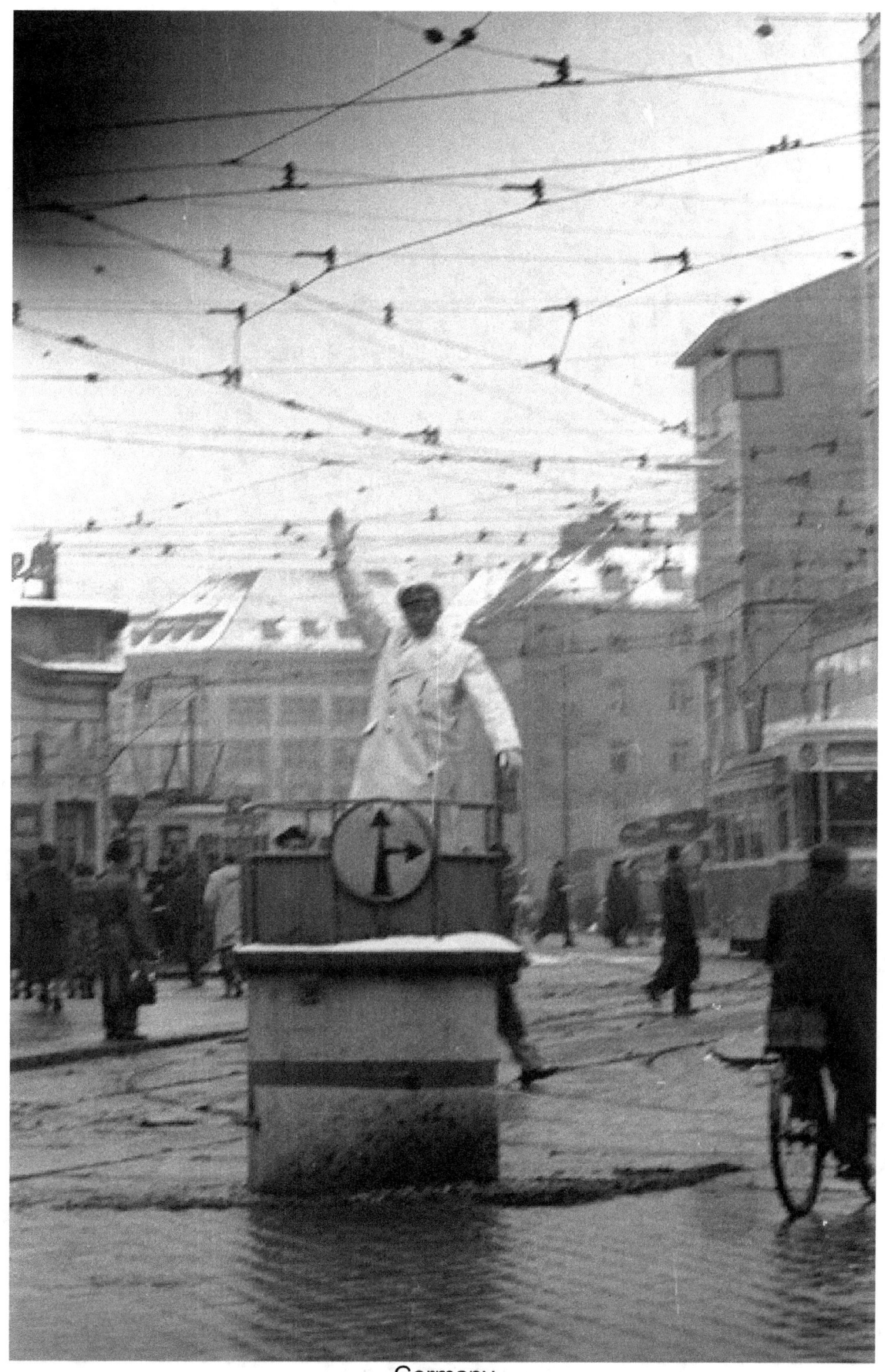

Germany

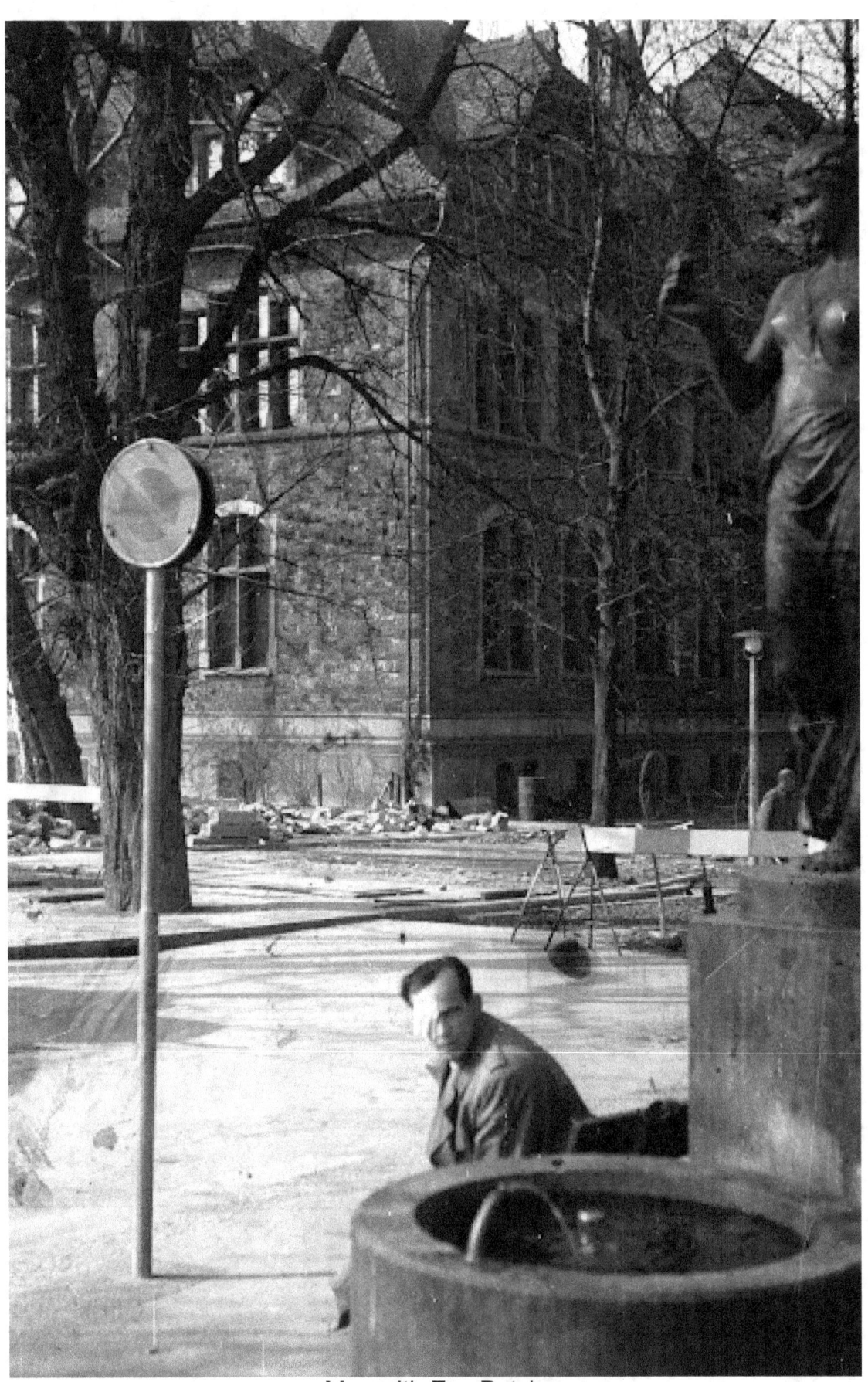
Man with Eye Patch

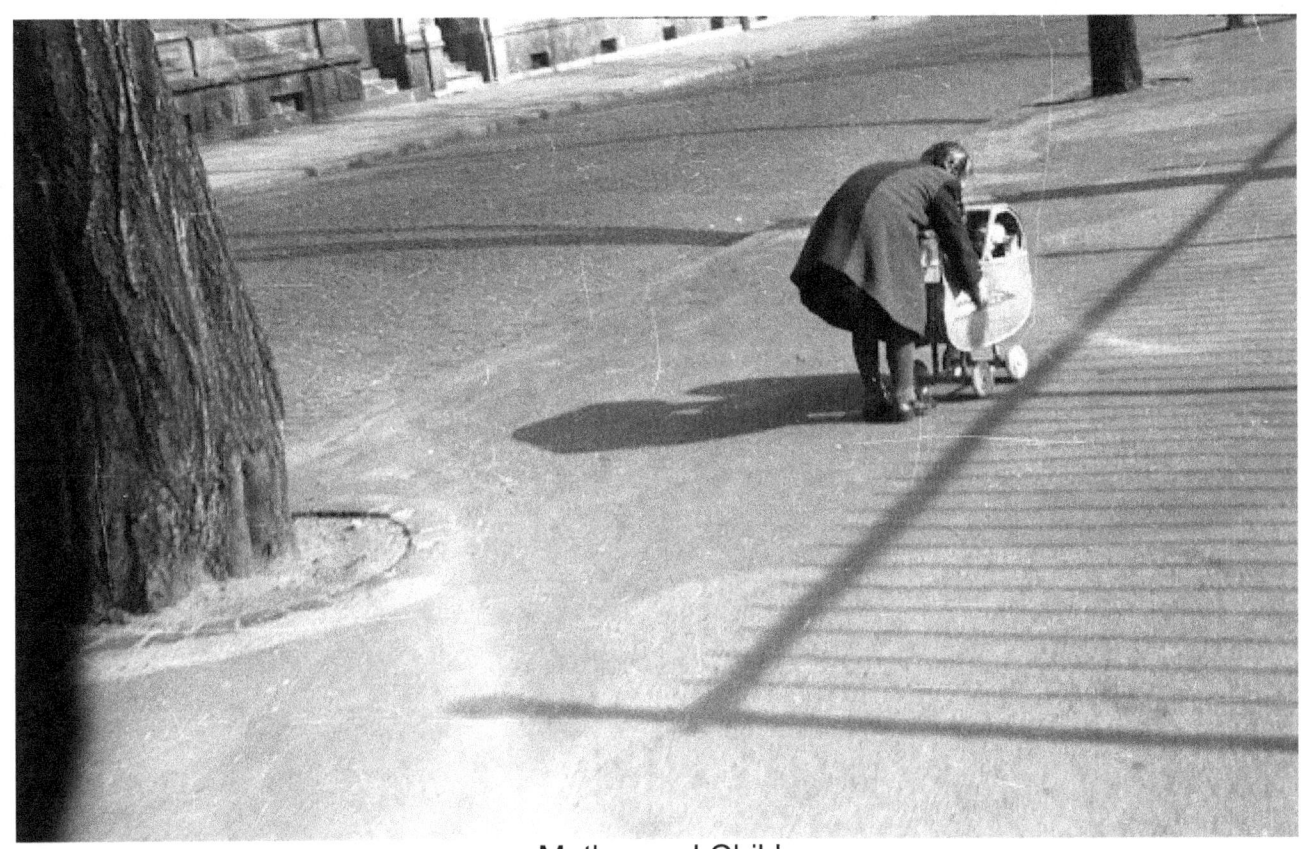
Mother and Child

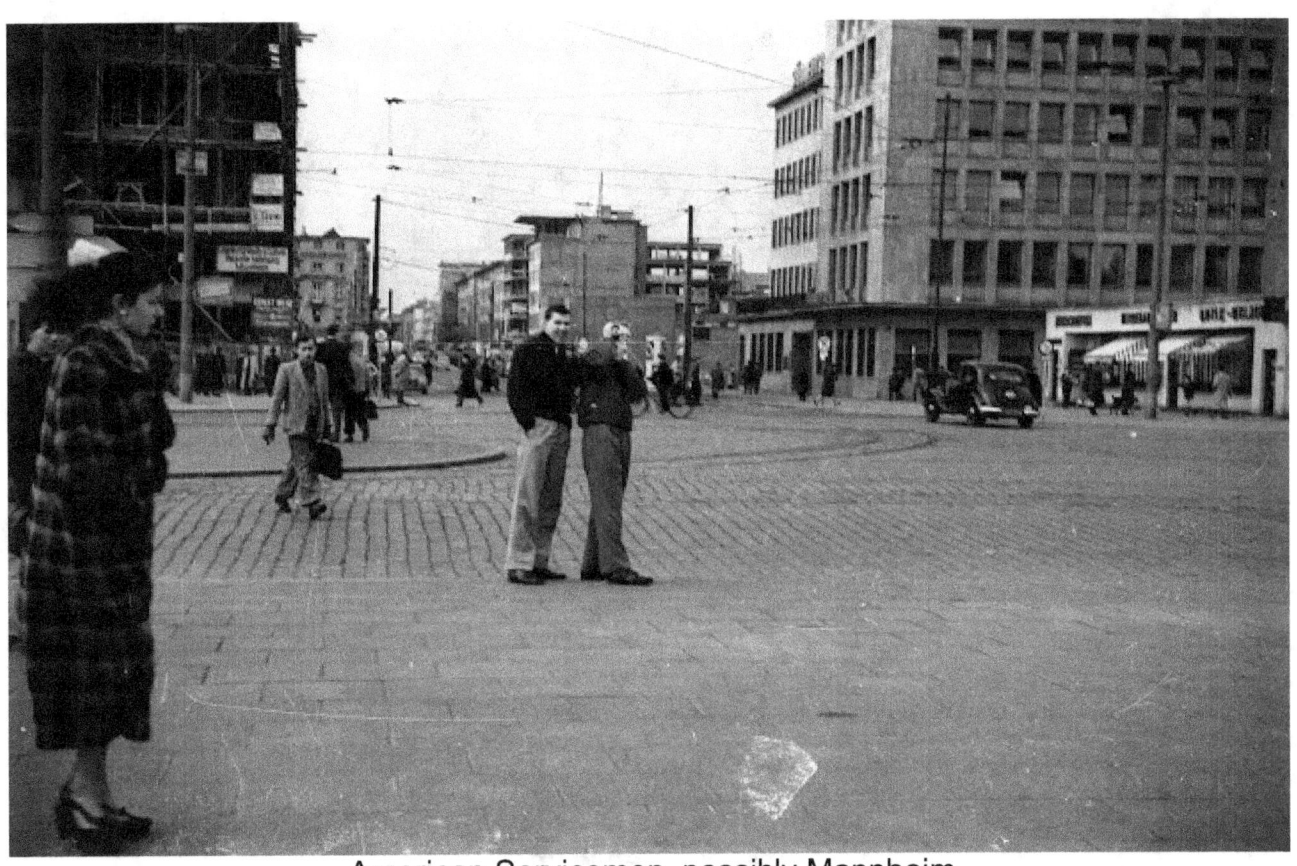
American Servicemen, possibly Mannheim

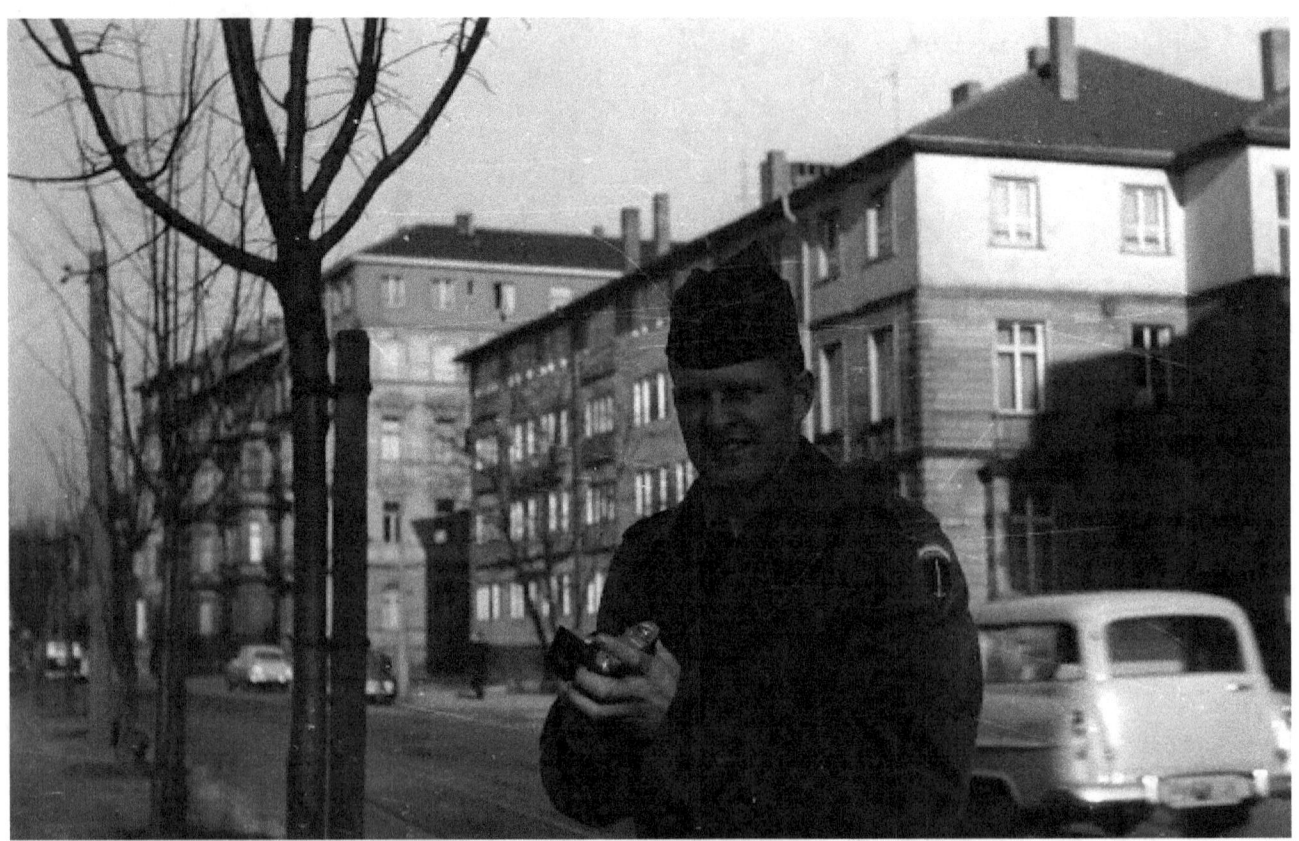
American Serviceman

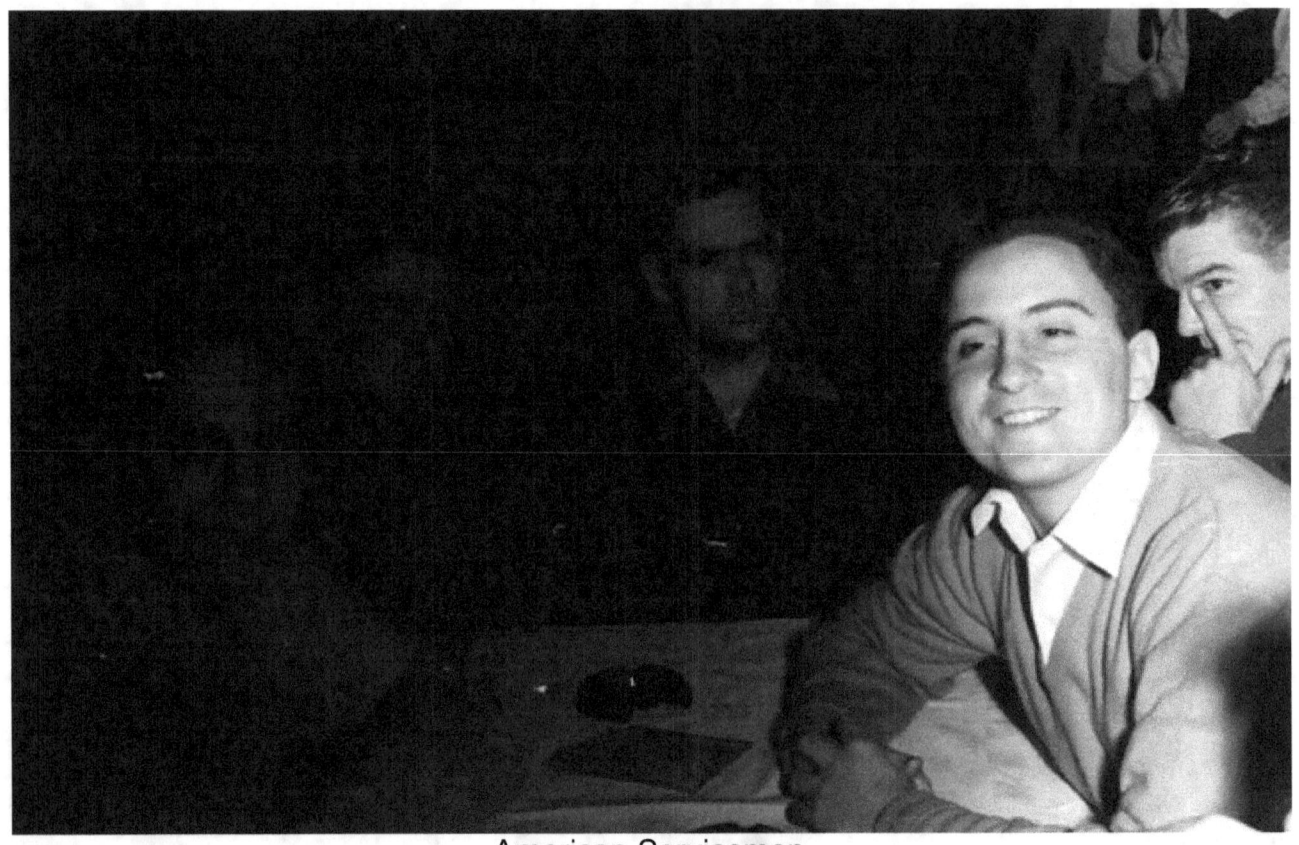
American Servicemen

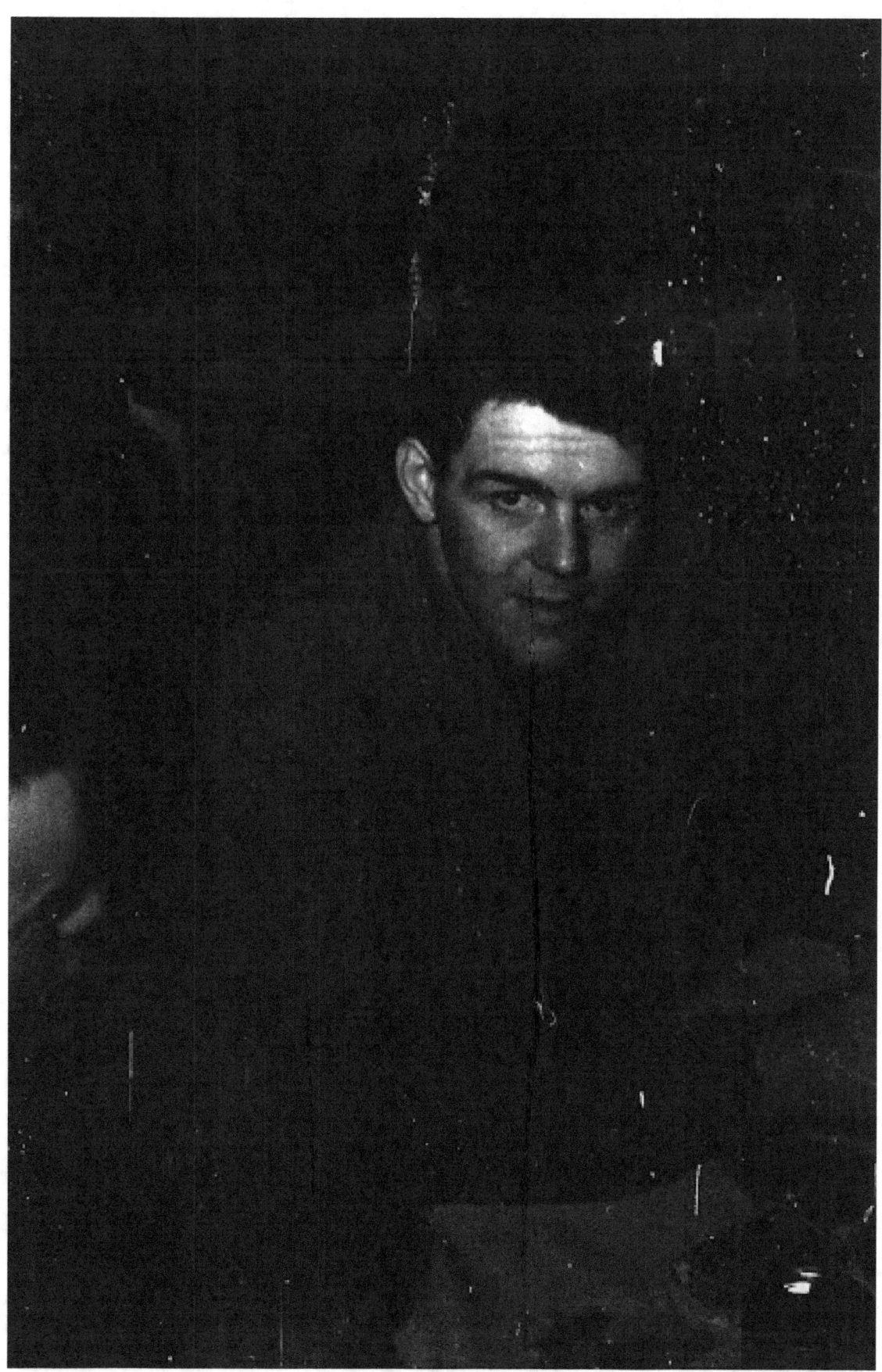
American Serviceman

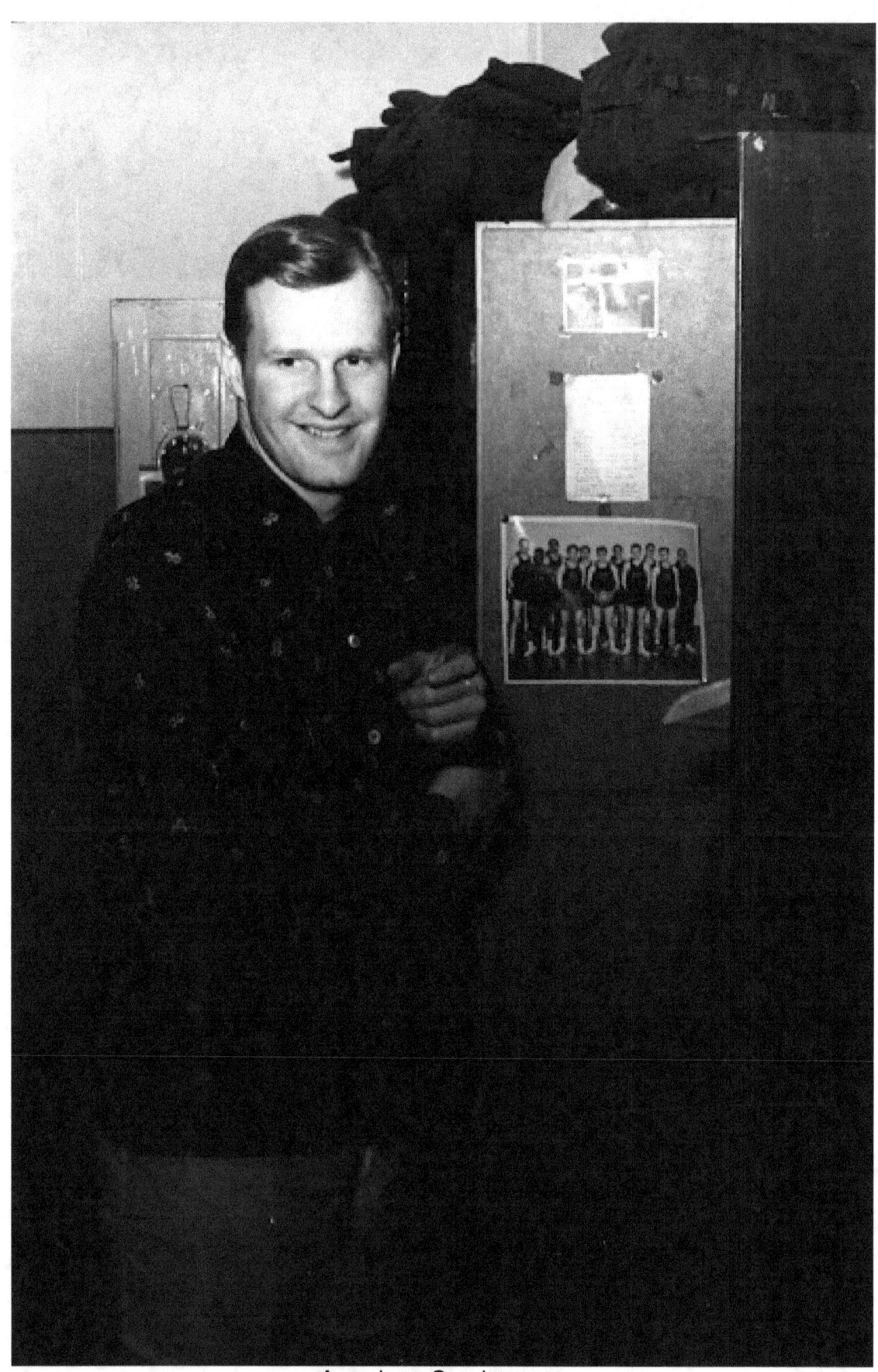

American Serviceman

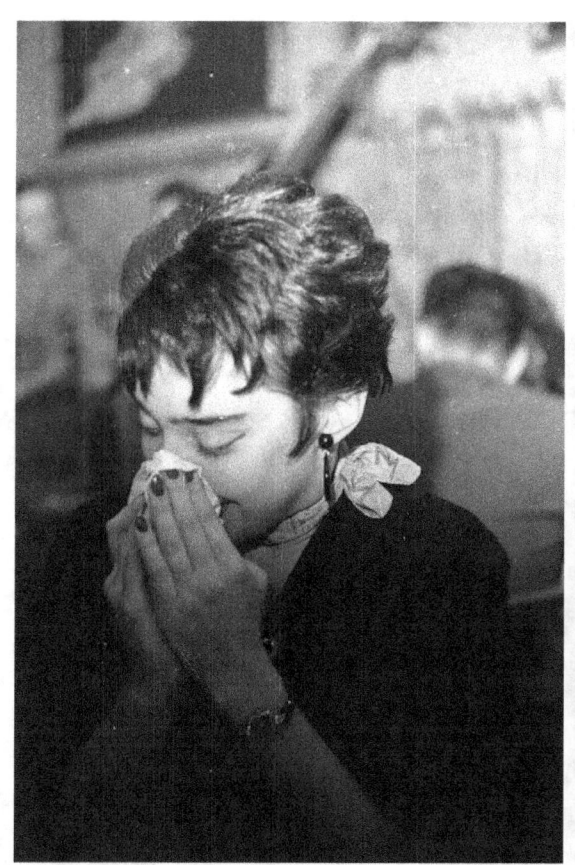
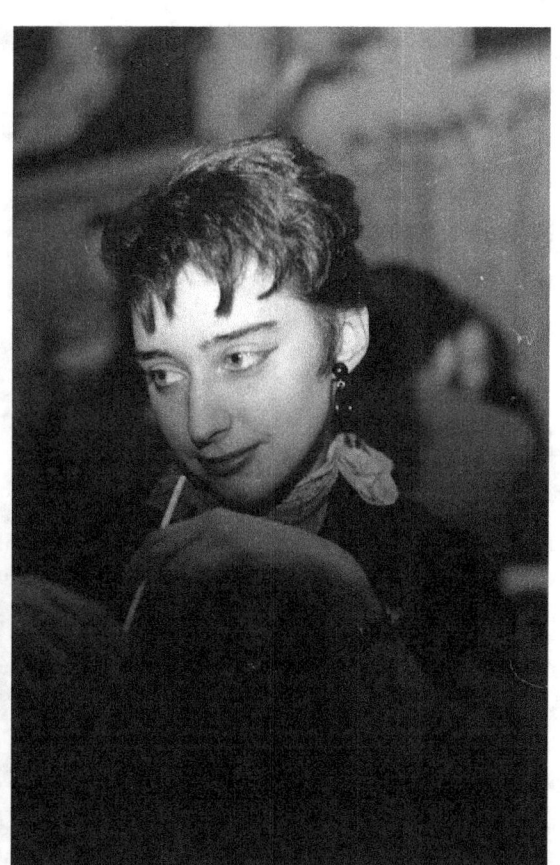

Singer

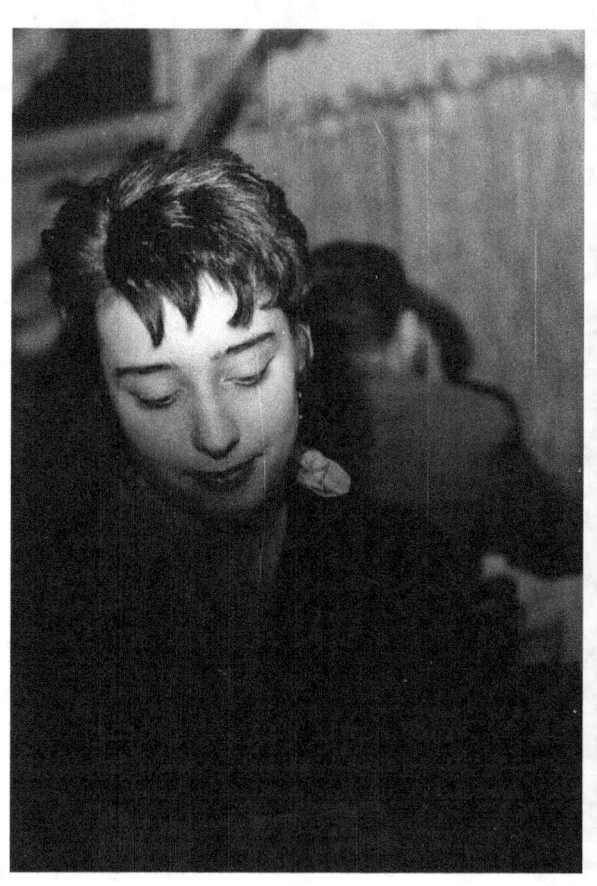
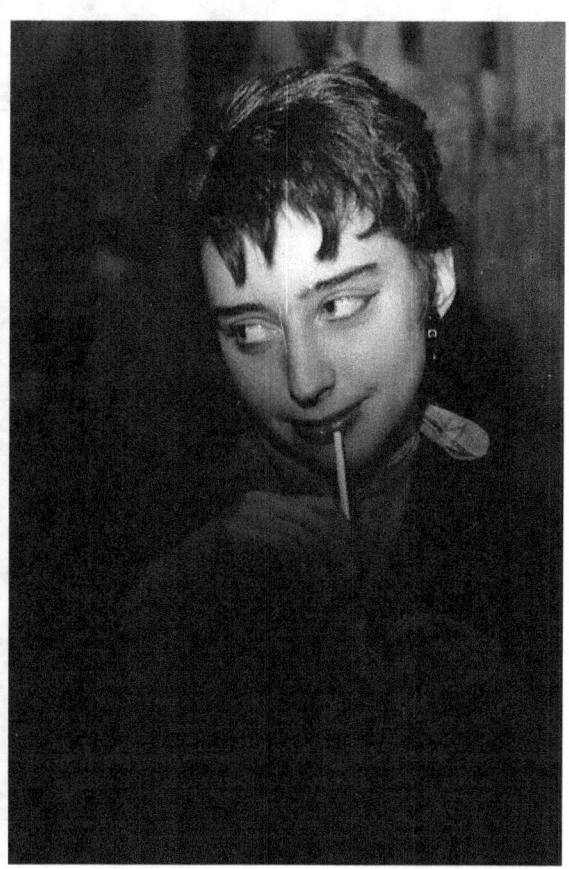

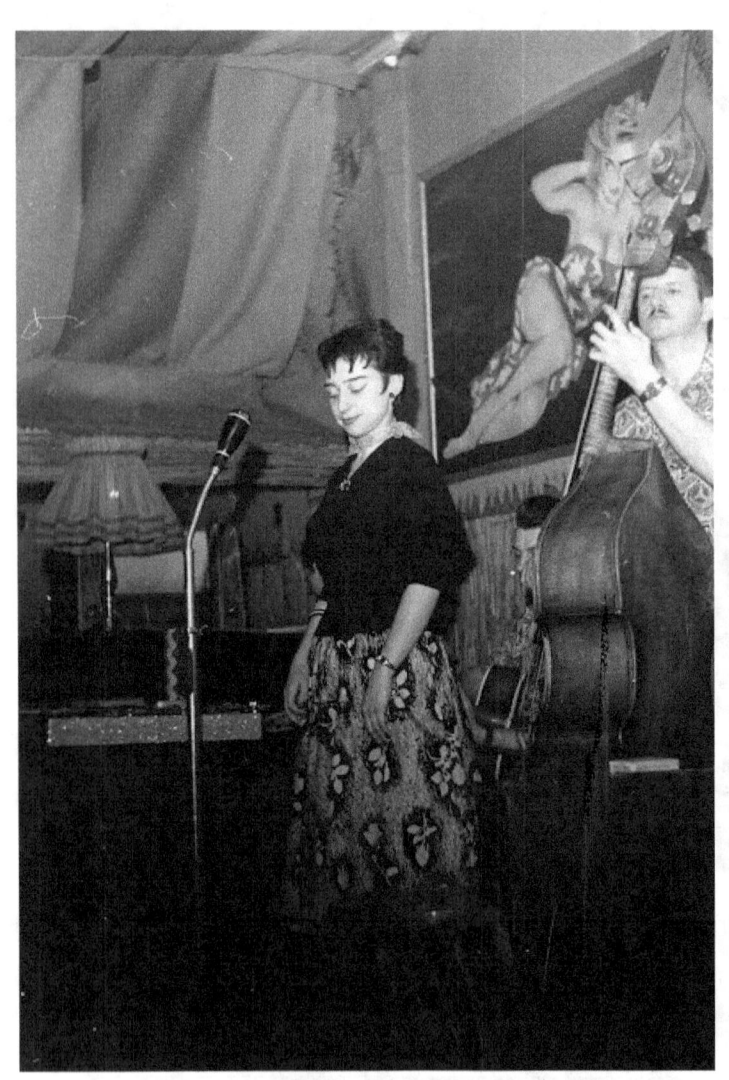 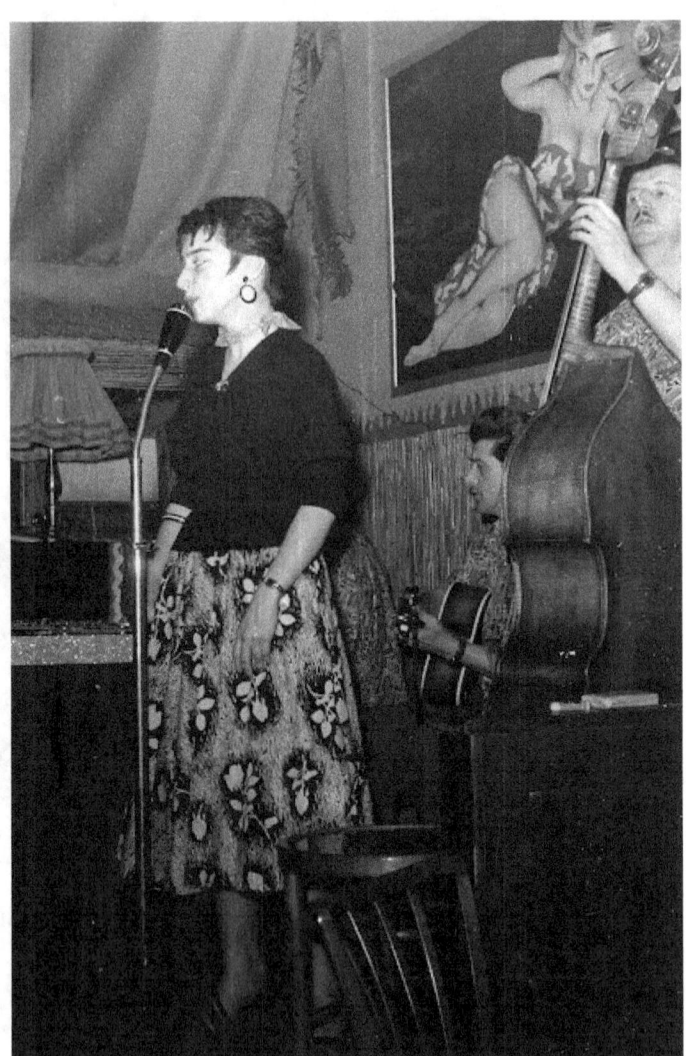

Singer

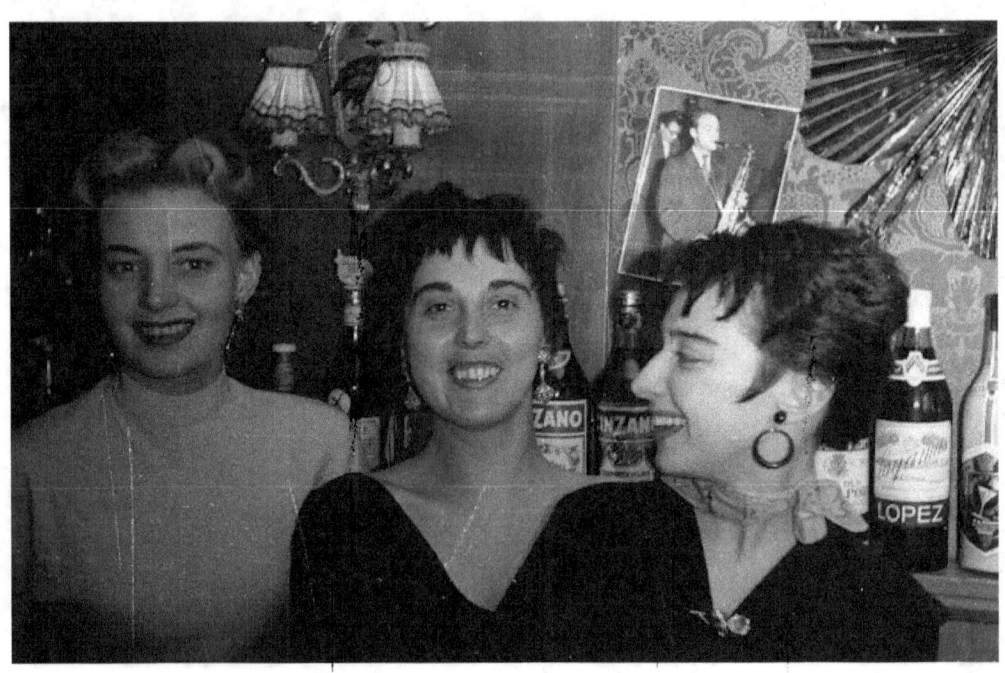

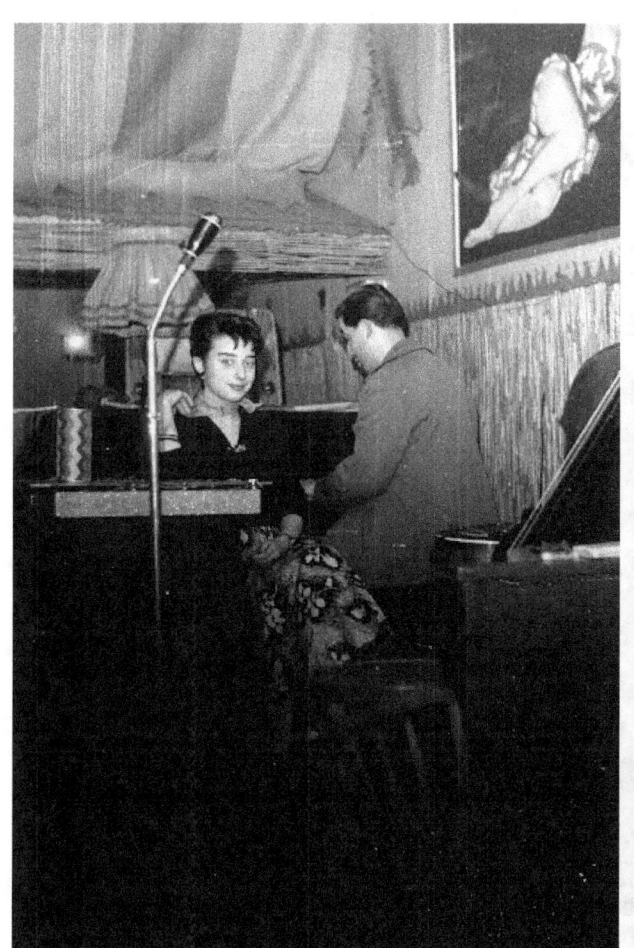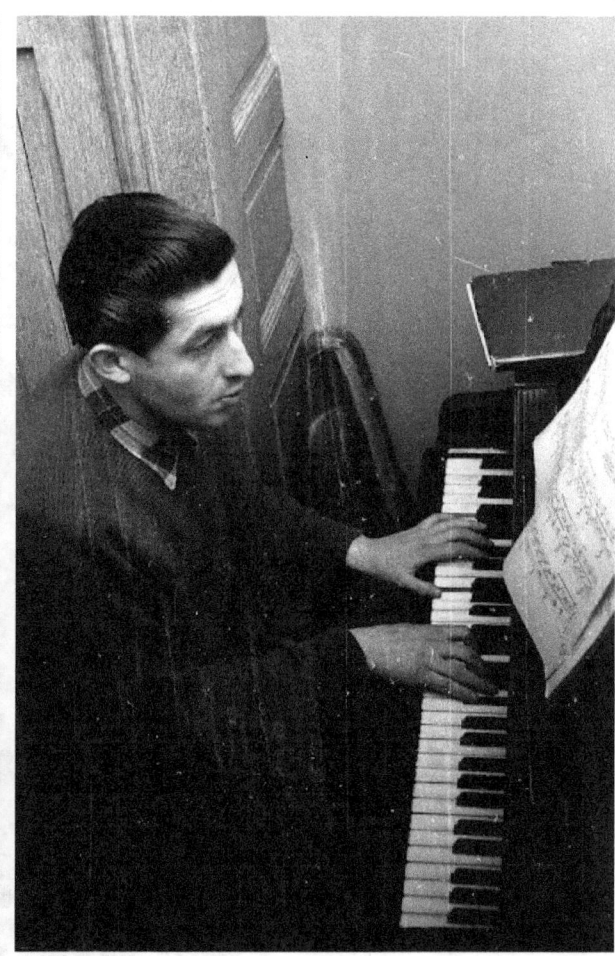

Singer and Pianist

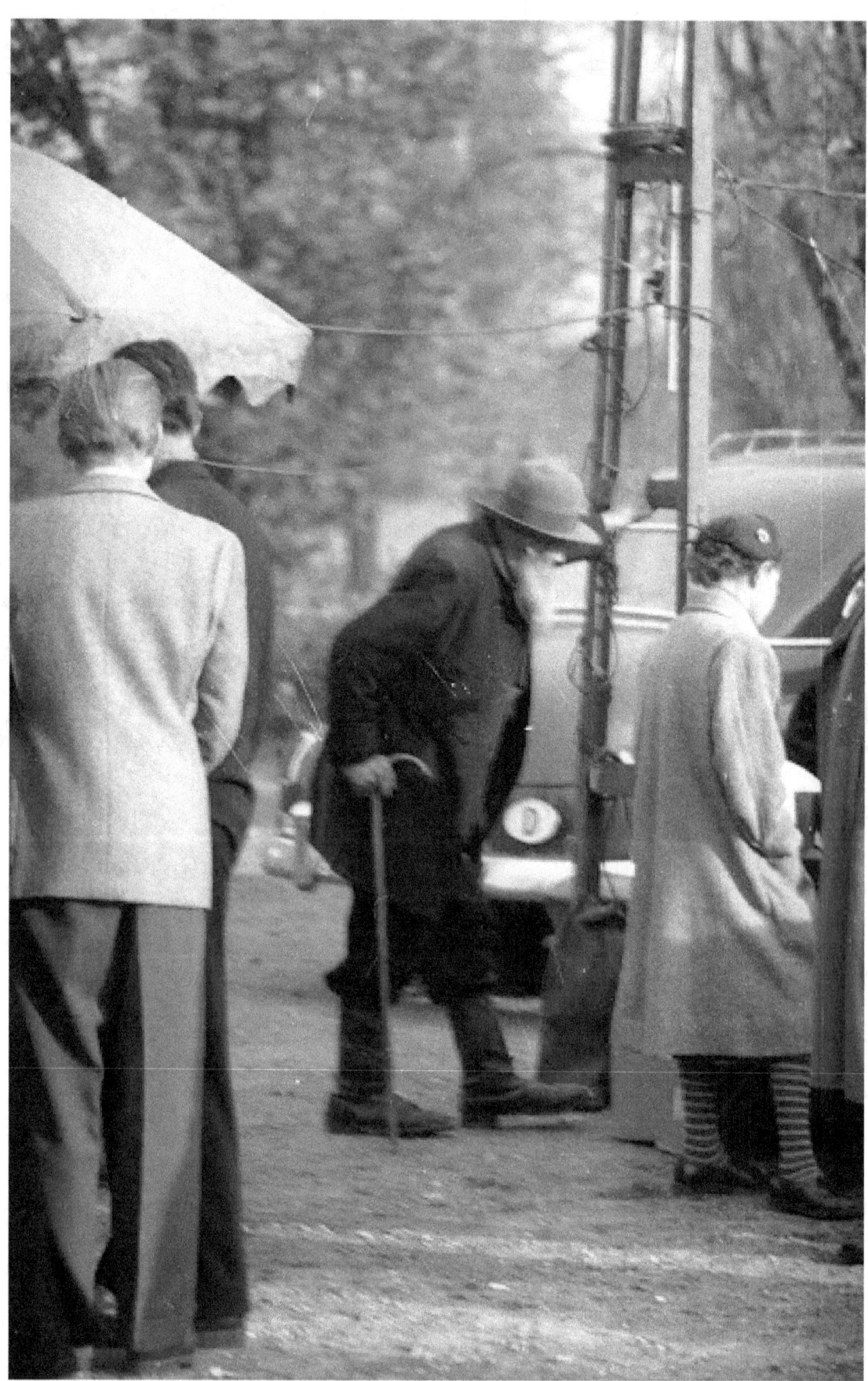
Man with Cane

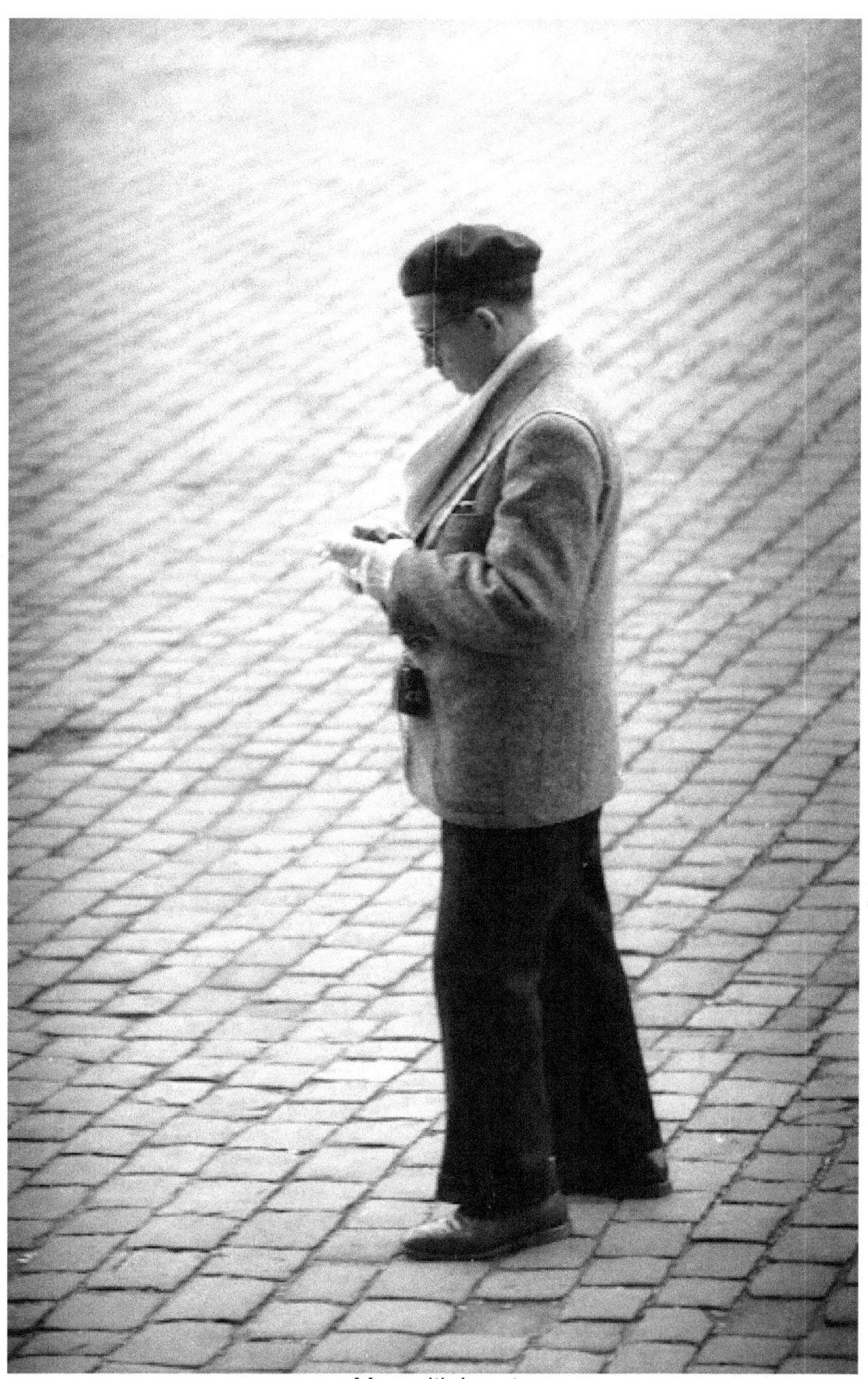

Man with beret

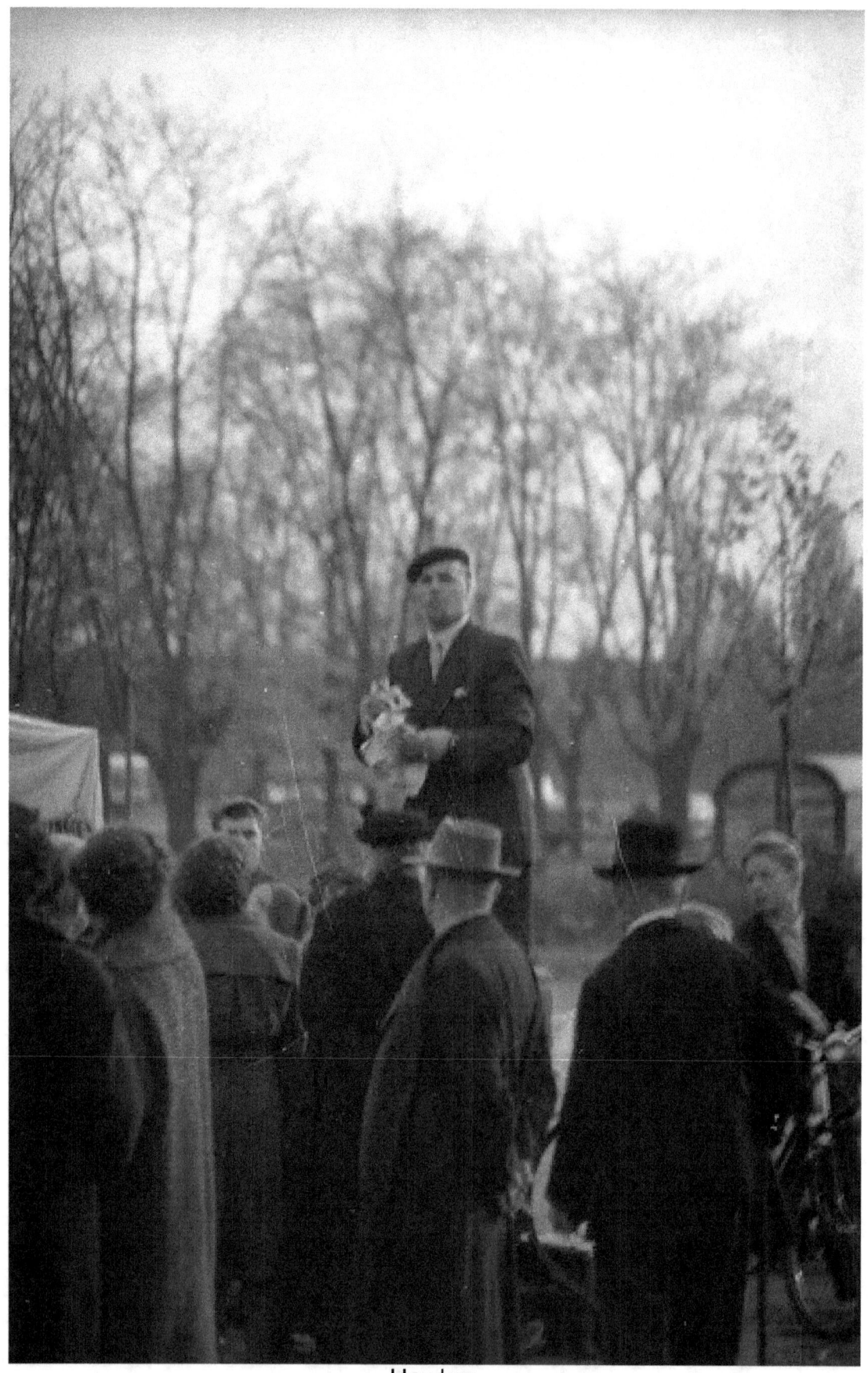
Hawker

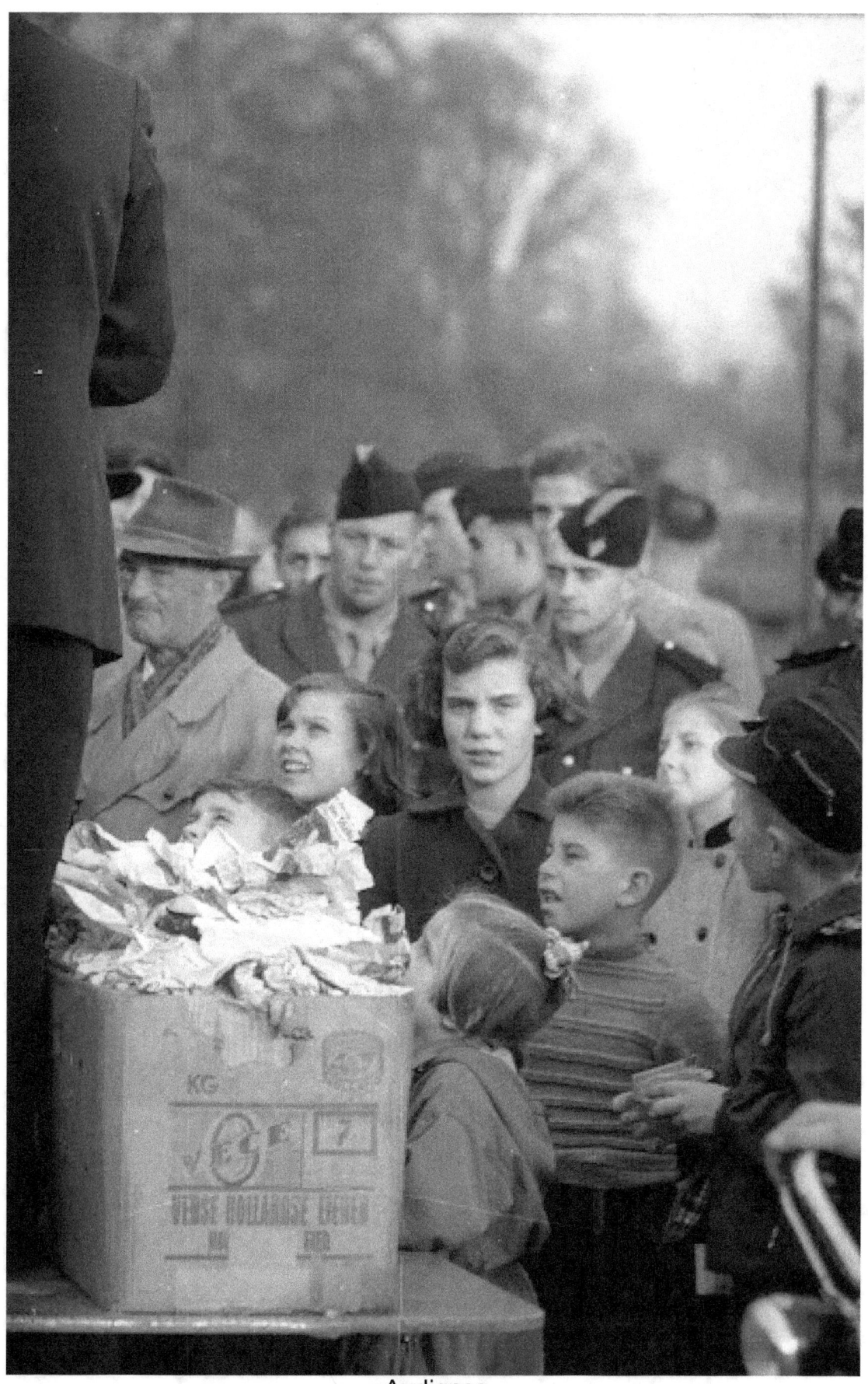
Audience

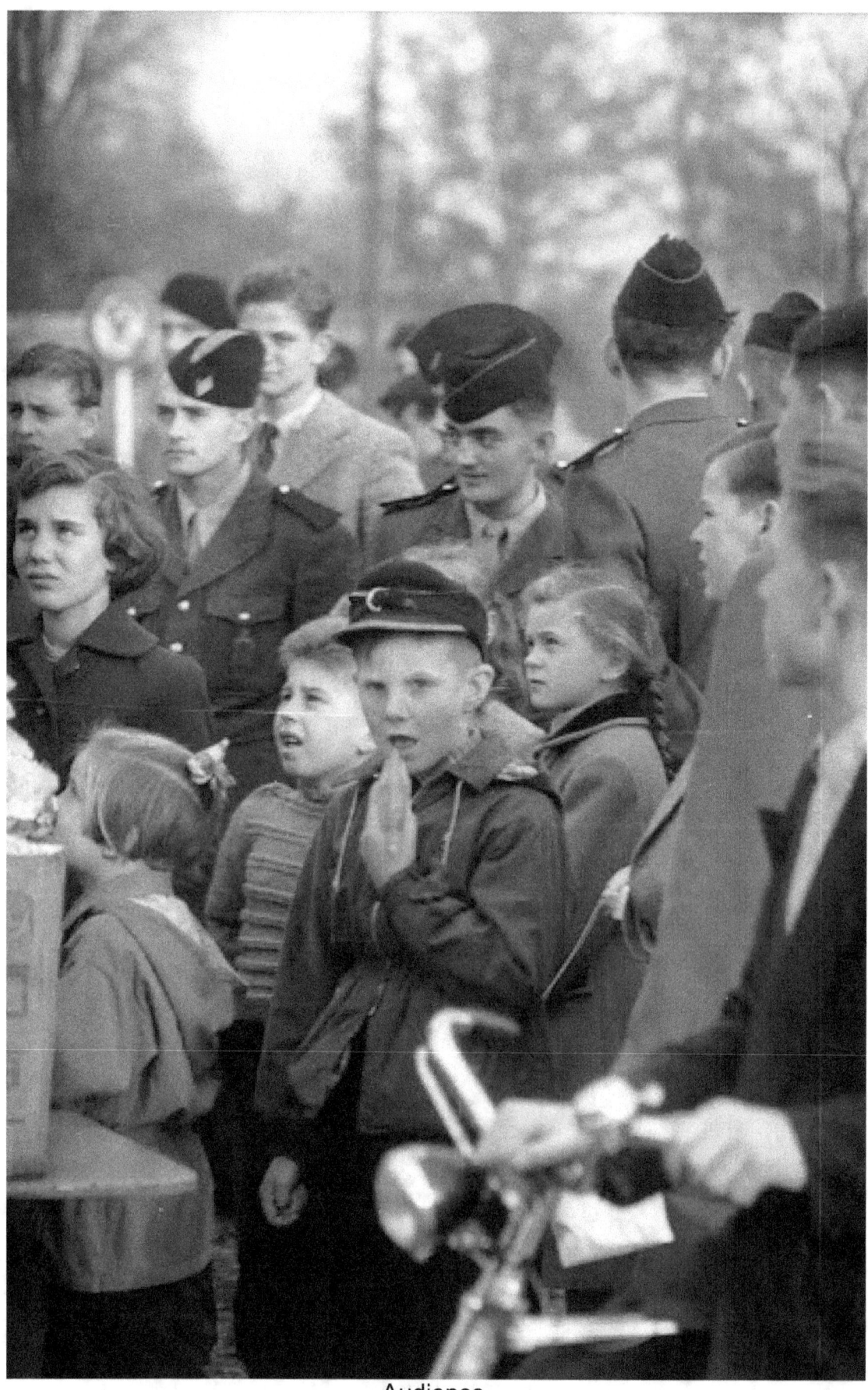
Audience

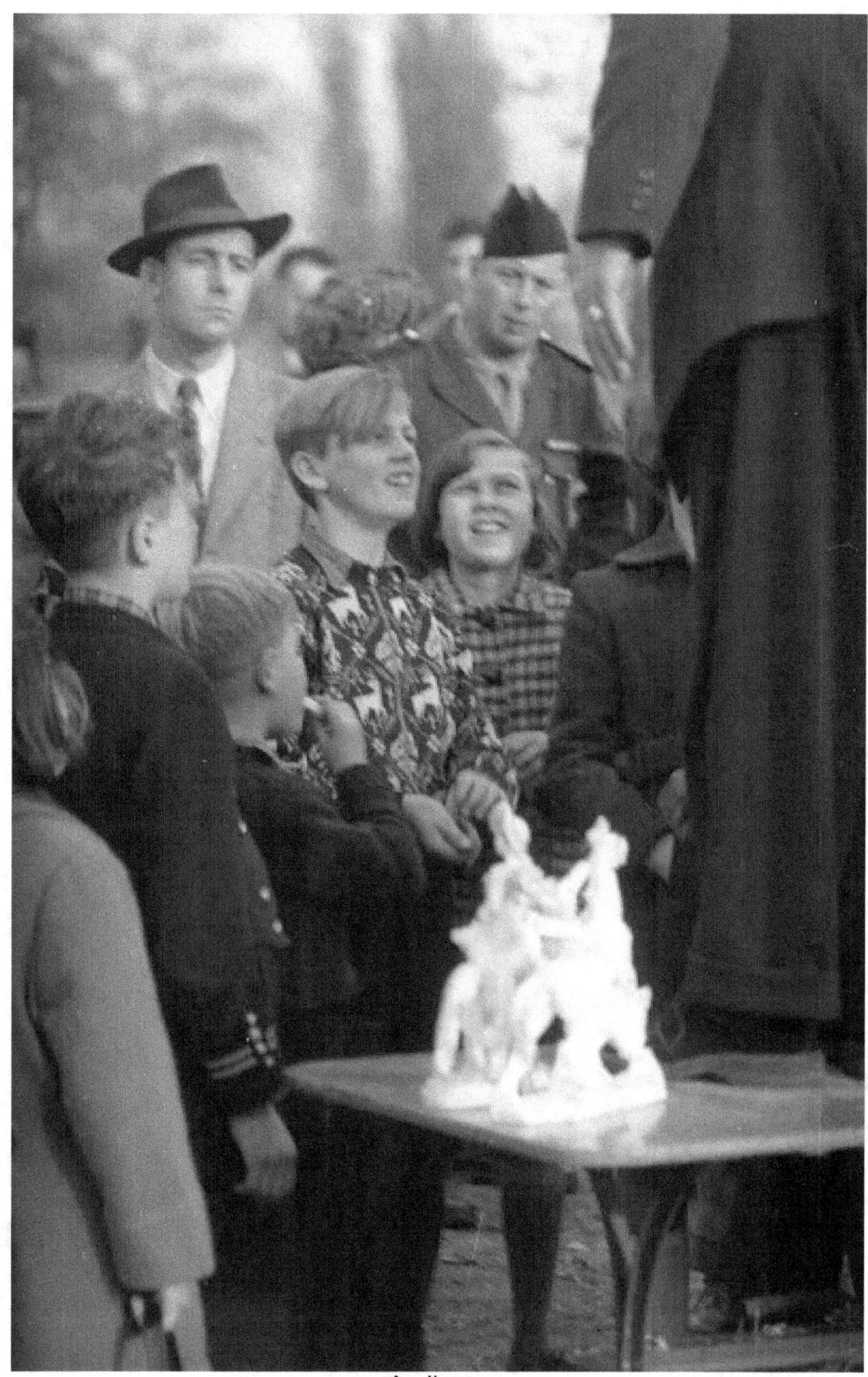
Audience

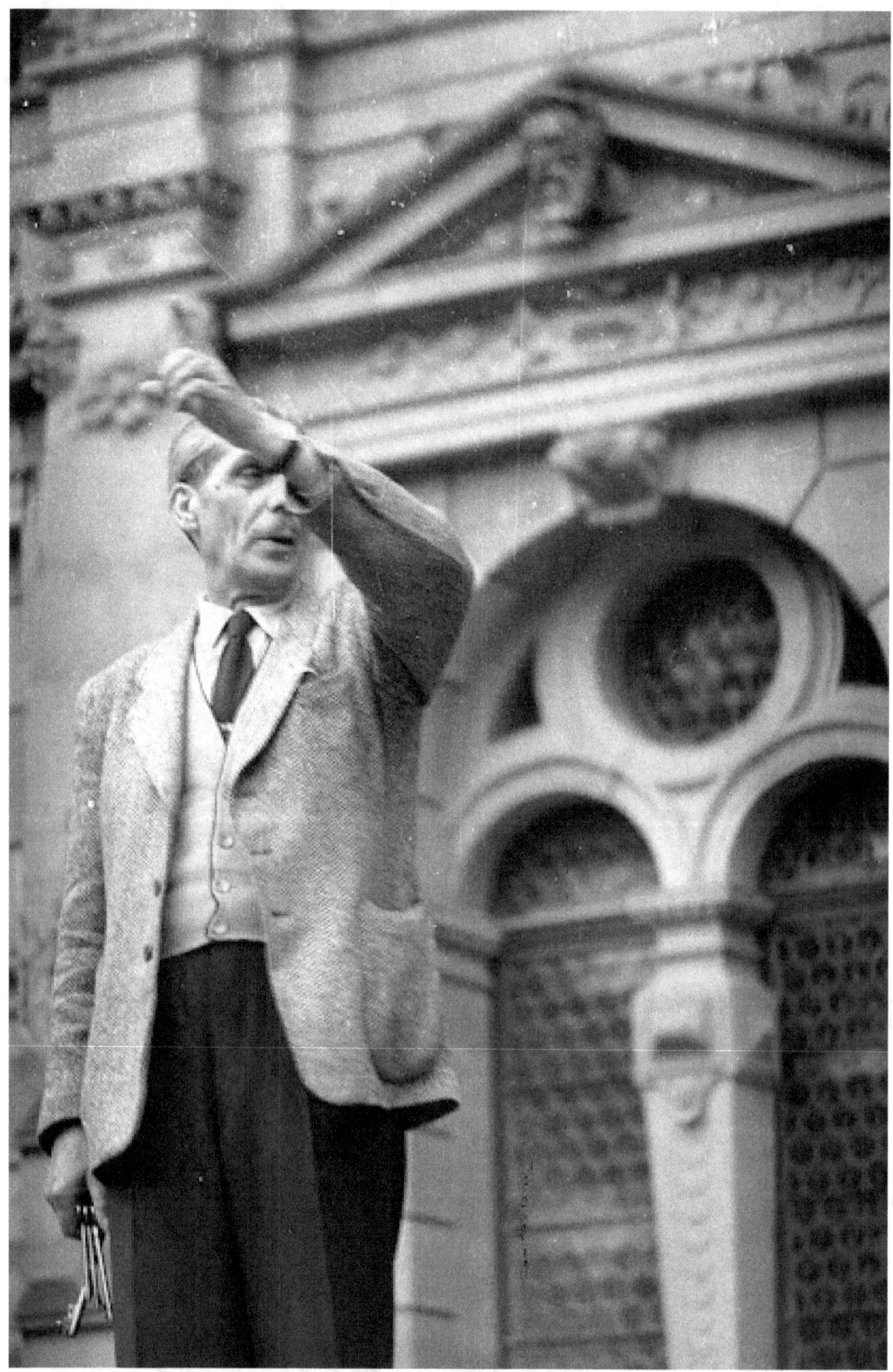
Hawker

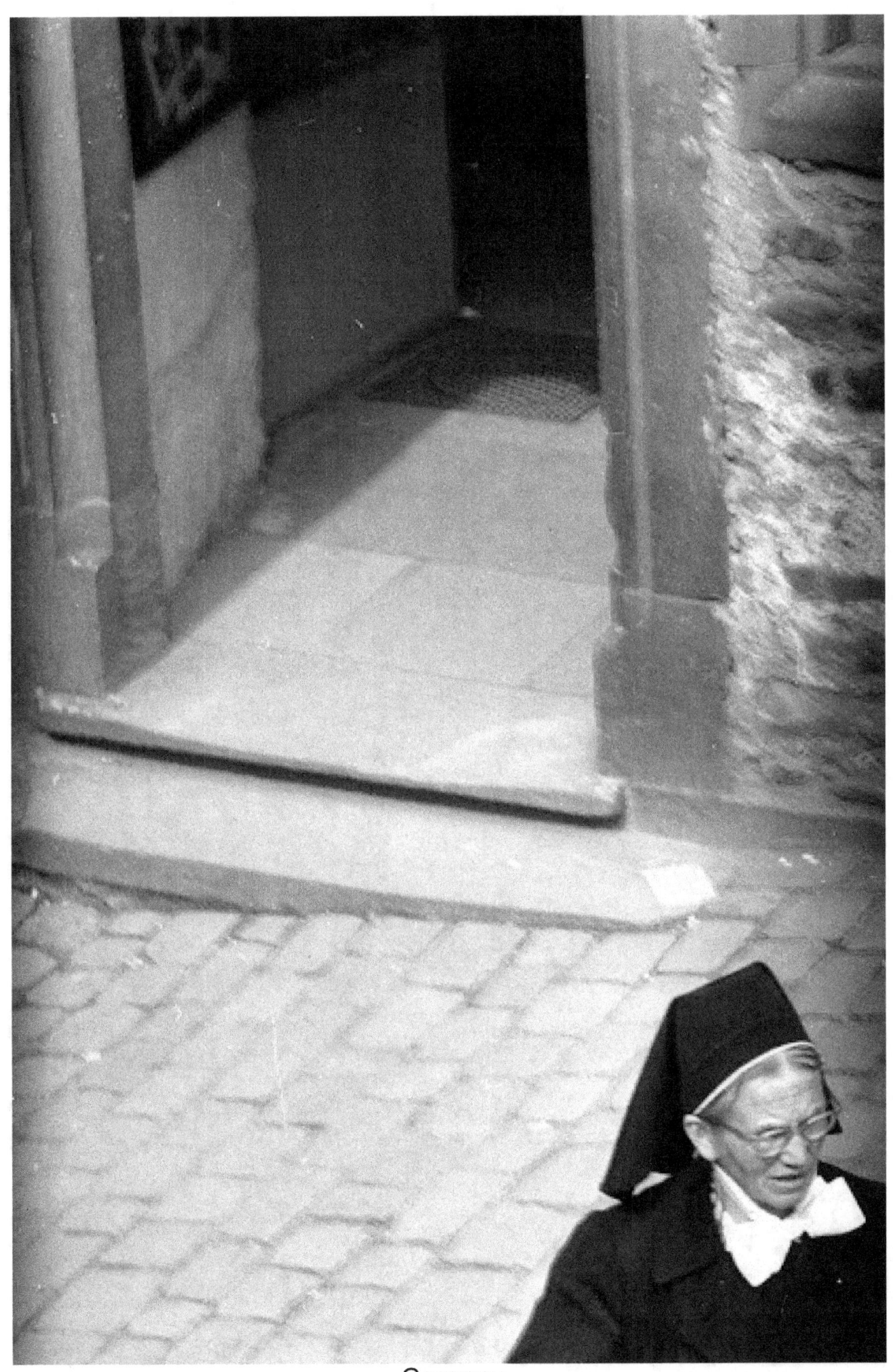

Germany

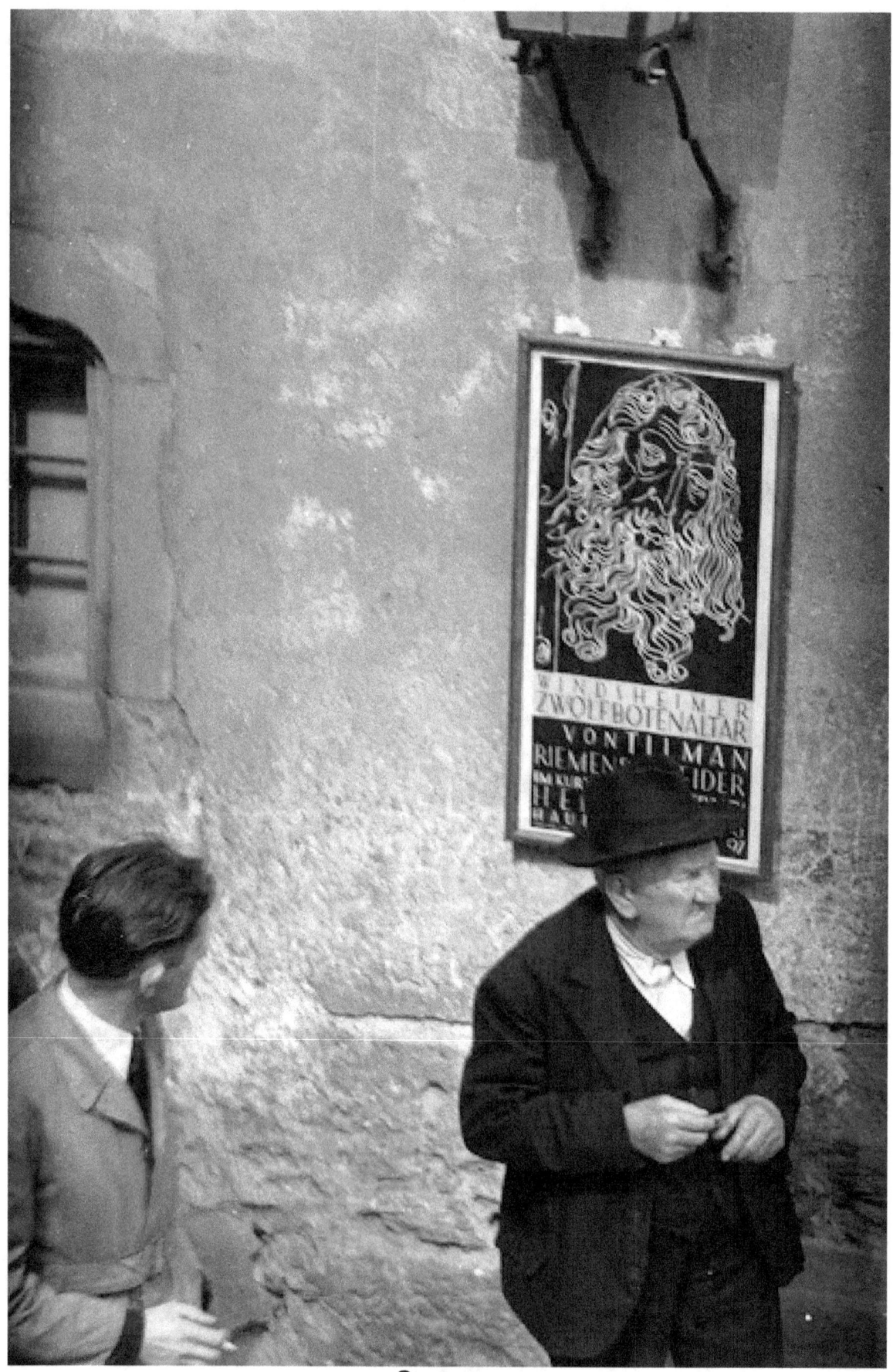

Germany

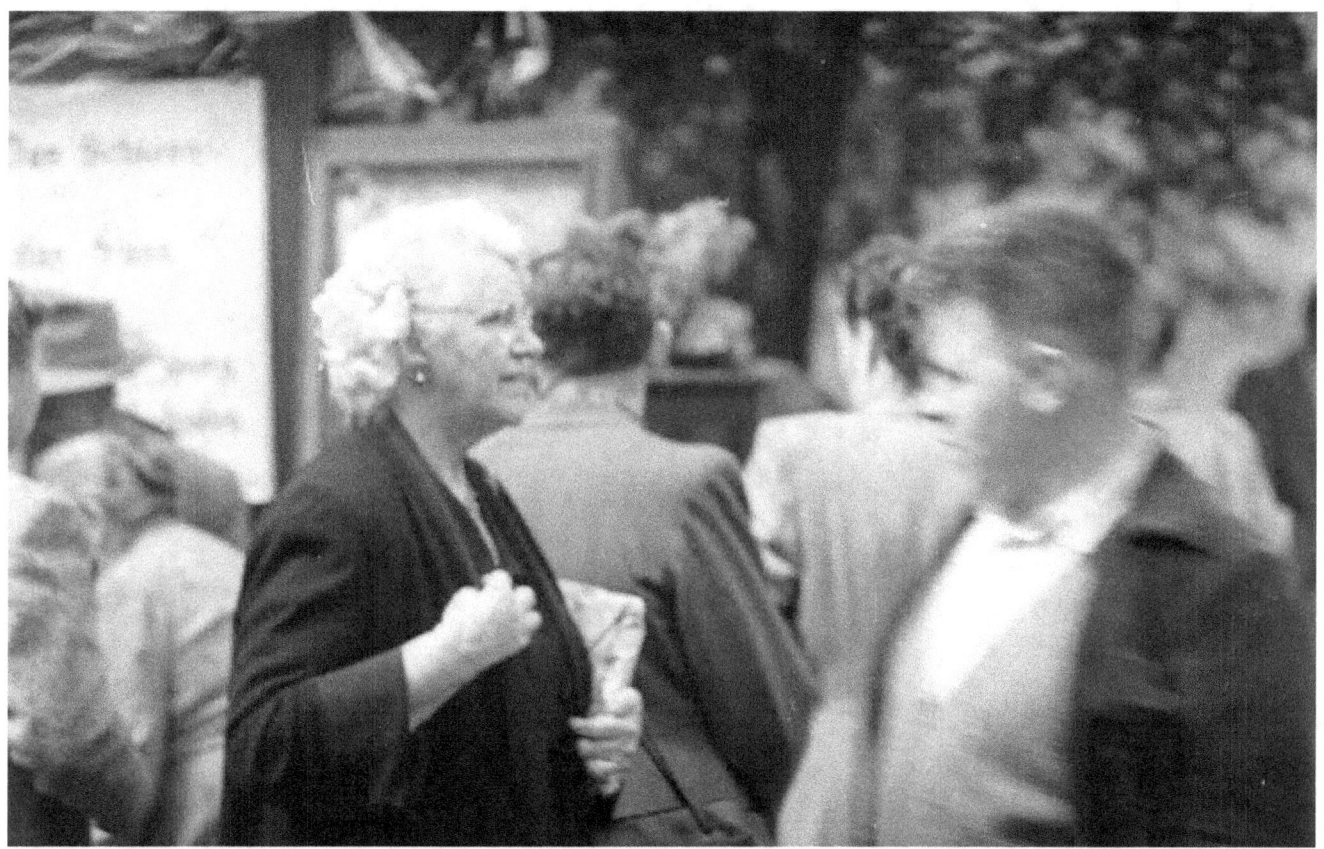
Germany

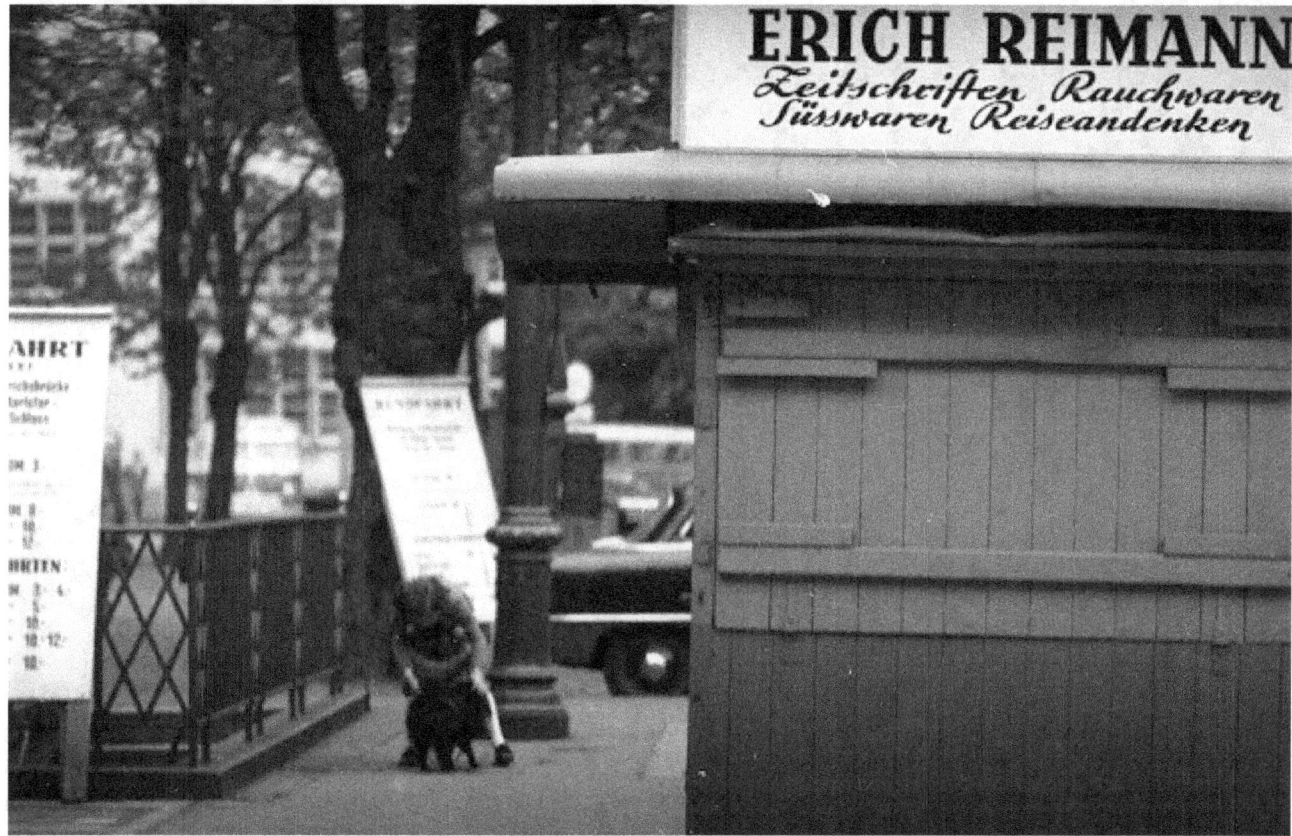
Girl with dog, Germany

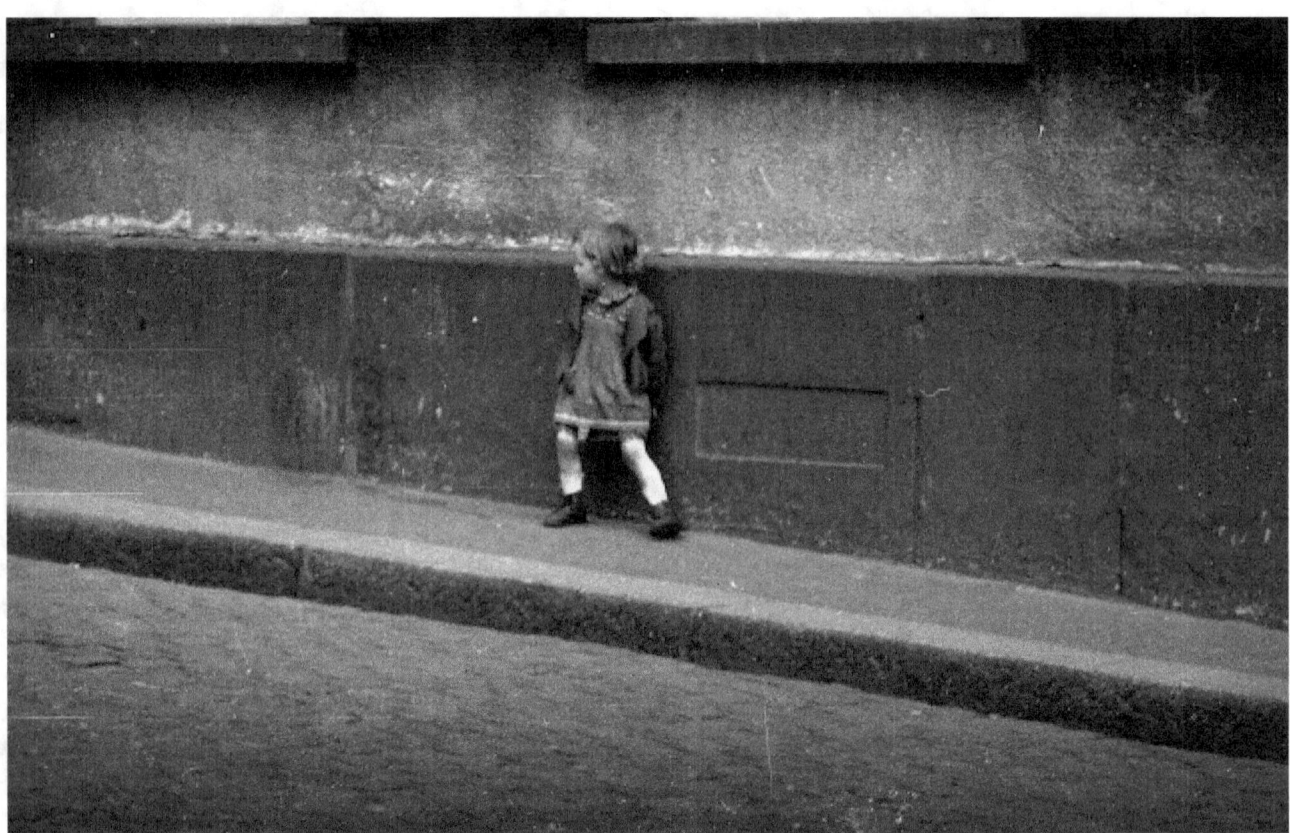
Girl

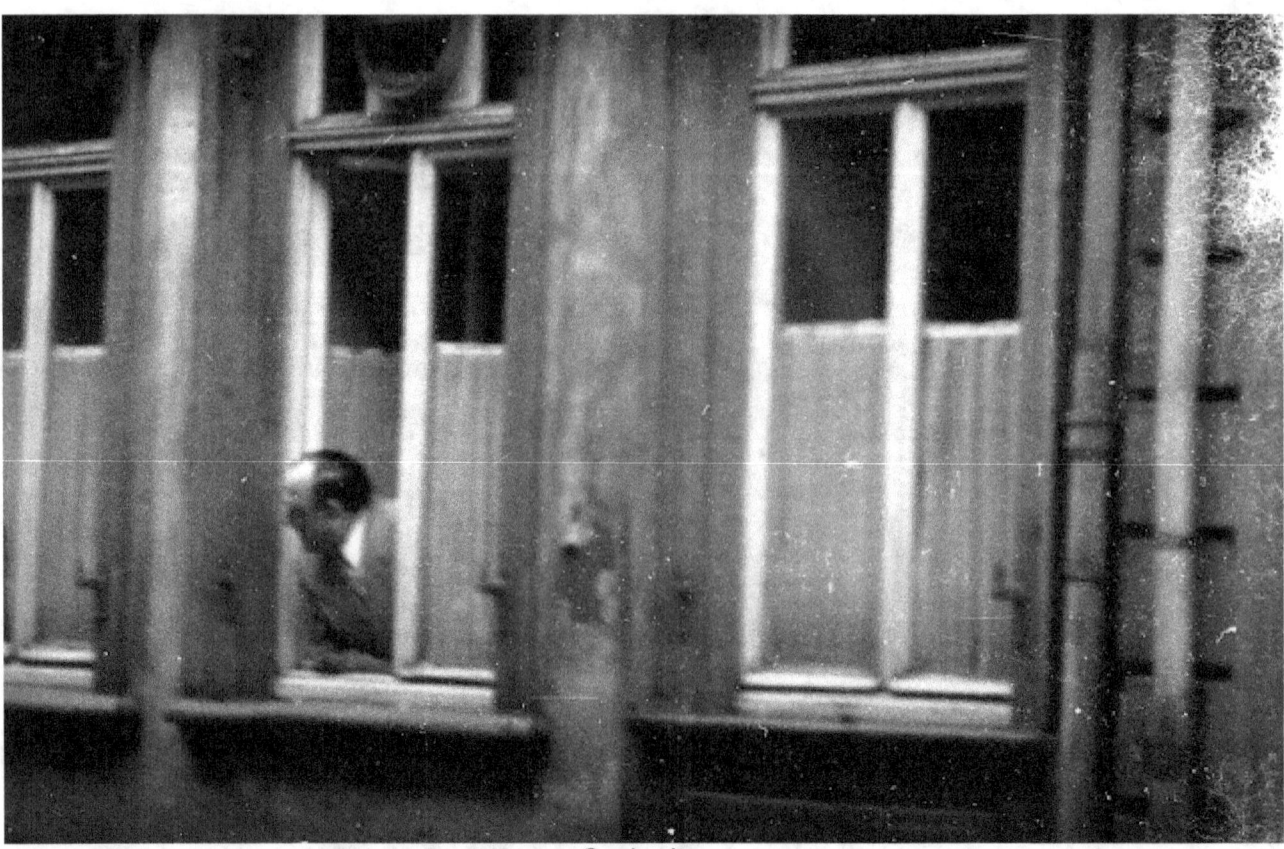
Curiosity

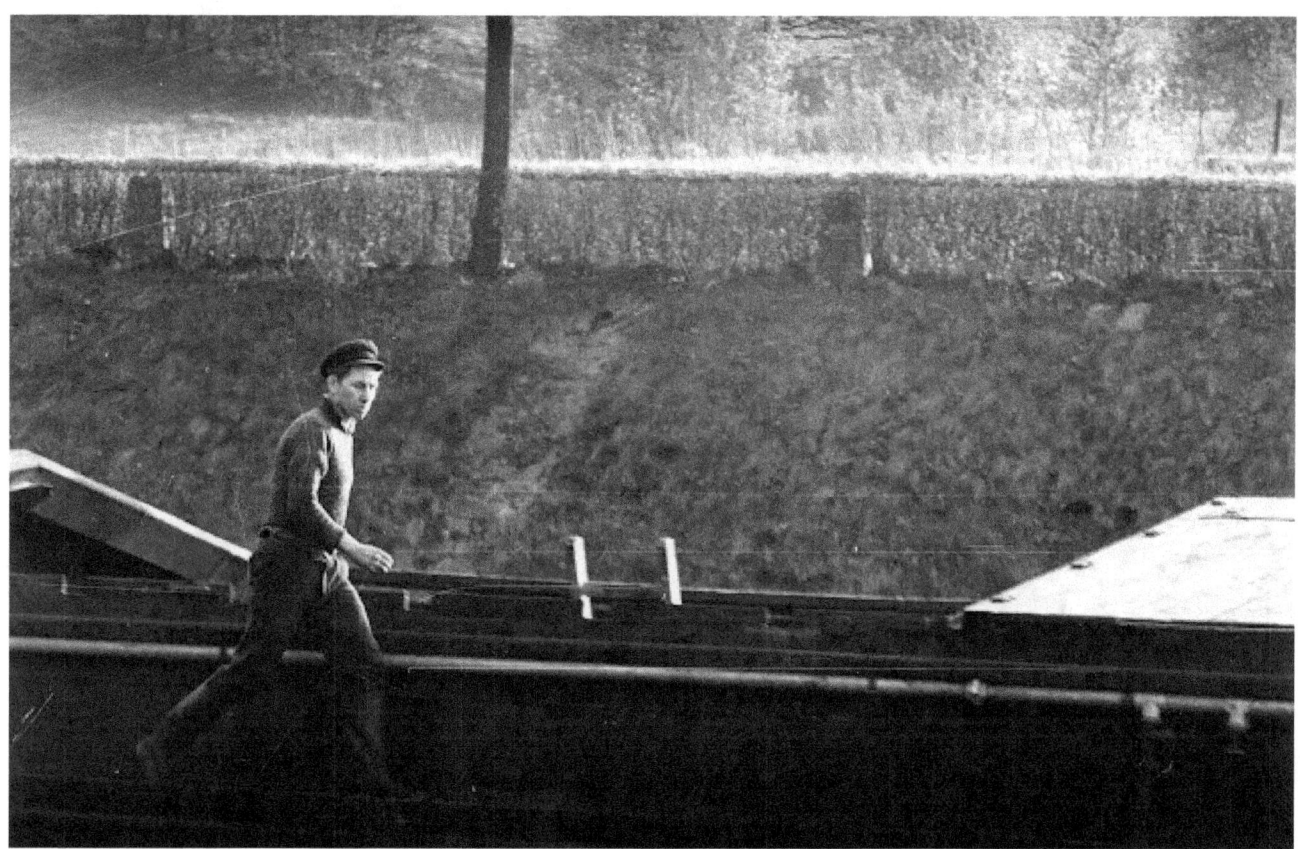
Along the Neckar River

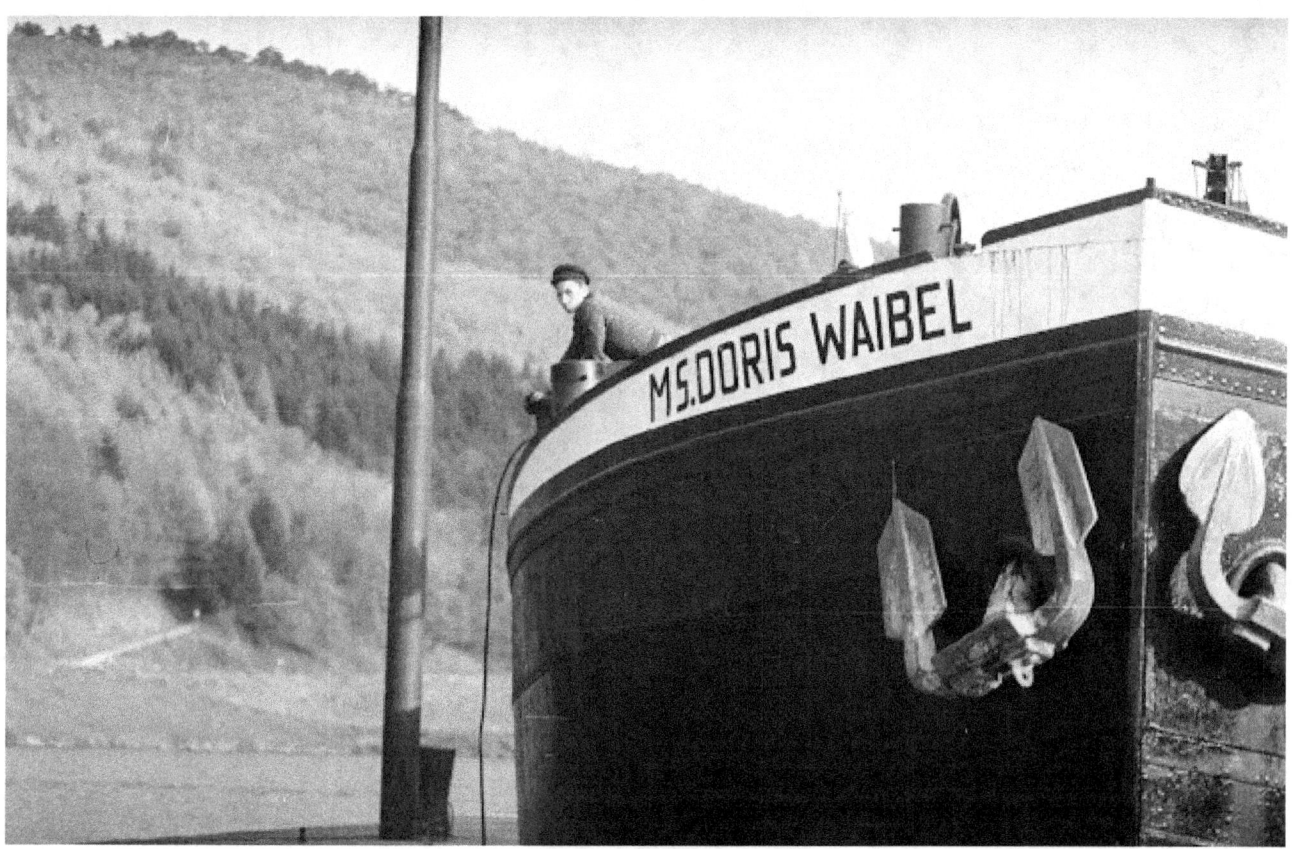
Neckar River boat

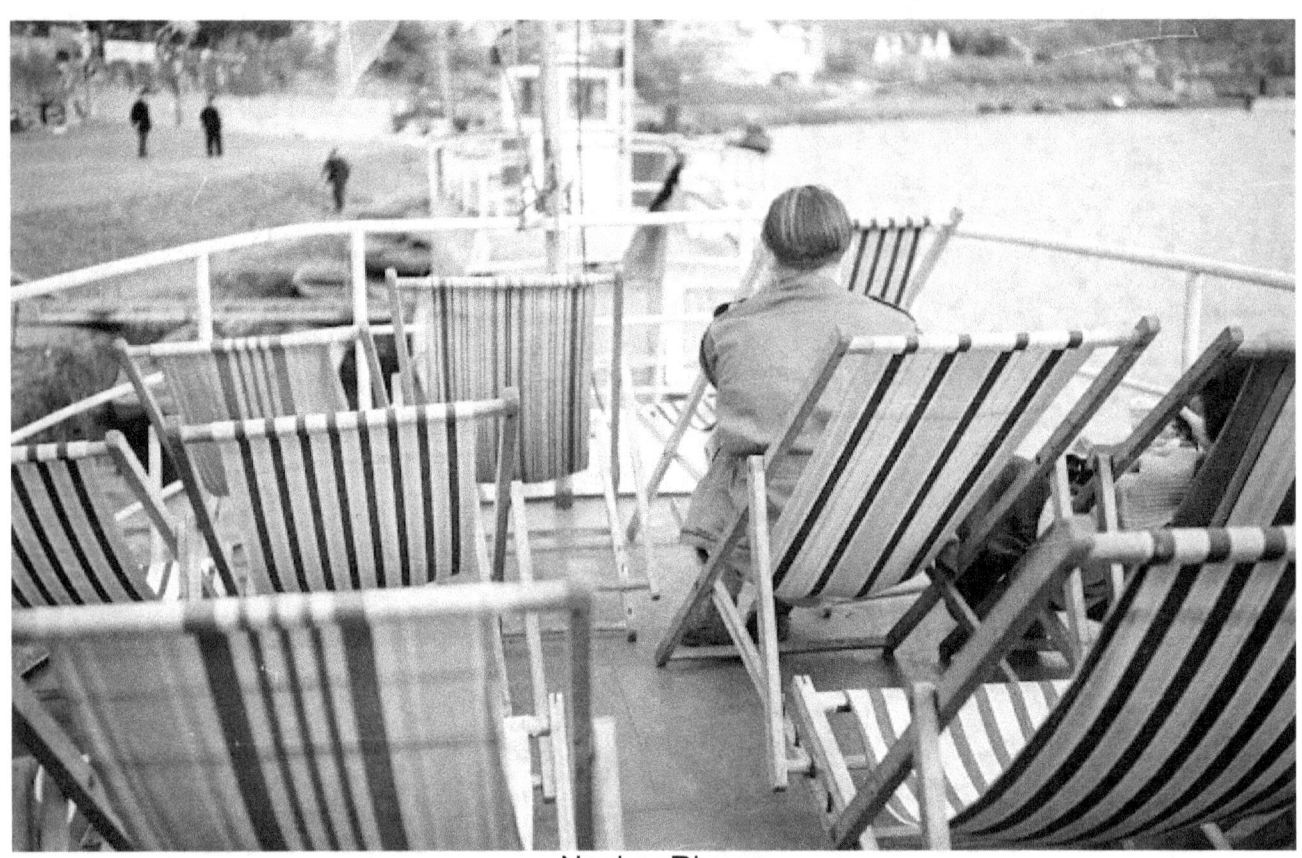
Neckar River

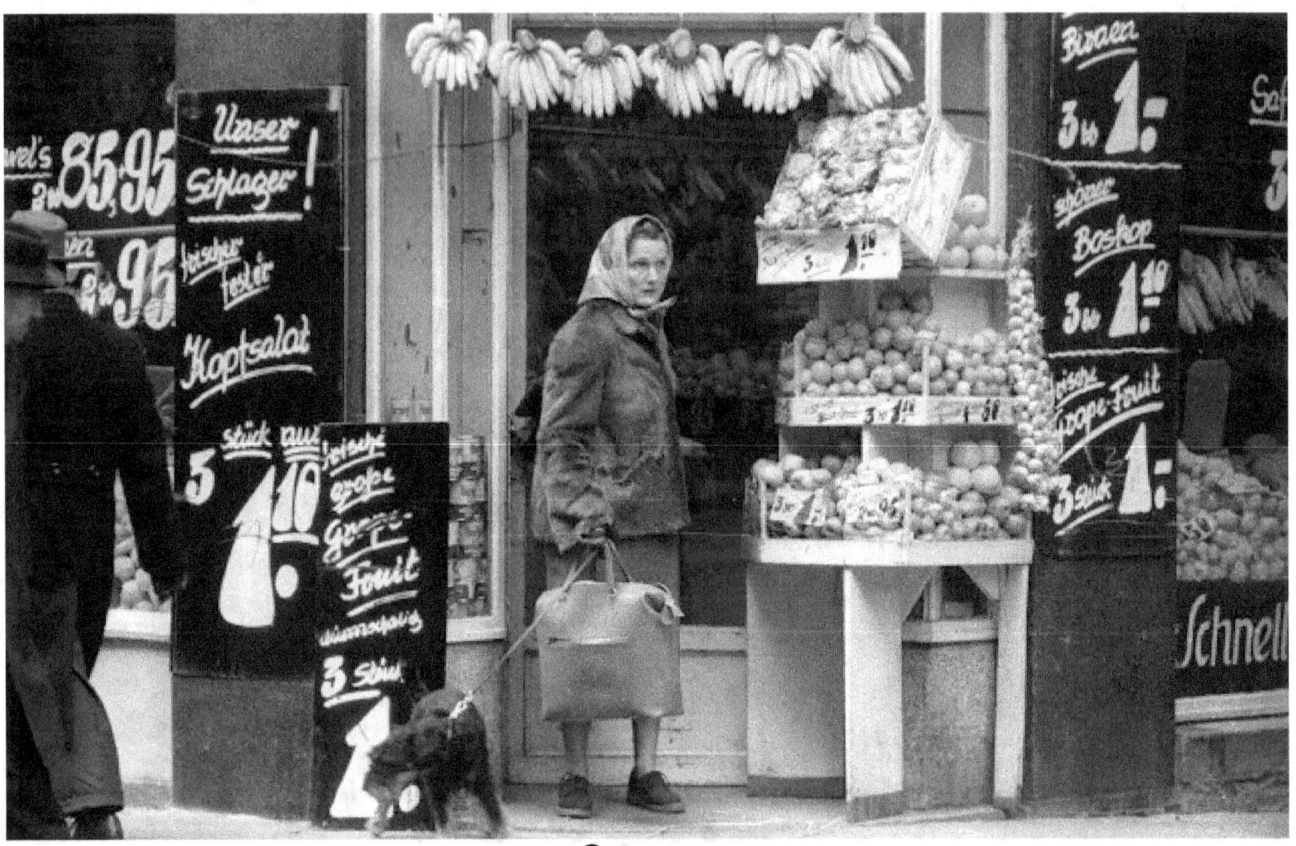
Germany

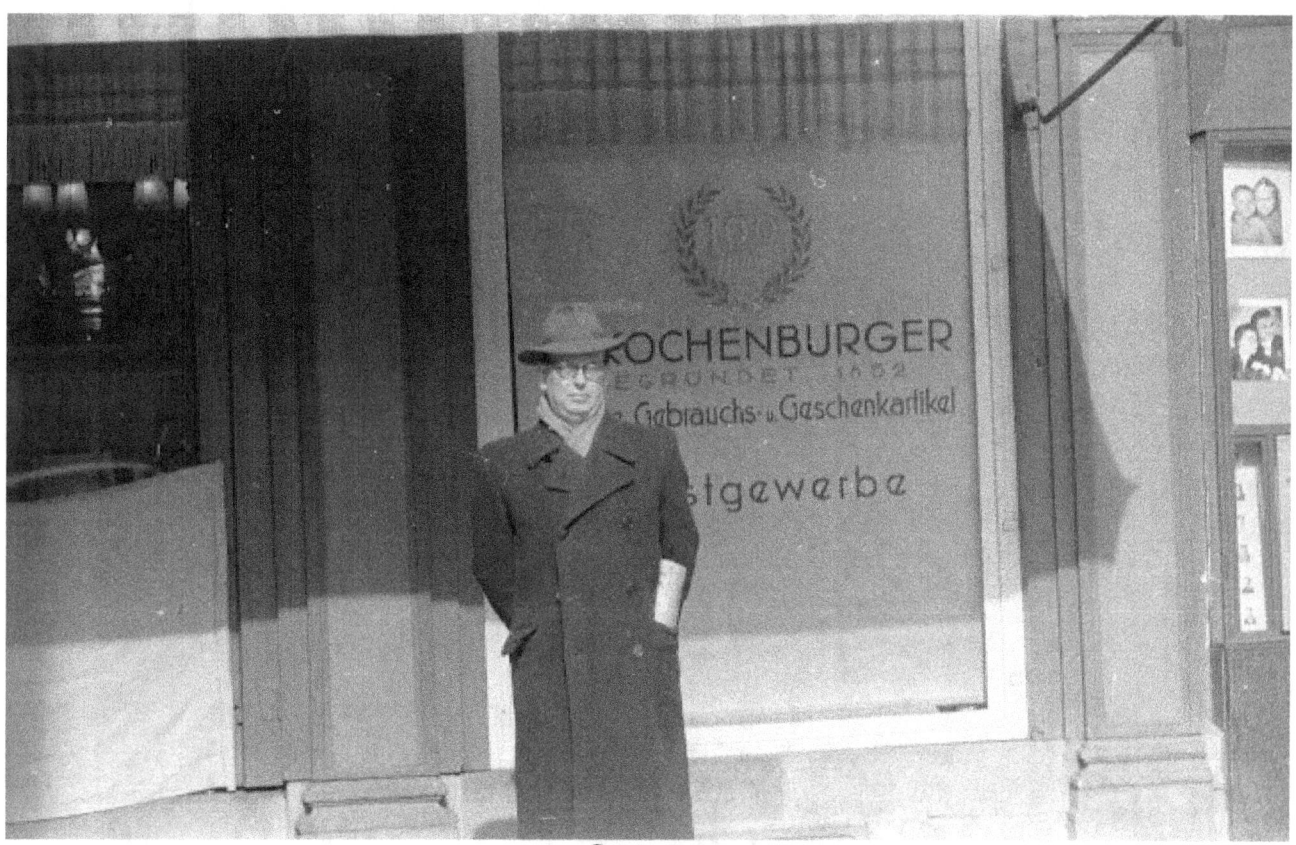
Germany

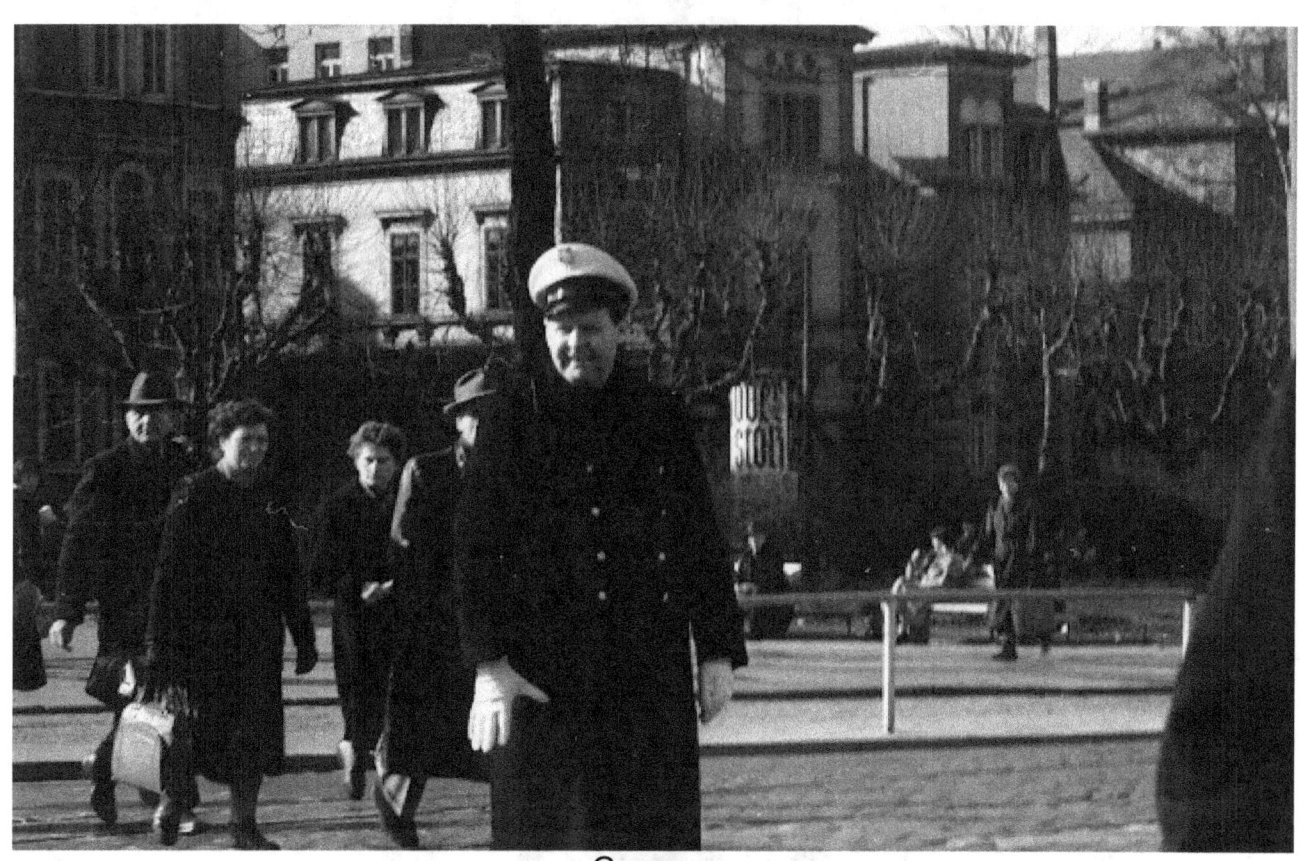
Germany

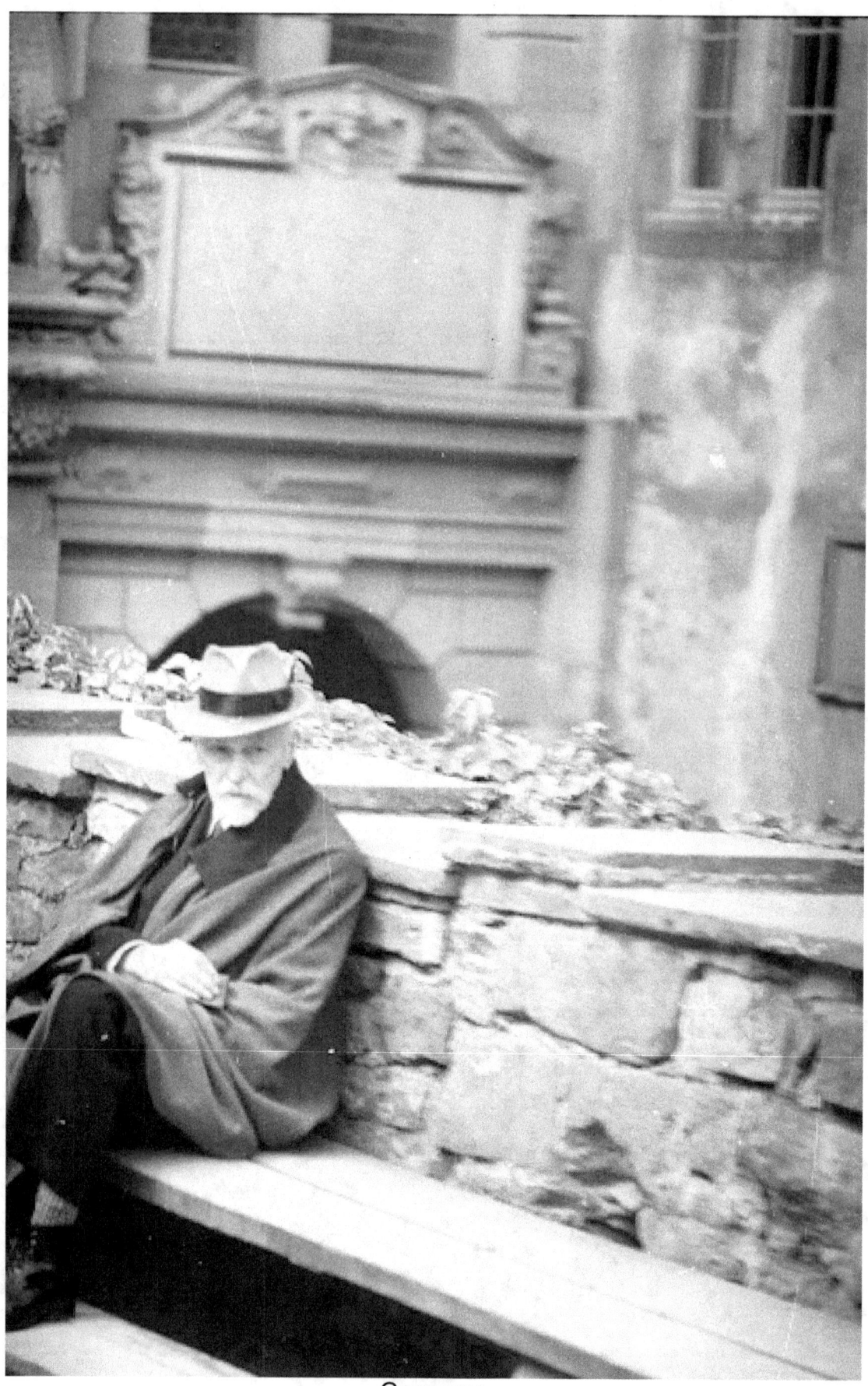
Germany

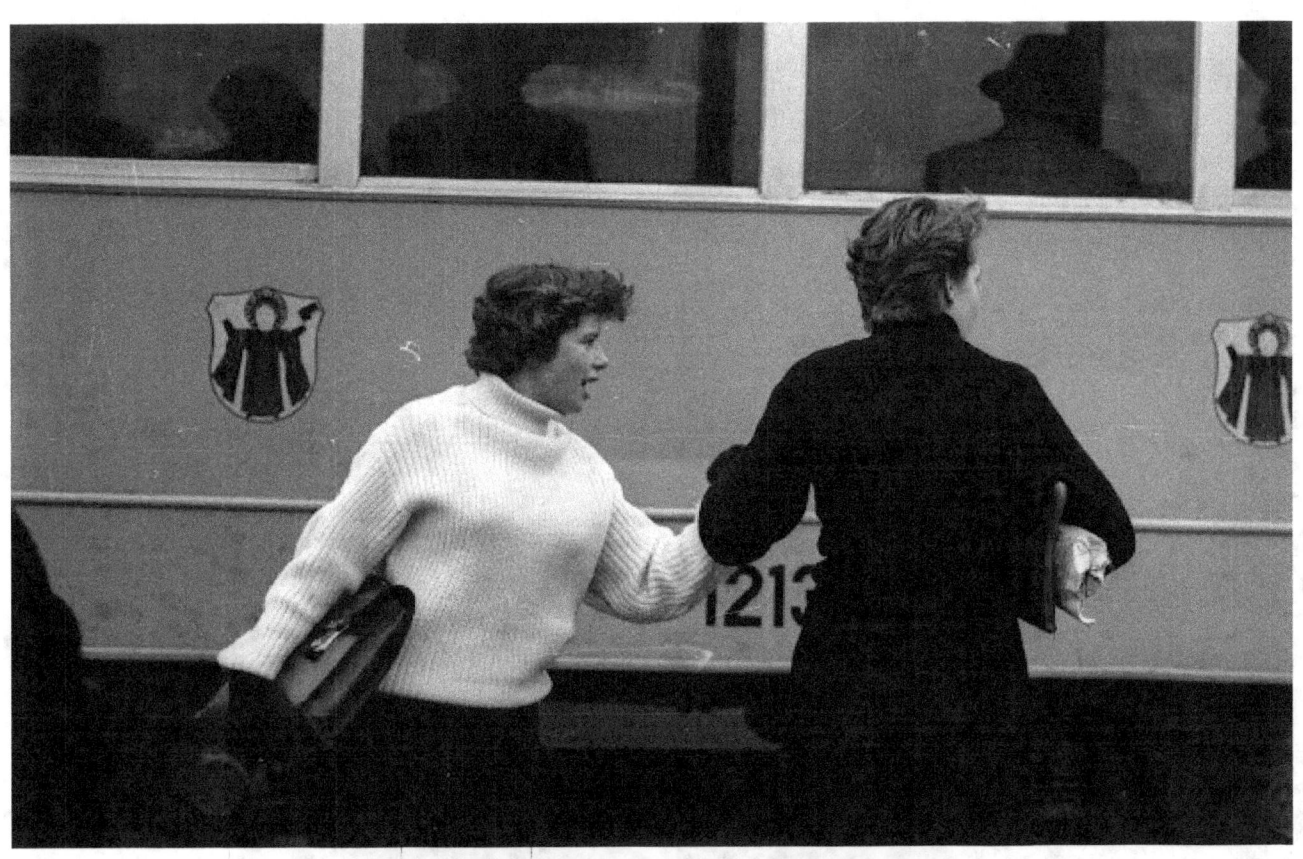
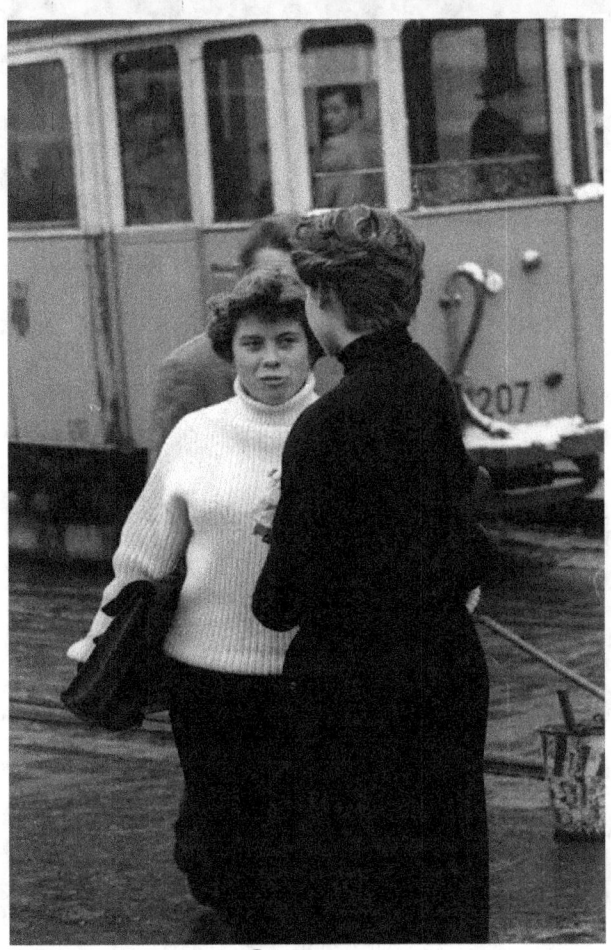

Germany

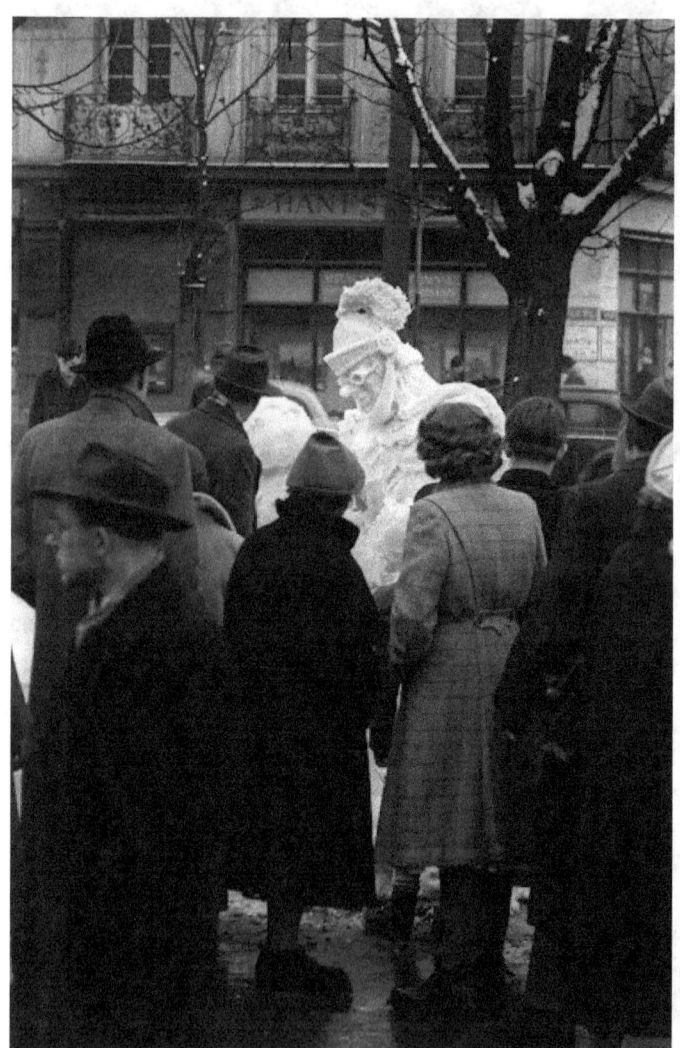
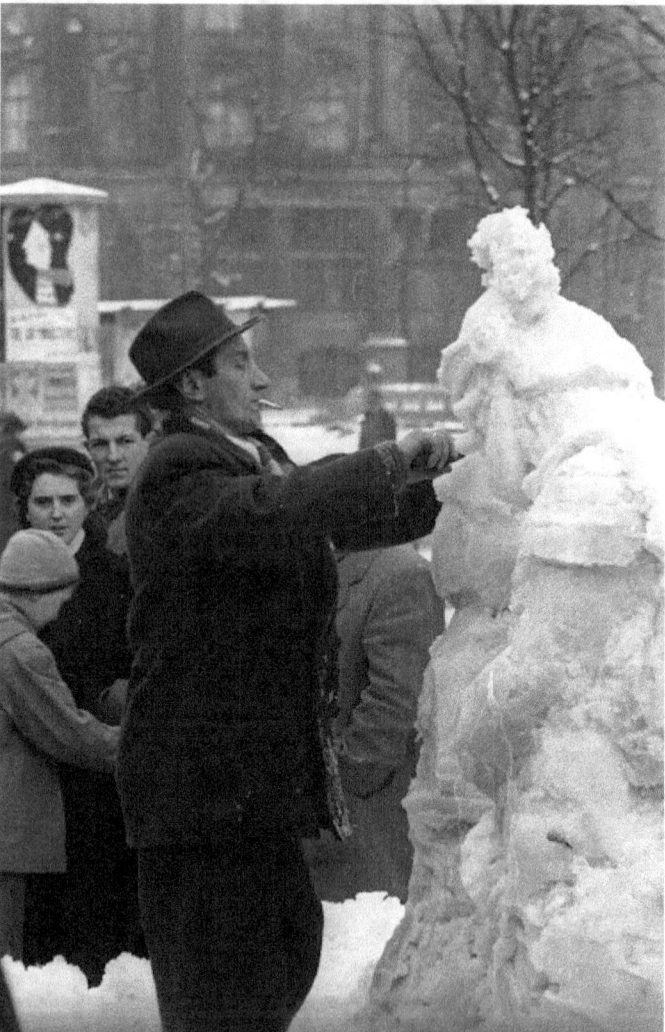
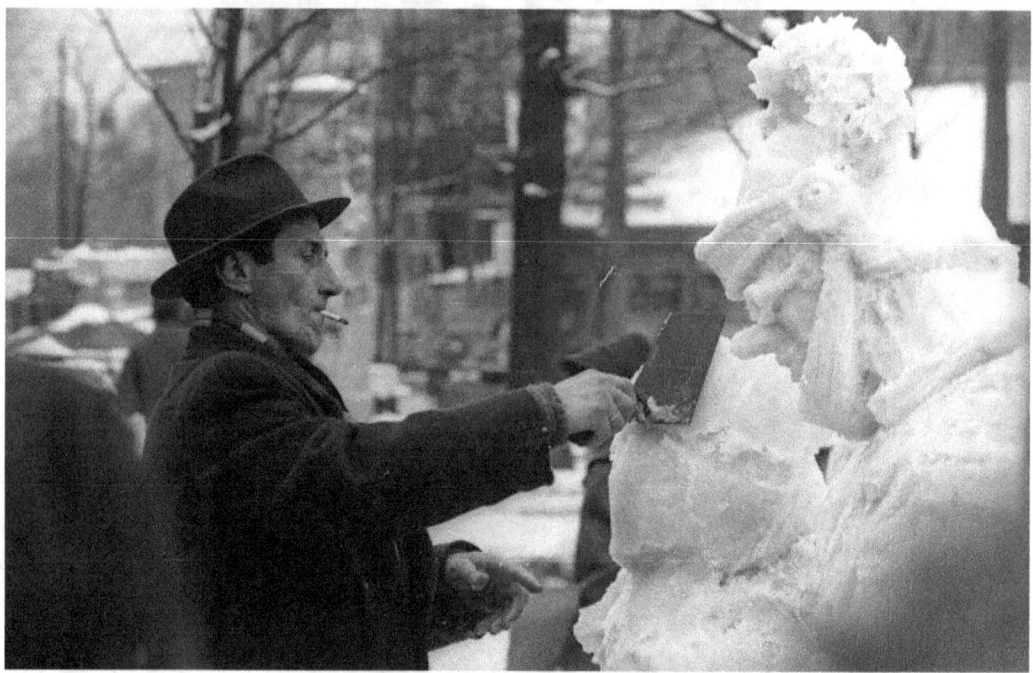

Ice Sculptor, Salzburg

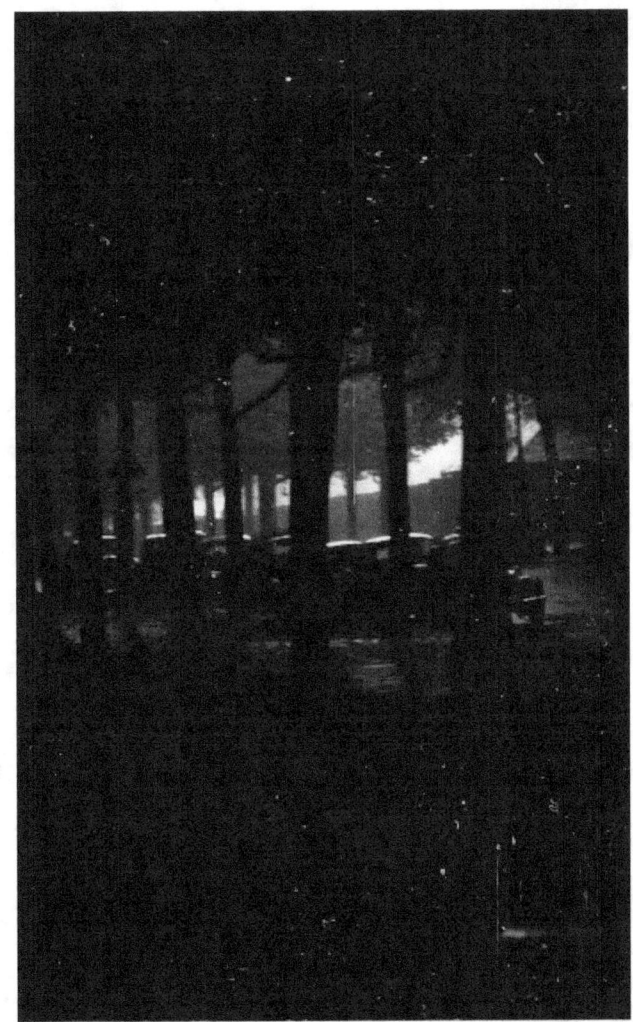
Germany

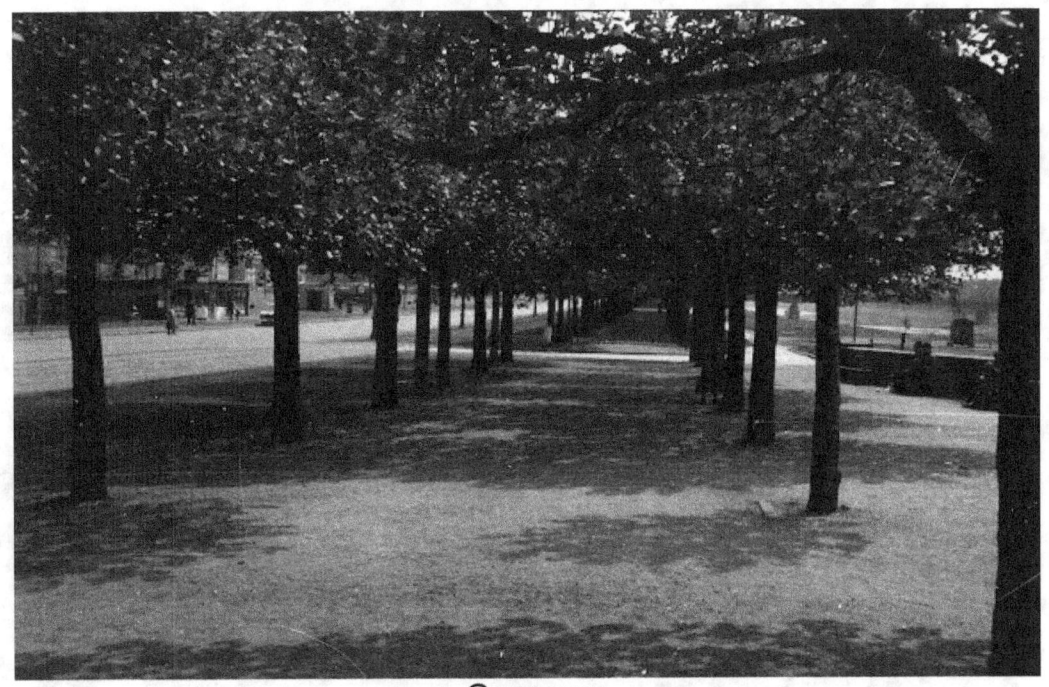
Germany

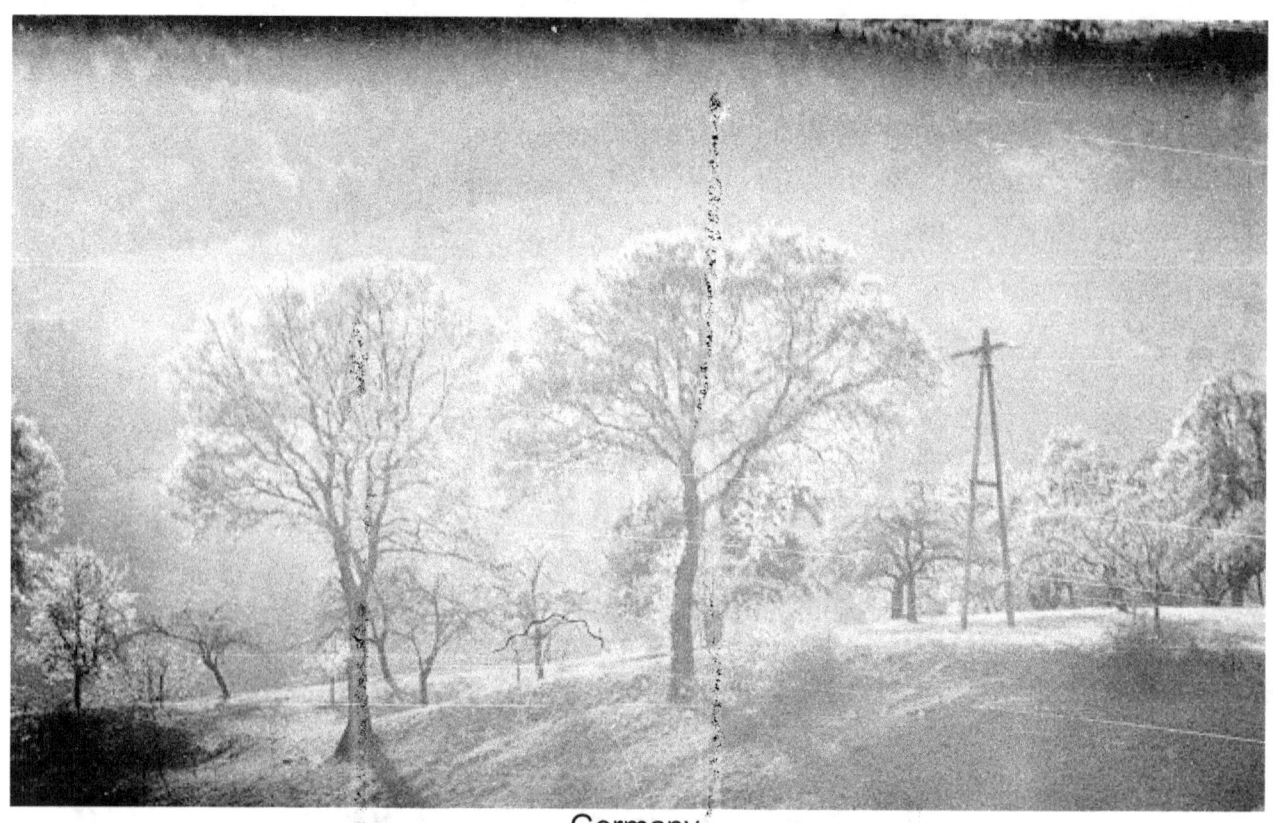

Germany

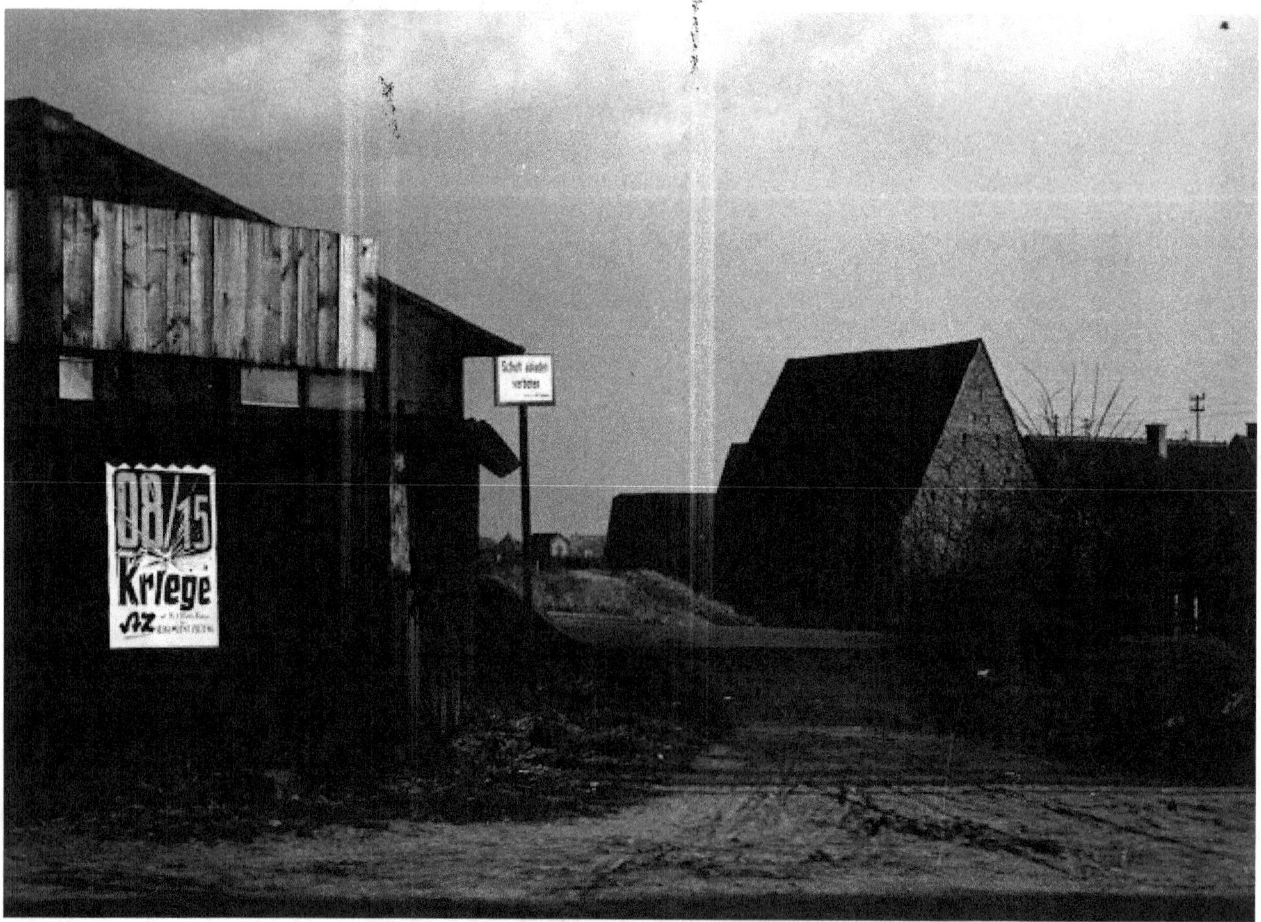

Germany (possibly near Seckenheim)

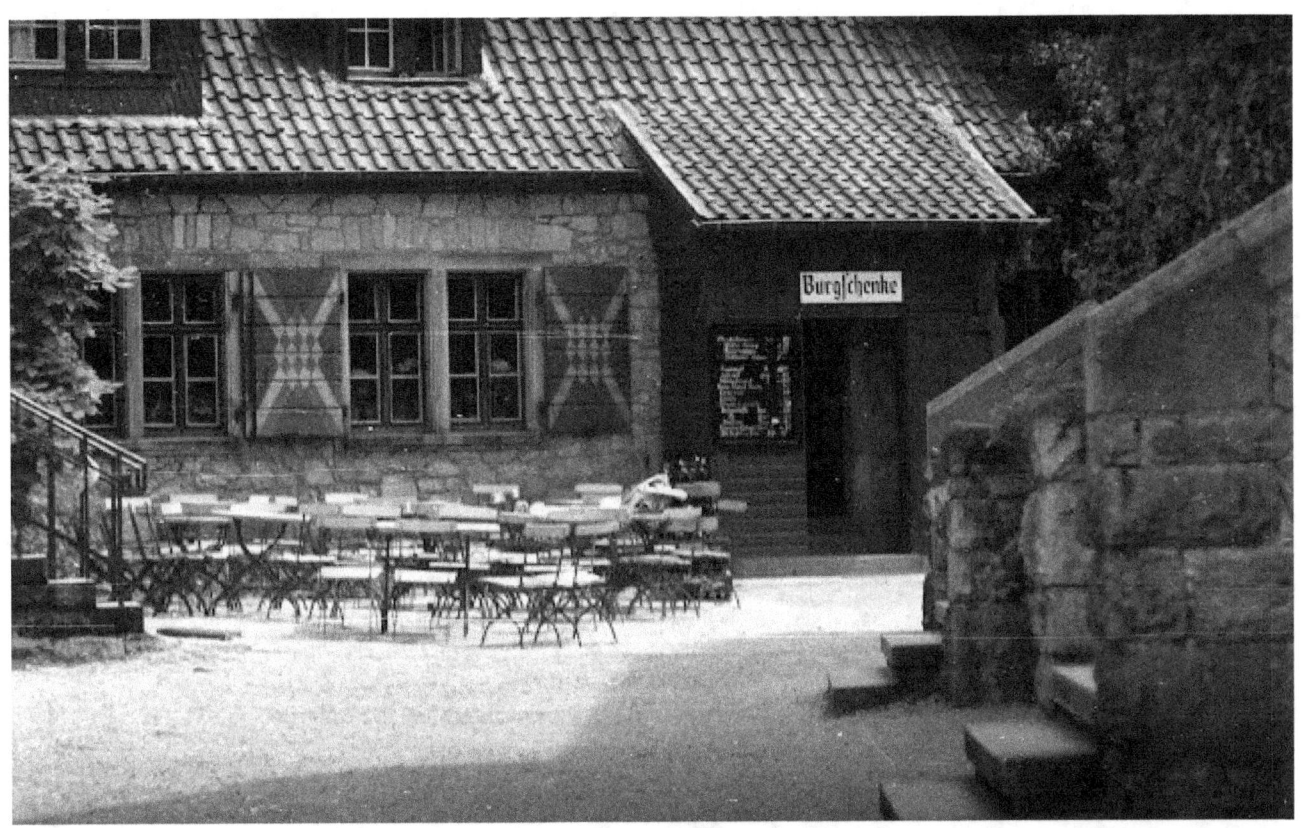
Germany

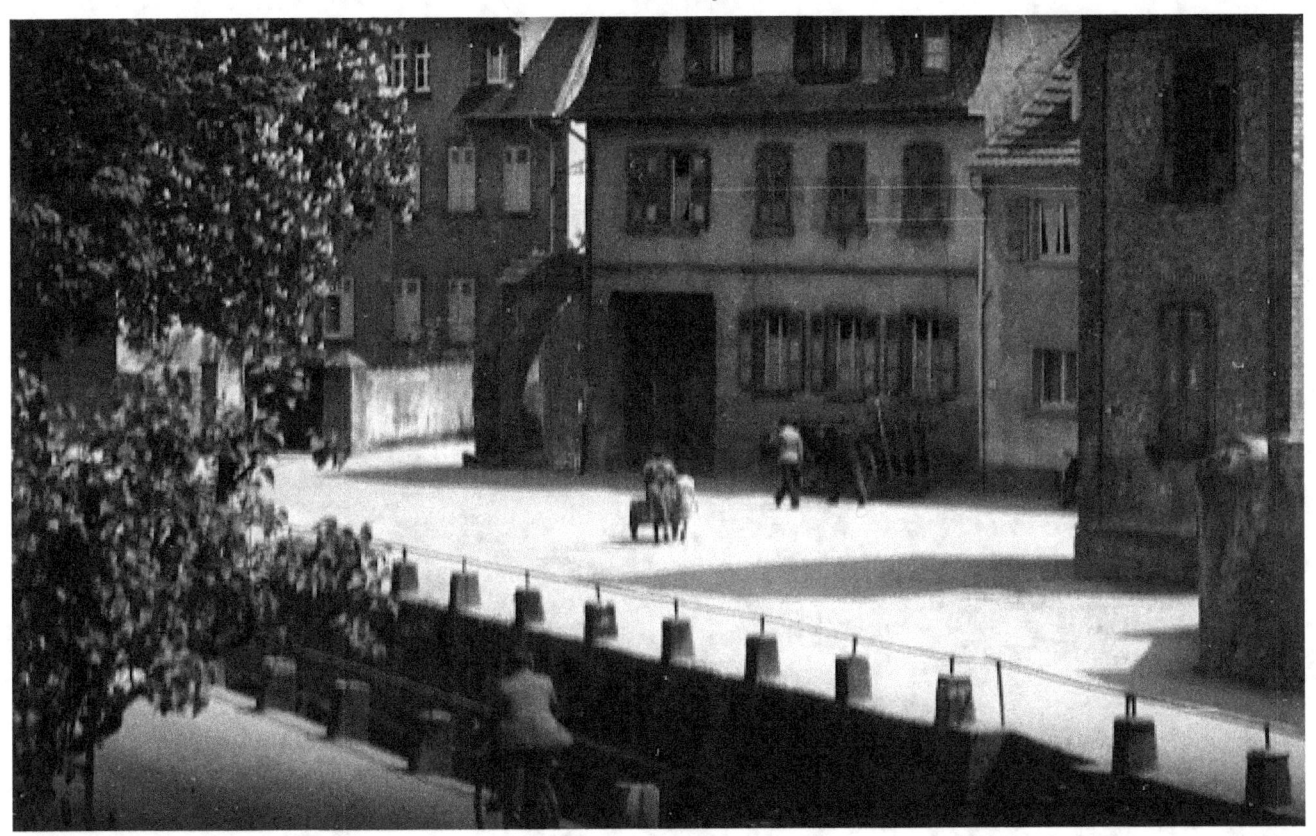
Germany

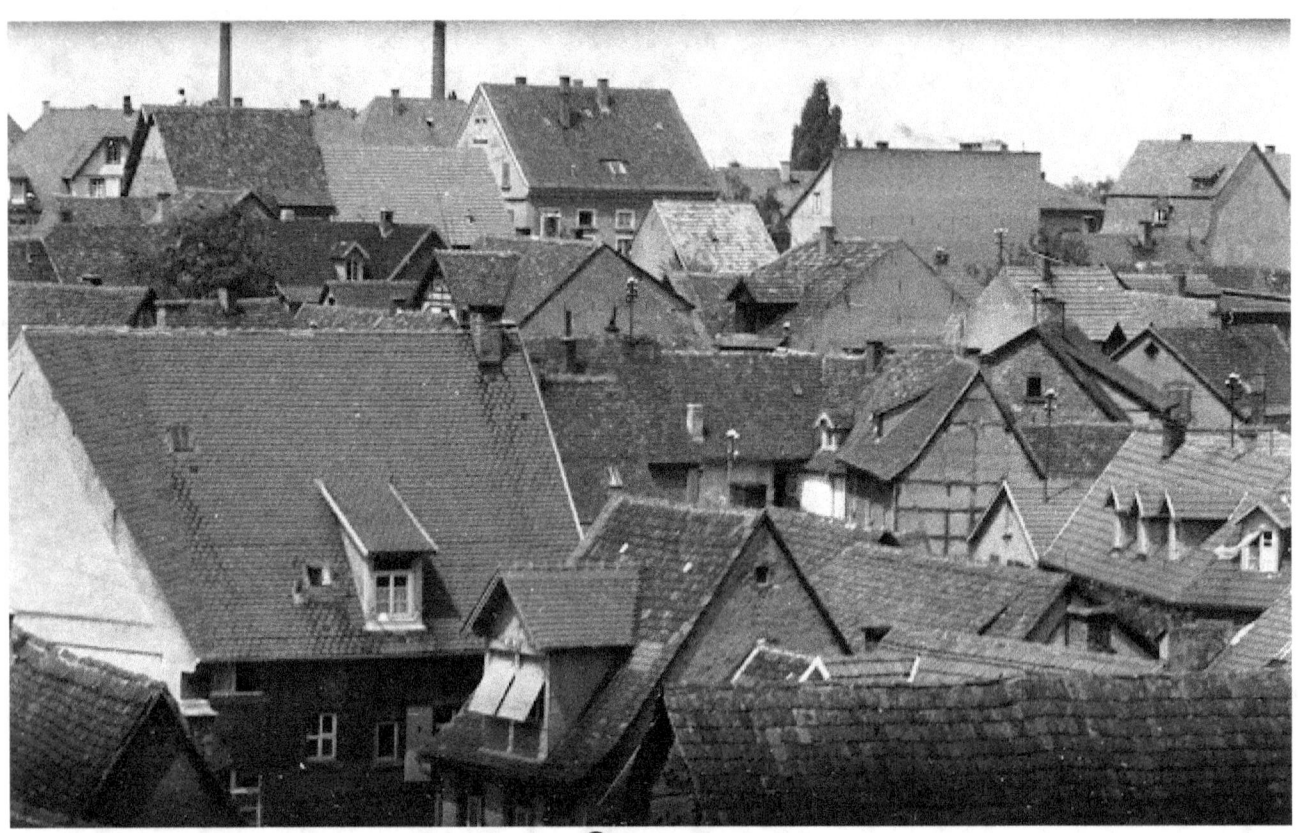
Germany

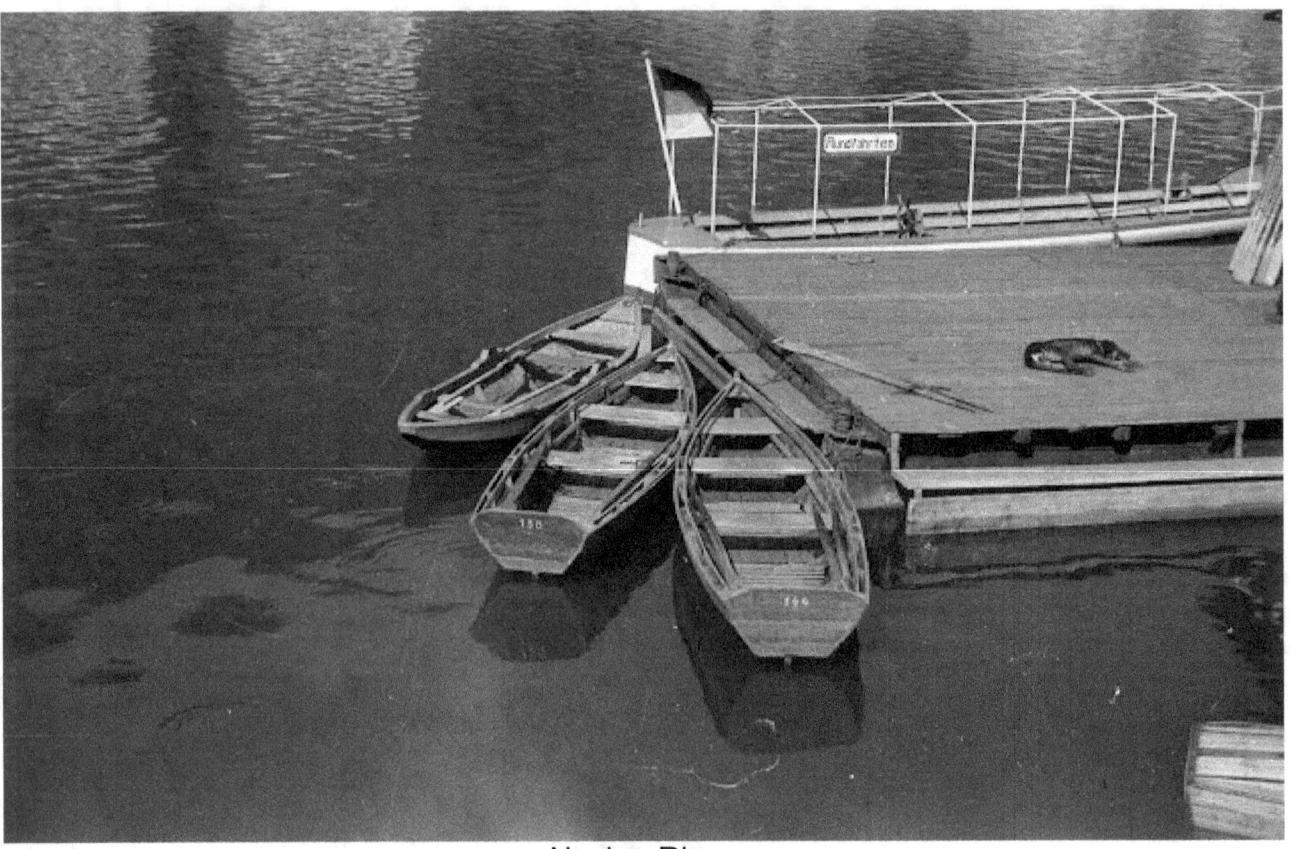
Neckar River

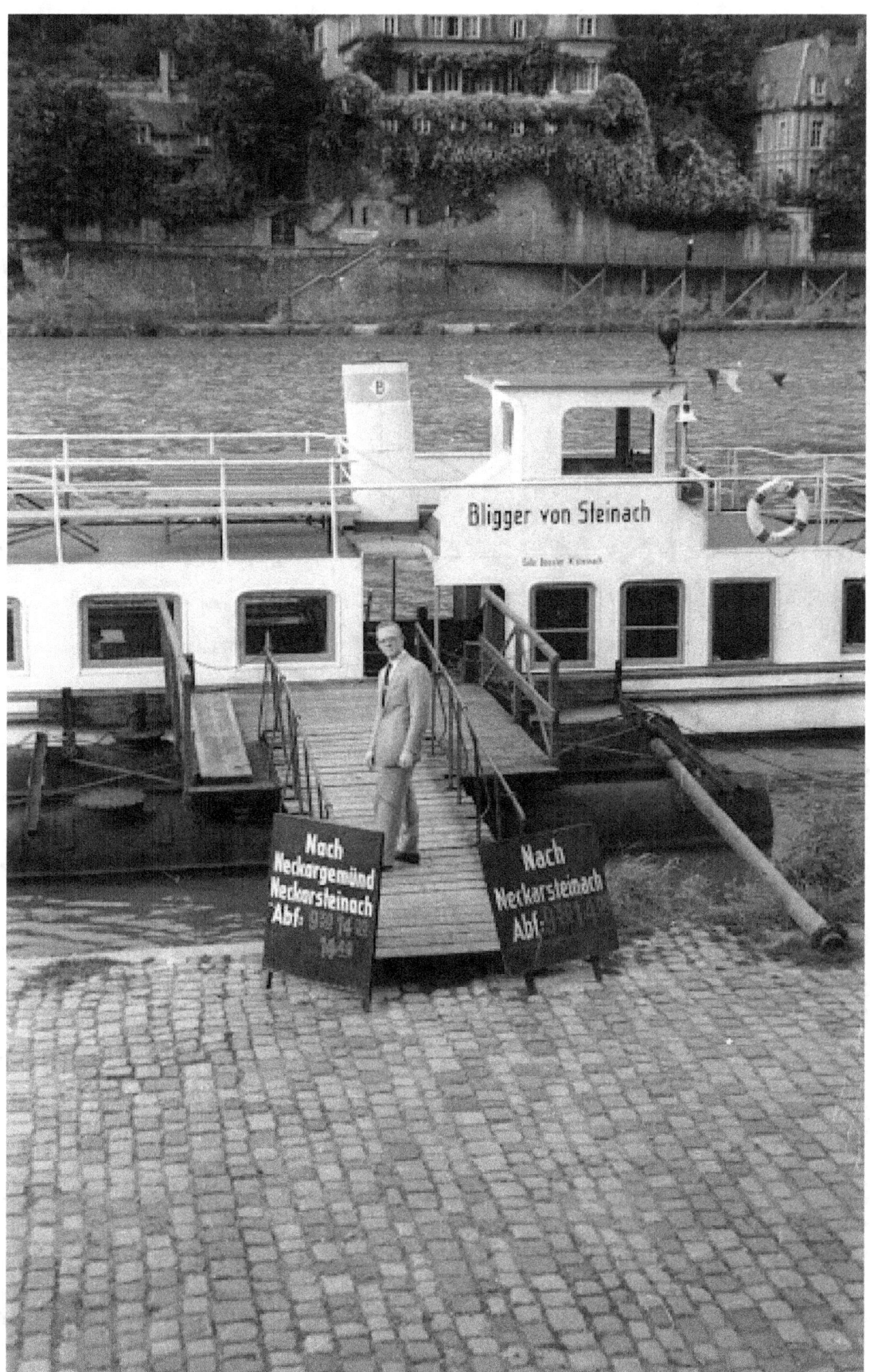

Neckar riverboat

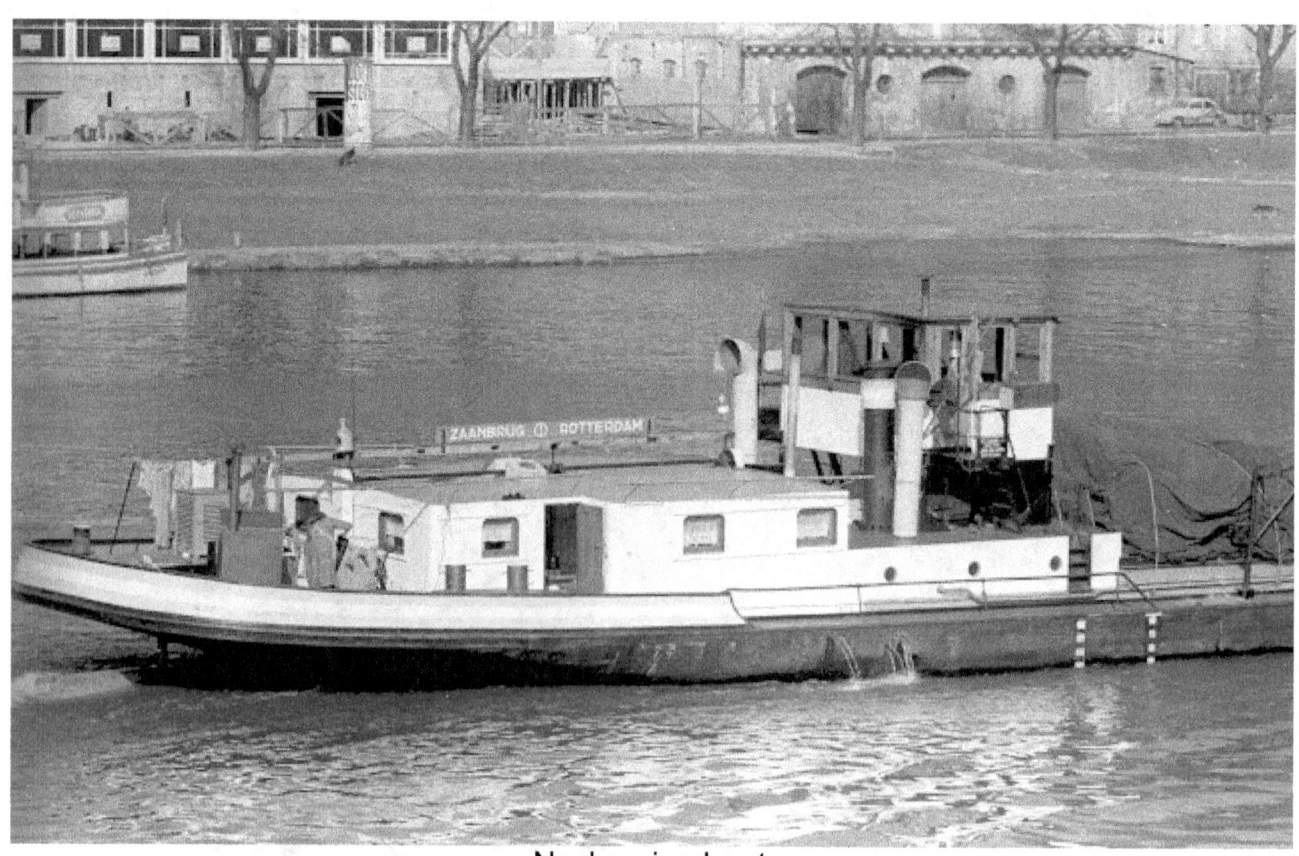

Neckar riverboat

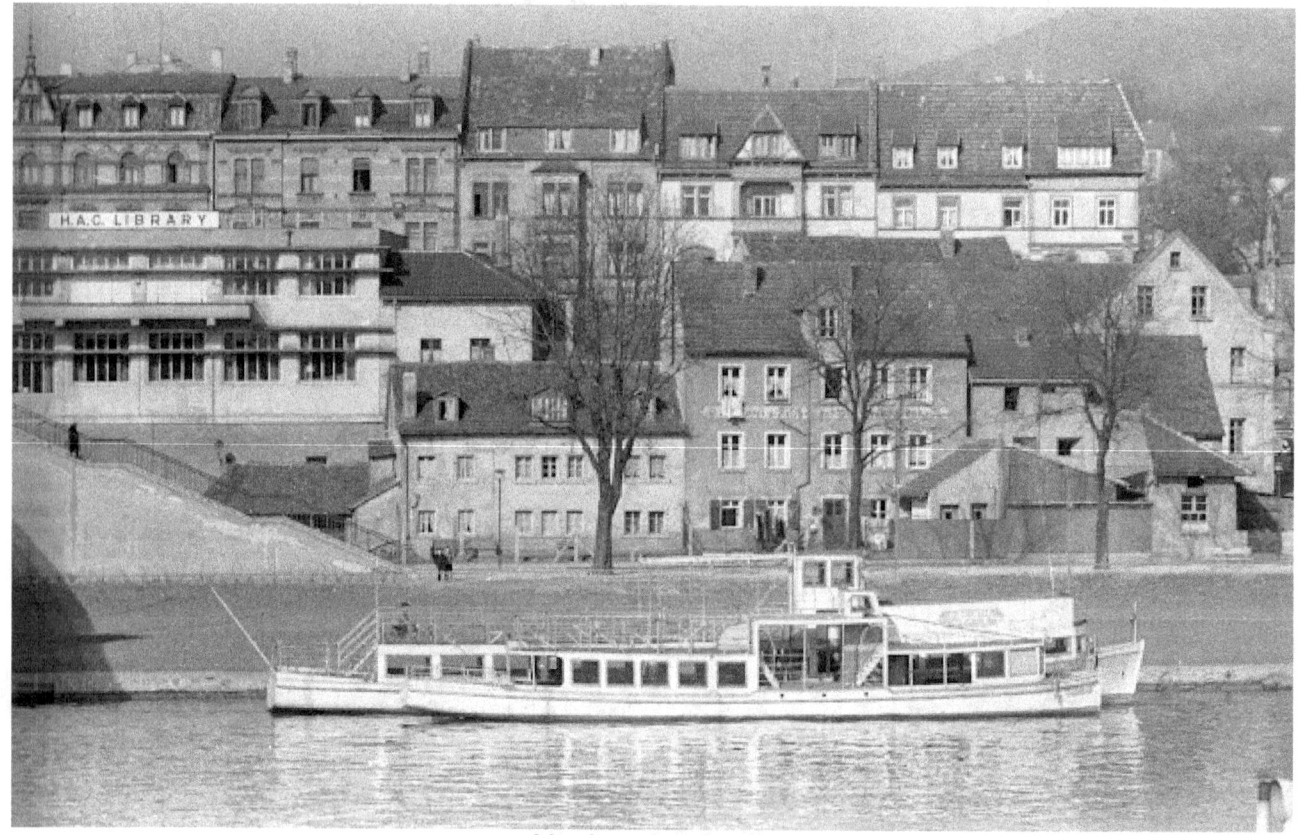

Neckar riverboat

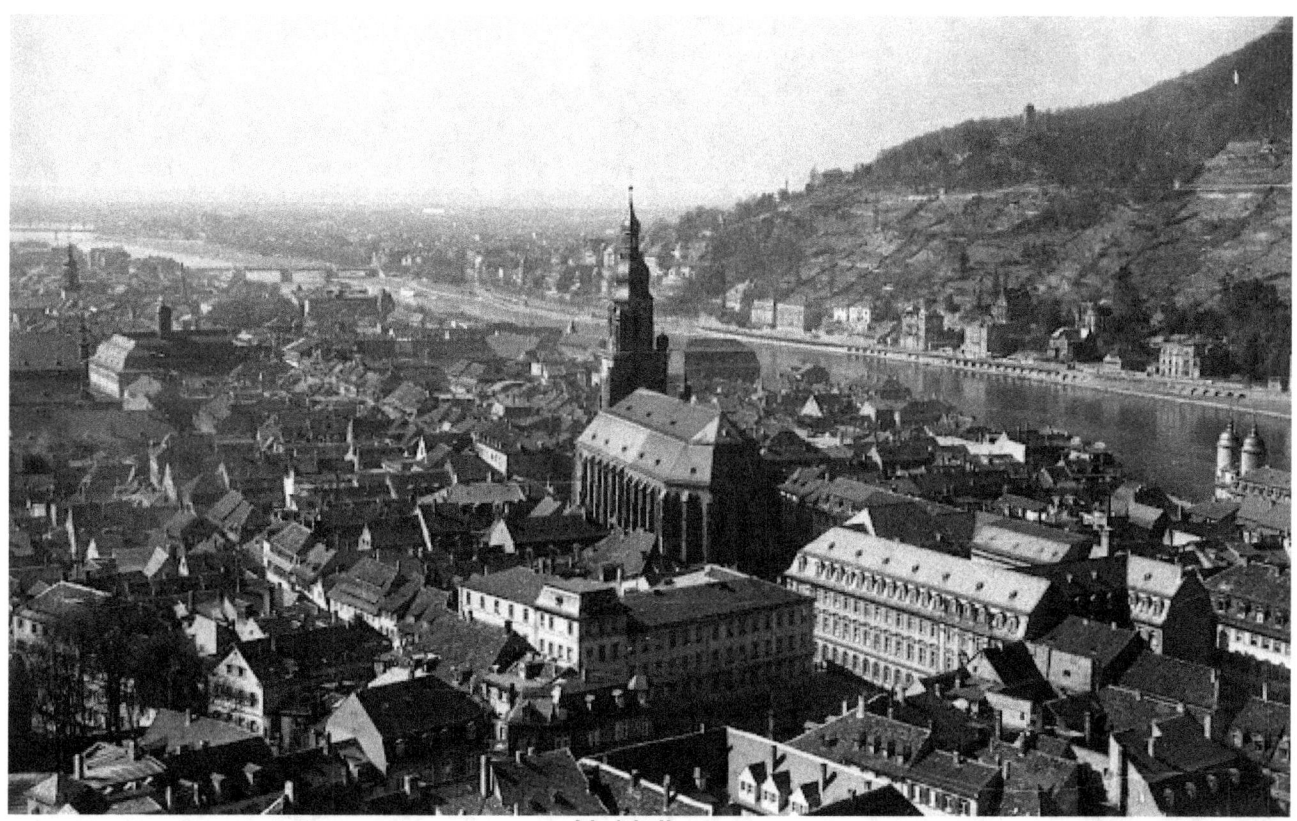
Heidelberg

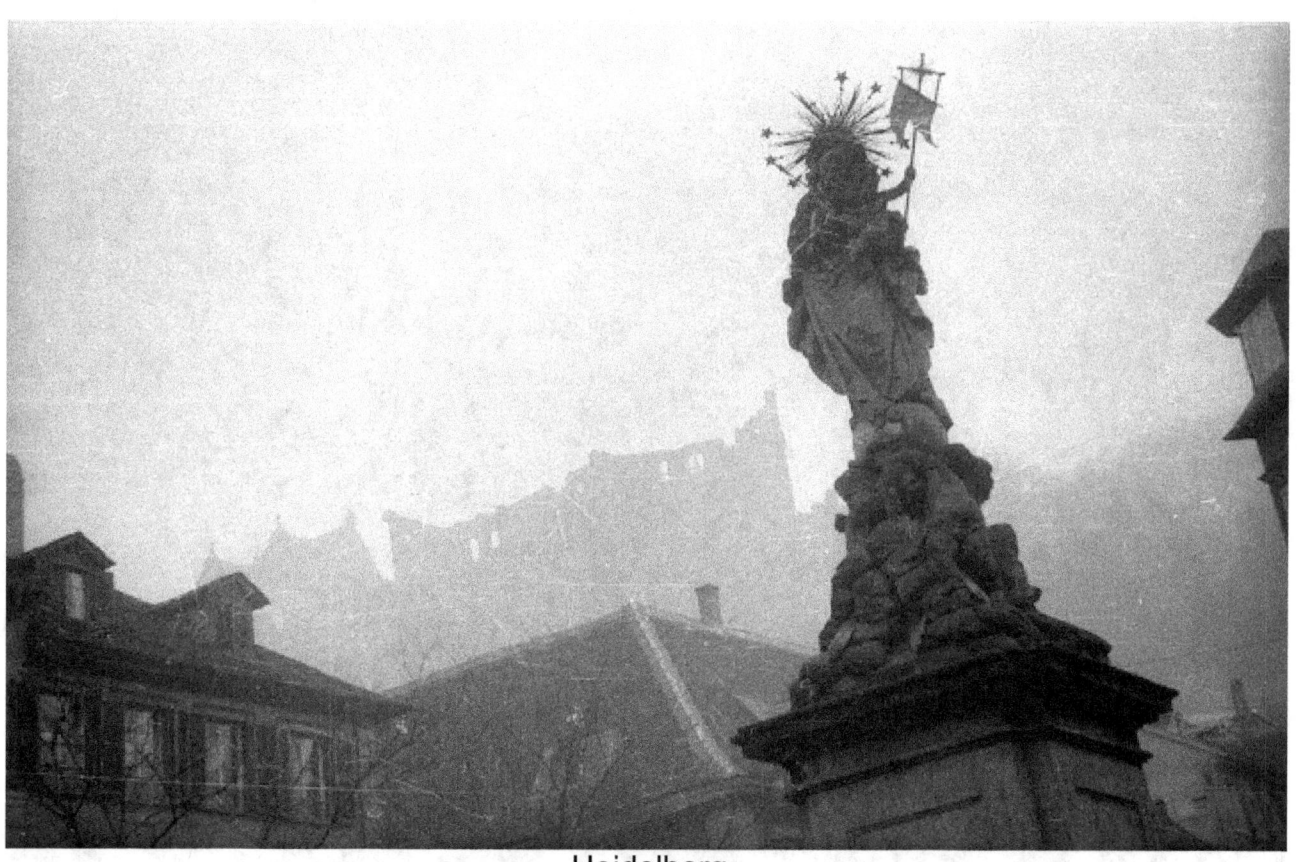
Heidelberg

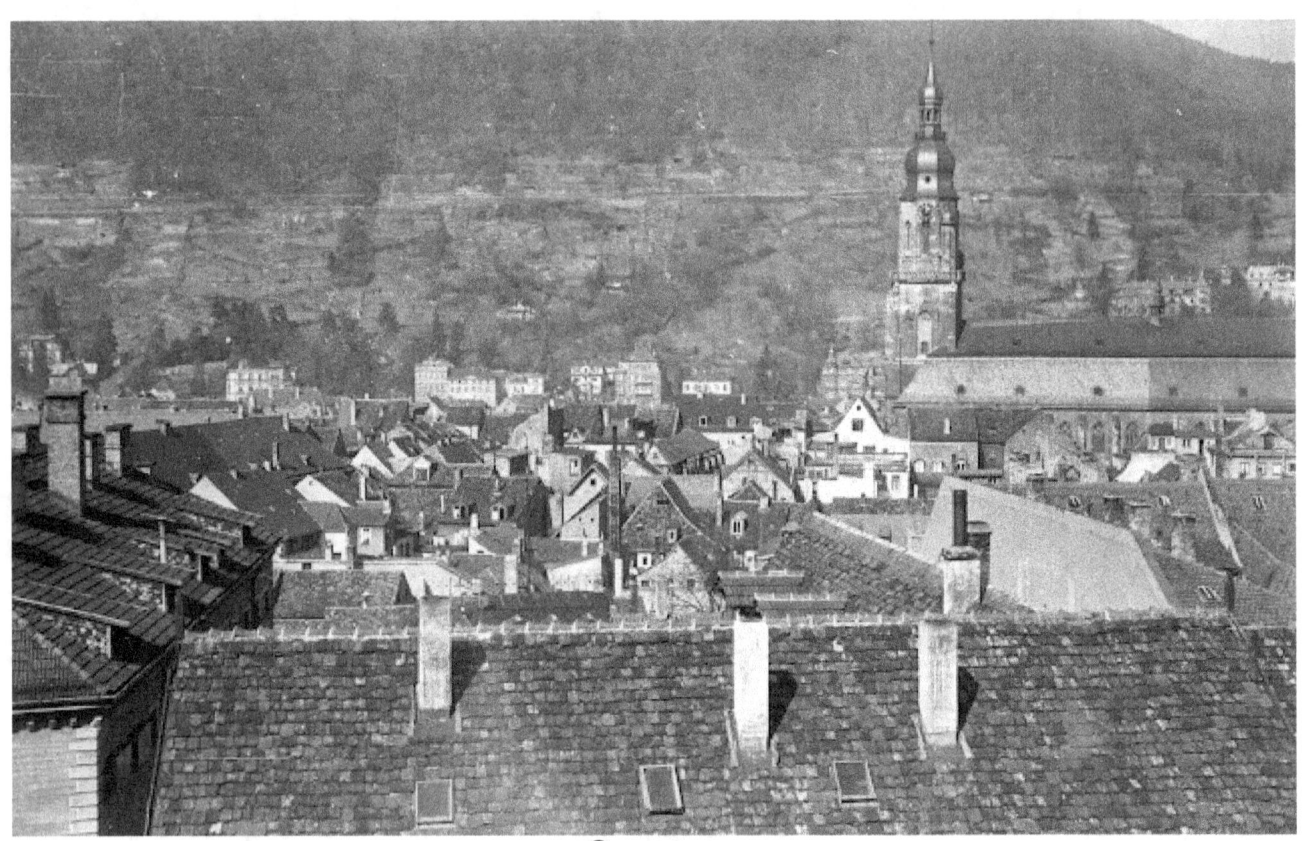
Germany

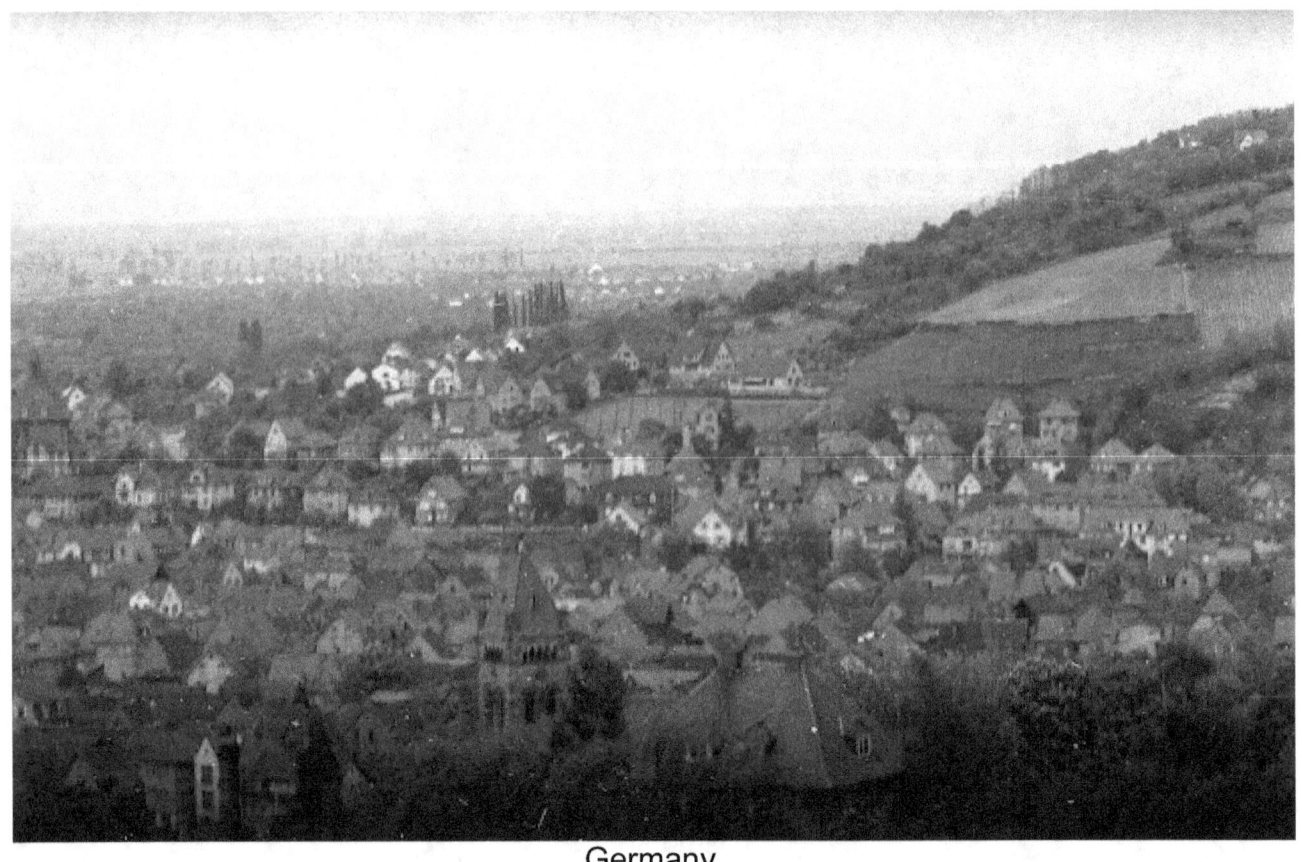
Germany

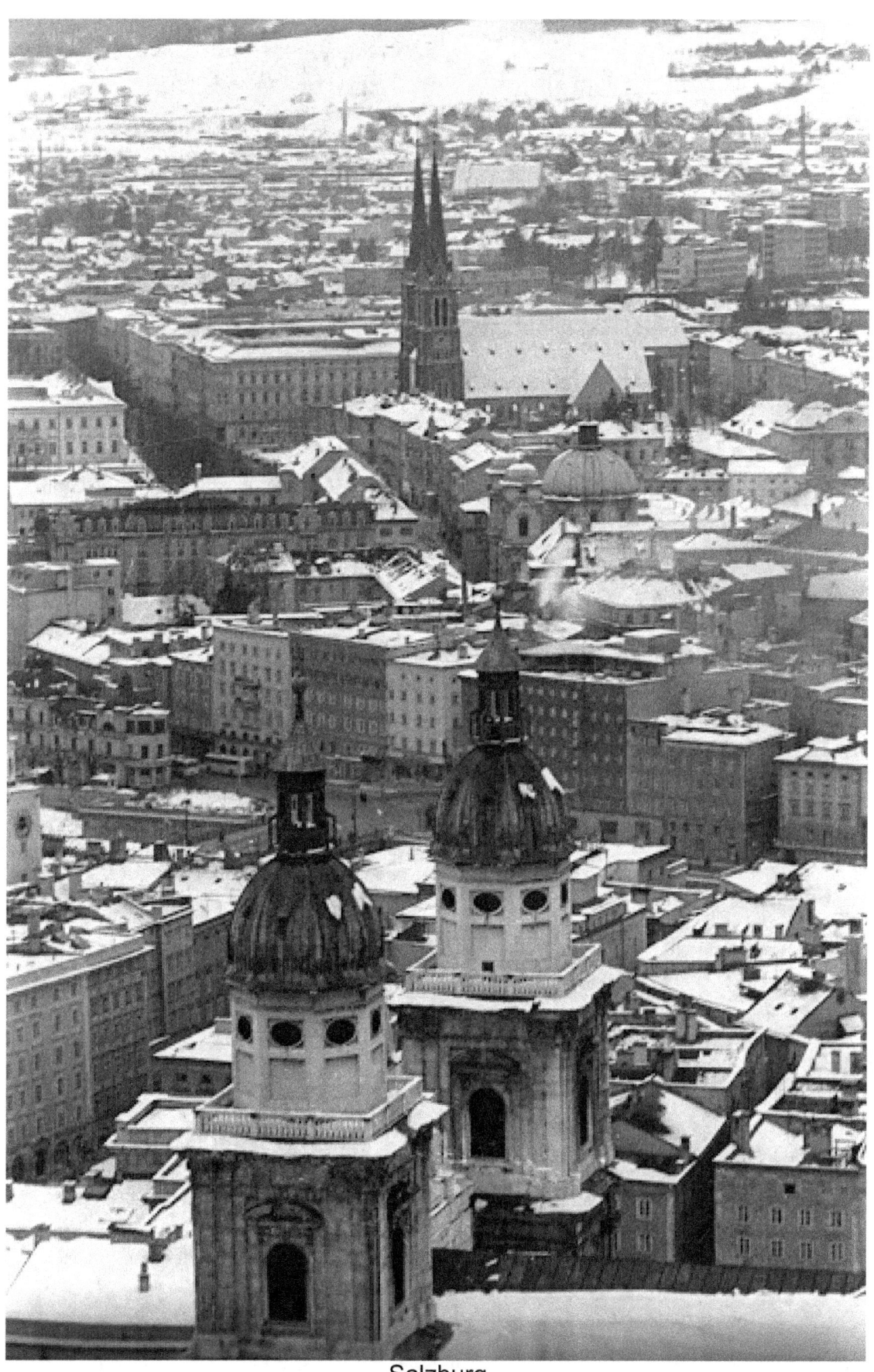
Salzburg

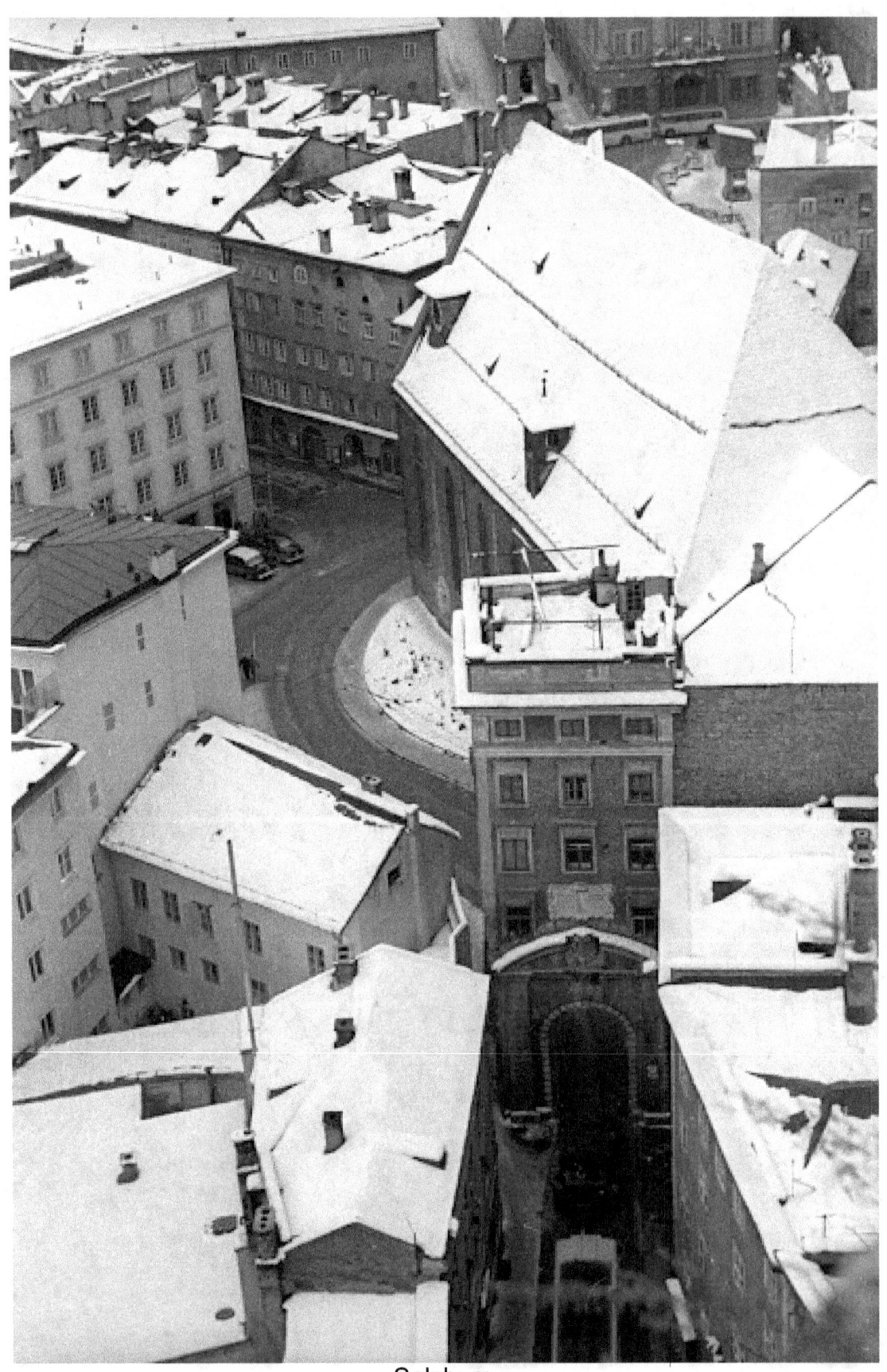
Salzburg

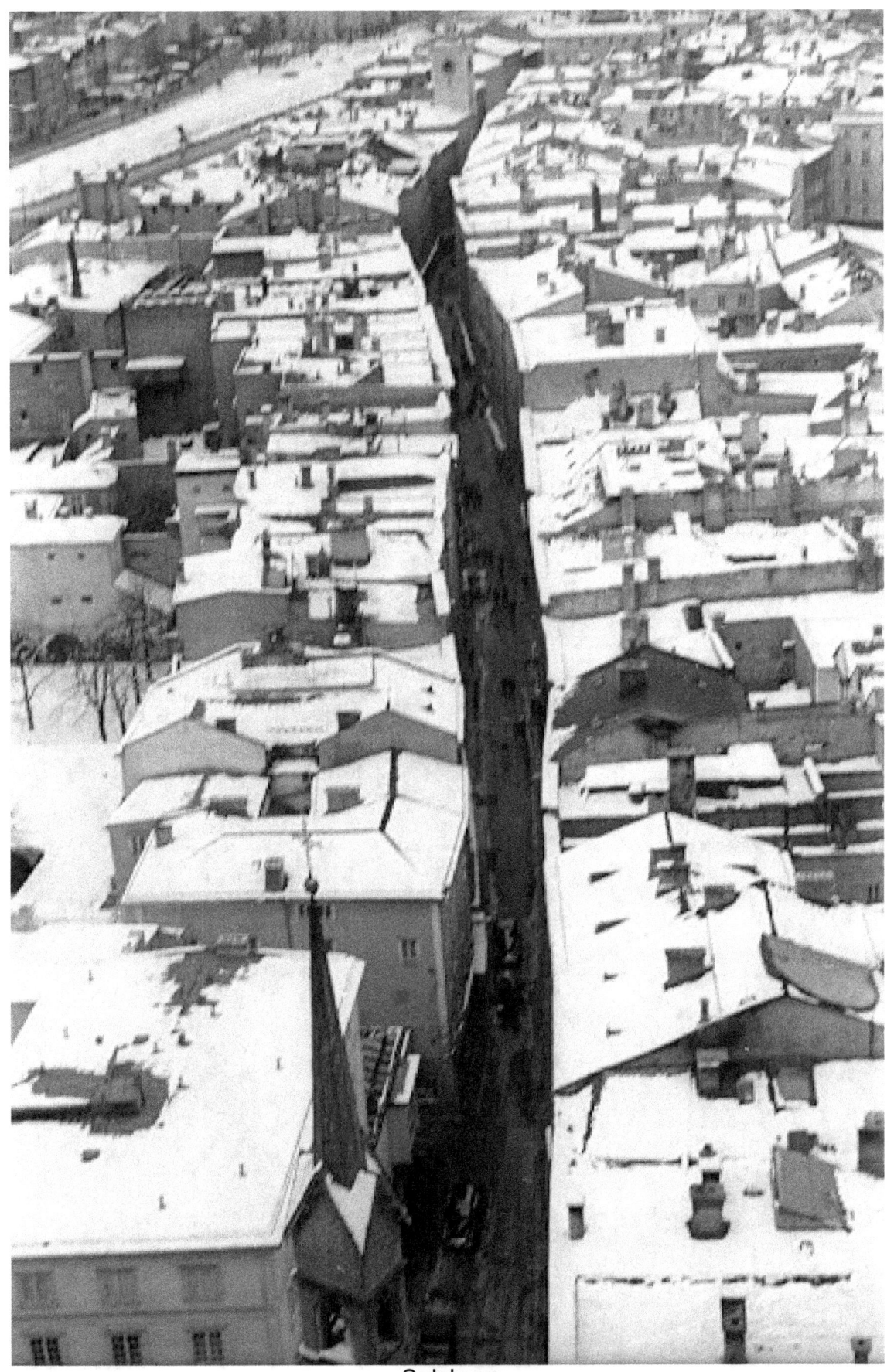
Salzburg

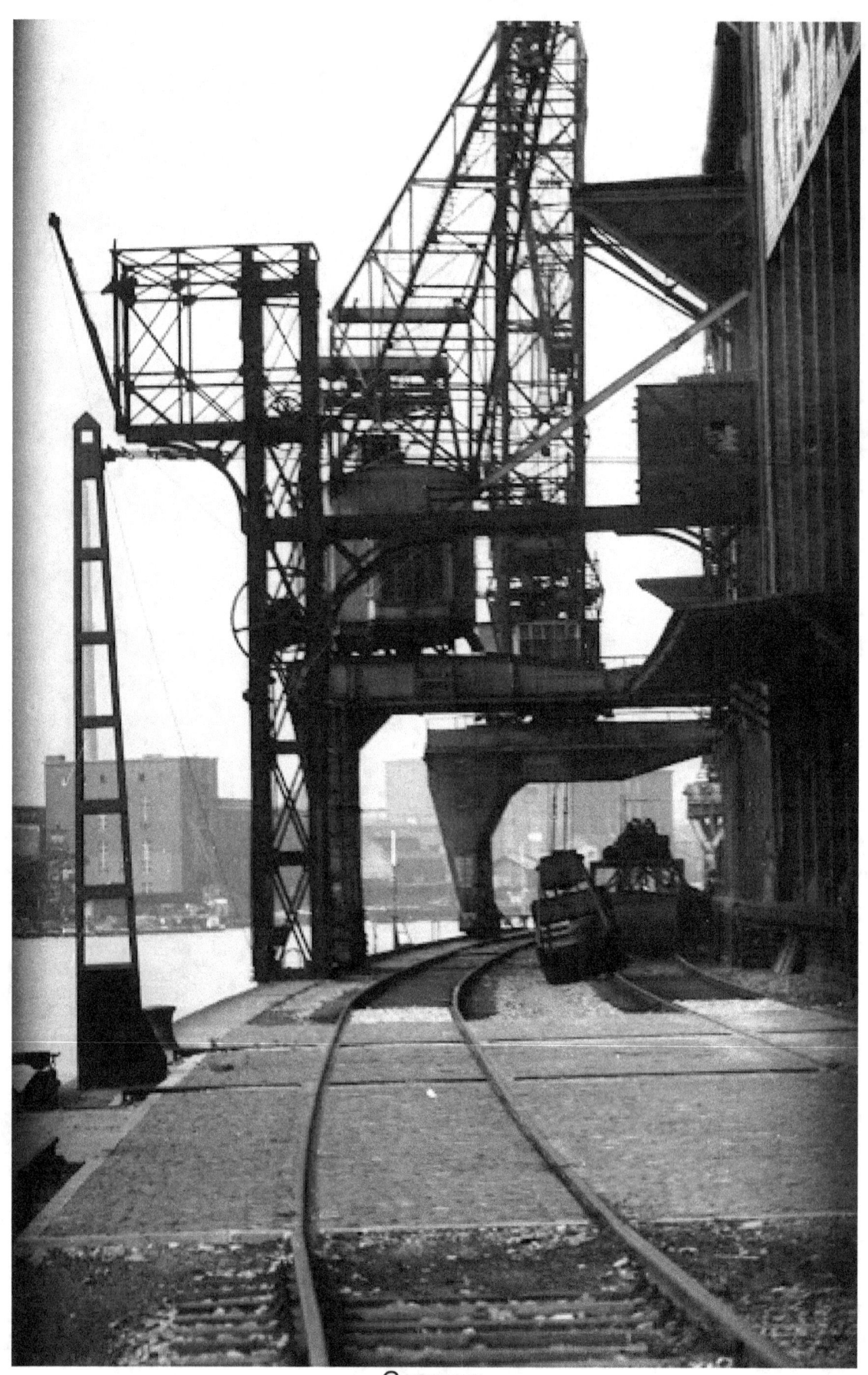

Germany

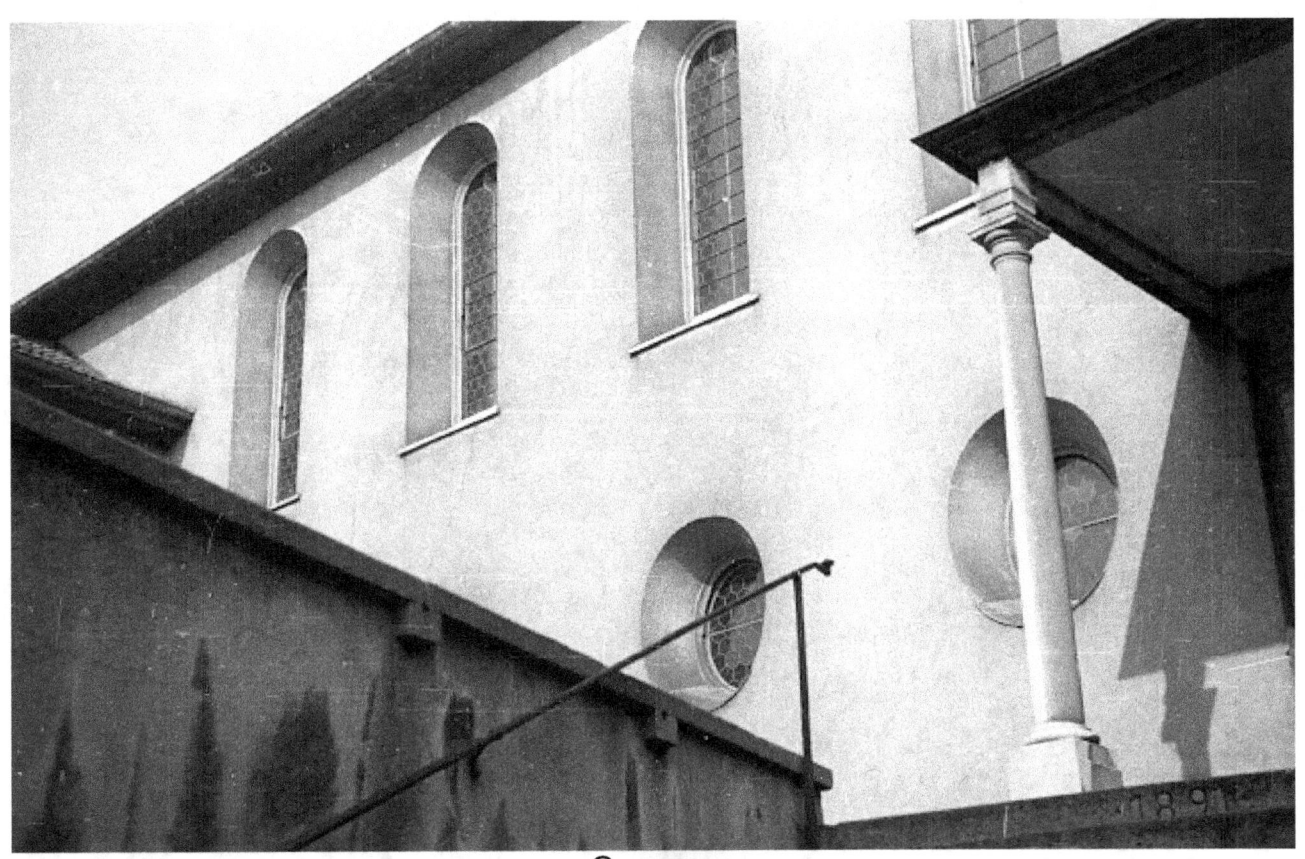
Germany

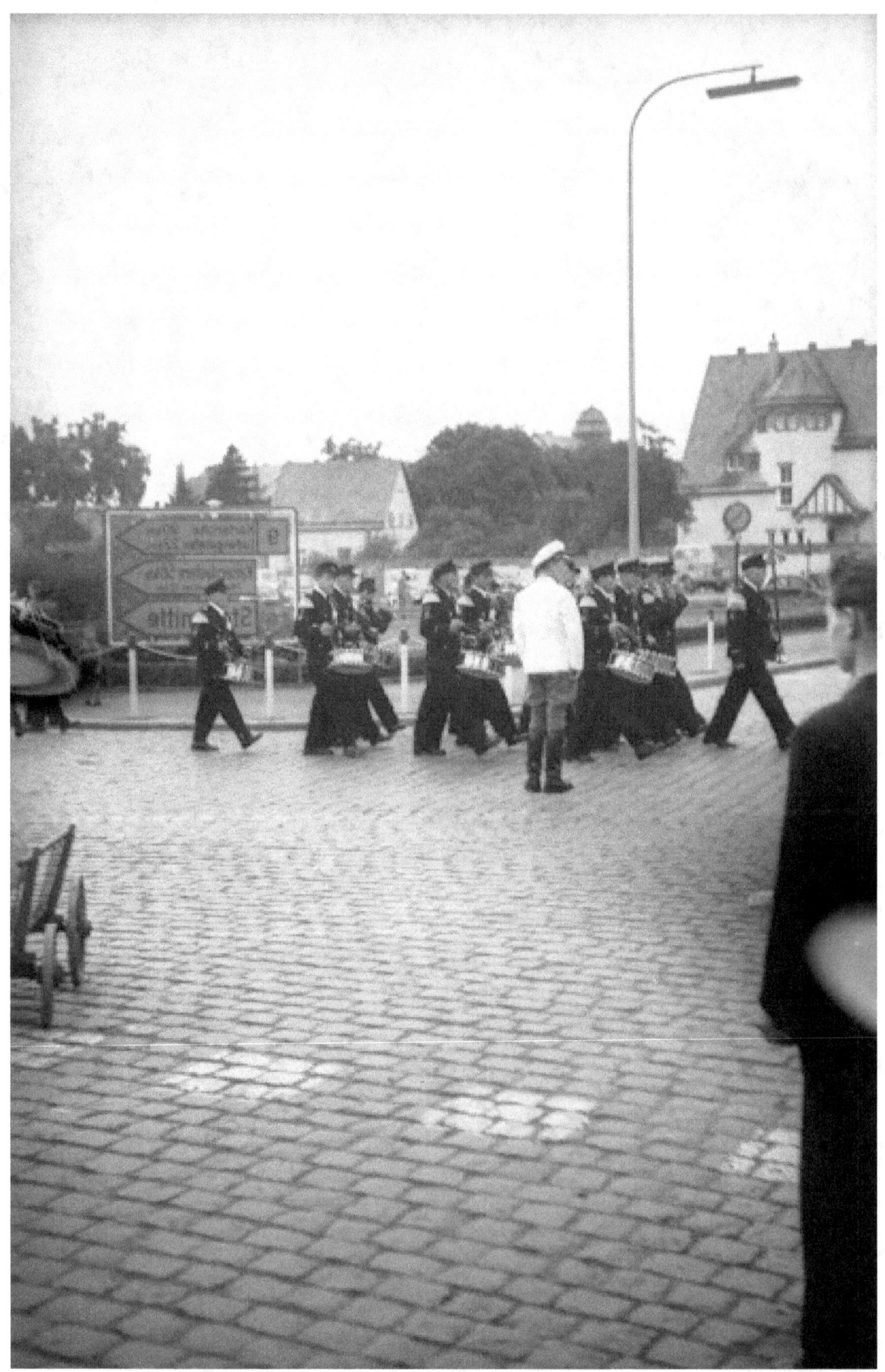
Parade

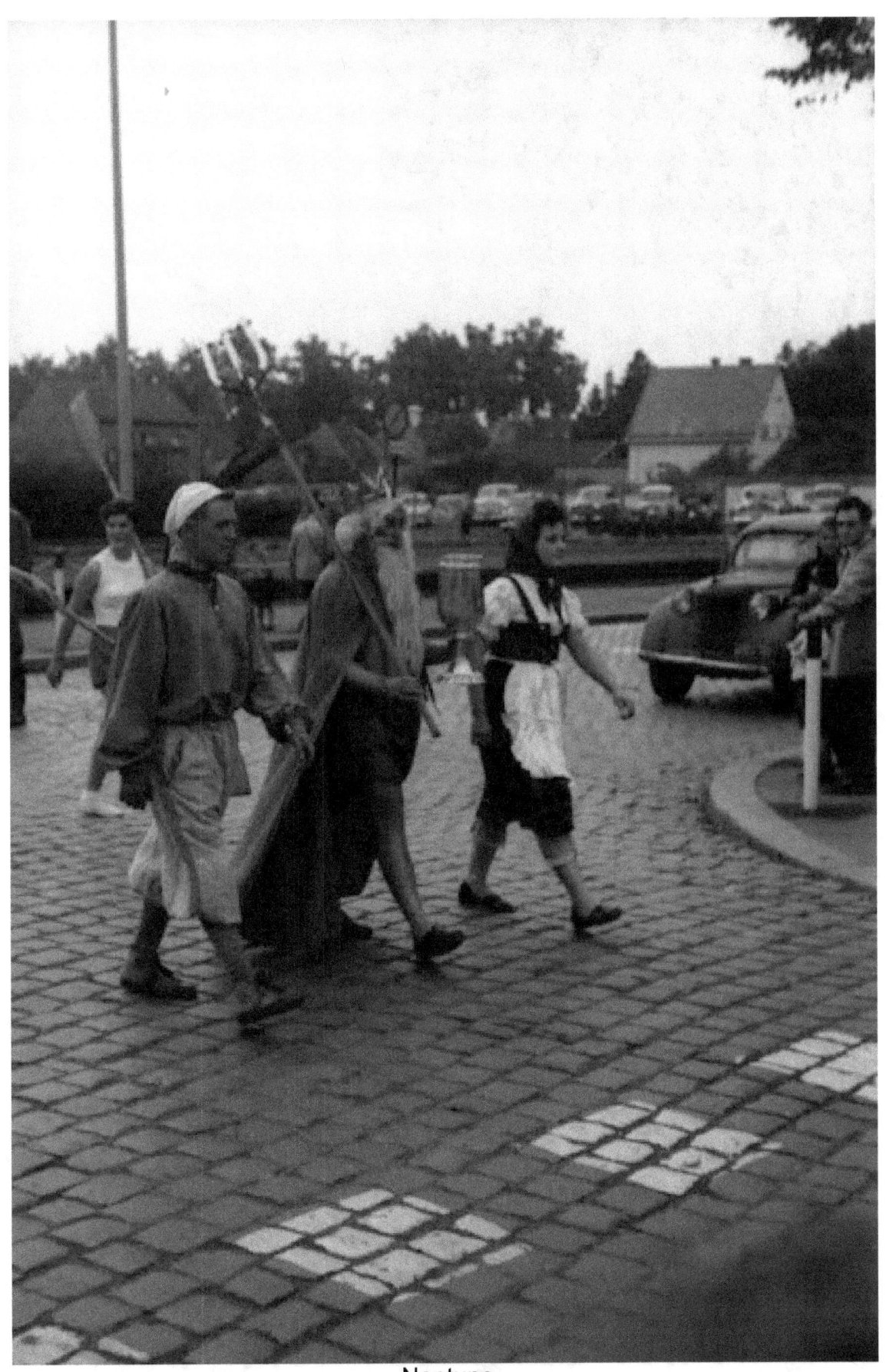
Neptune

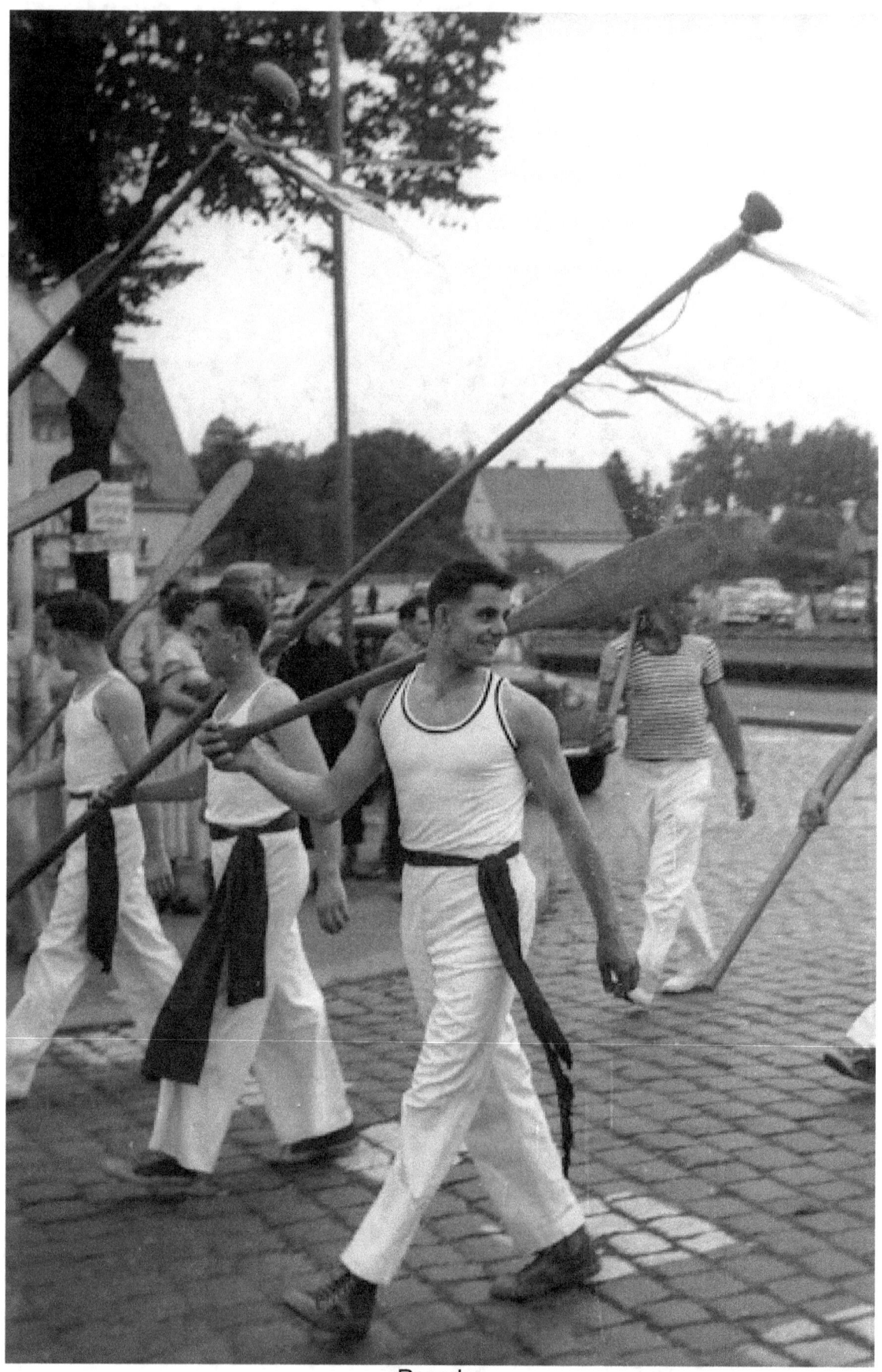
Parade

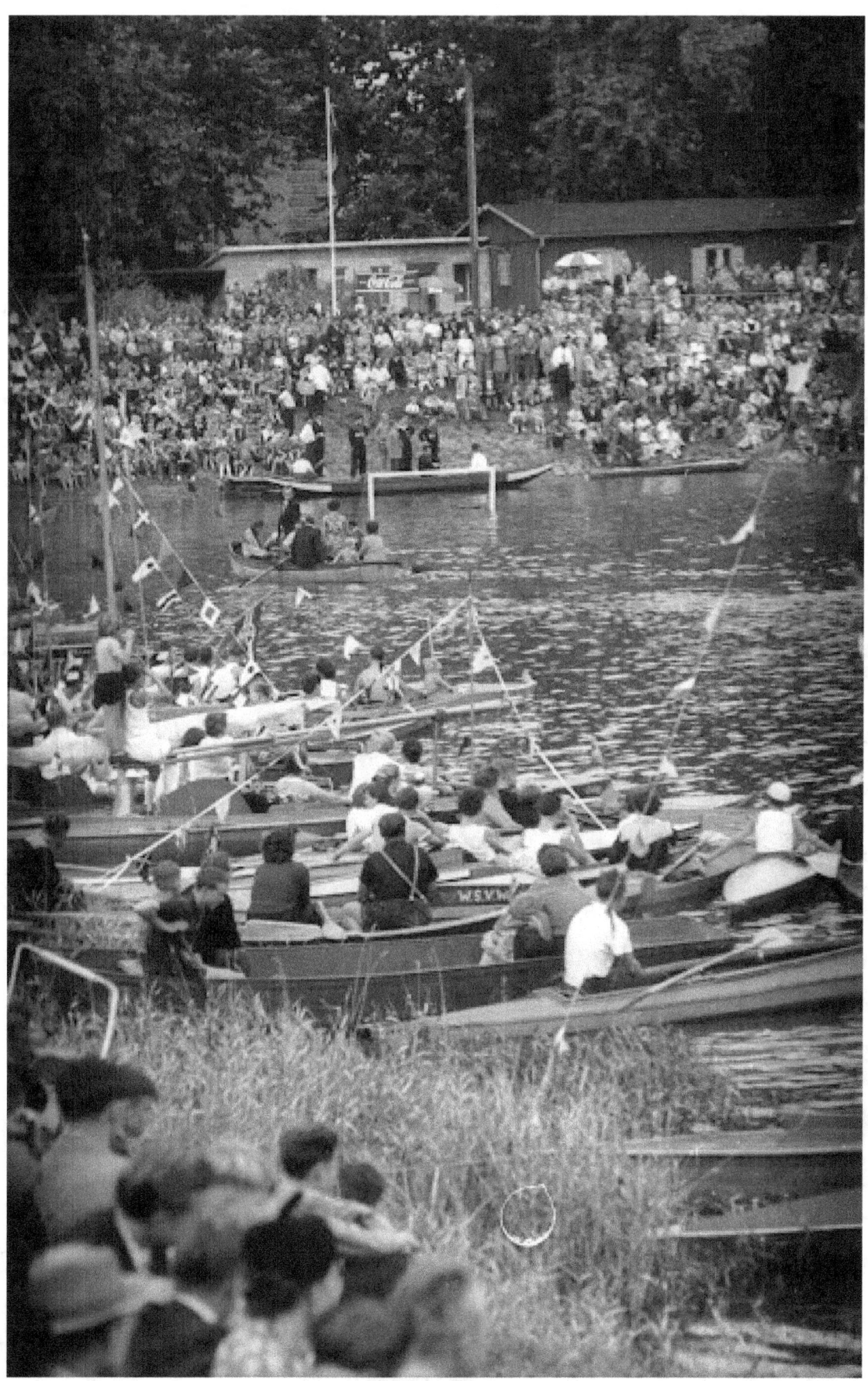
Neckar River

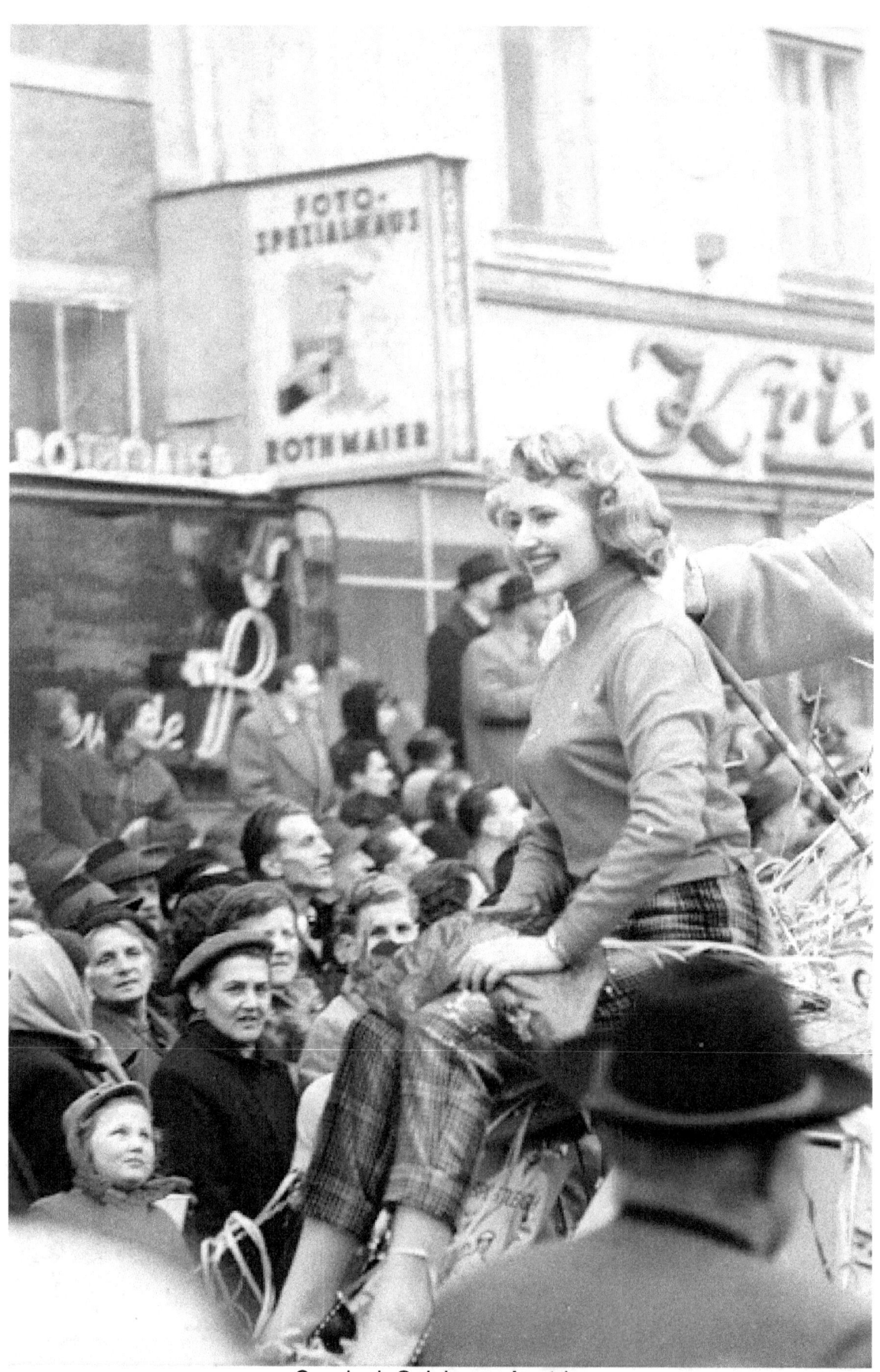
Carnival, Salzburg, Austria

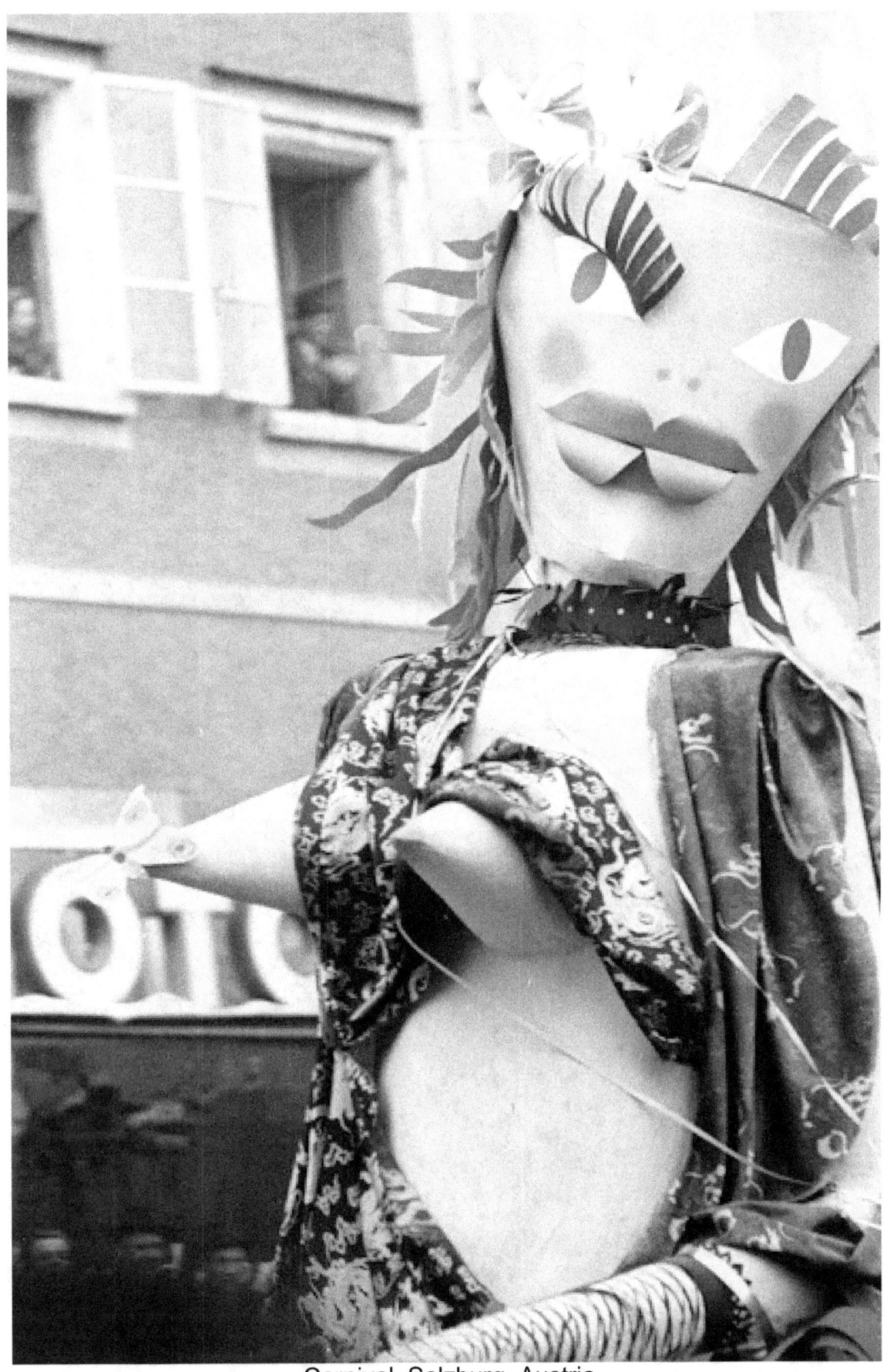
Carnival, Salzburg, Austria

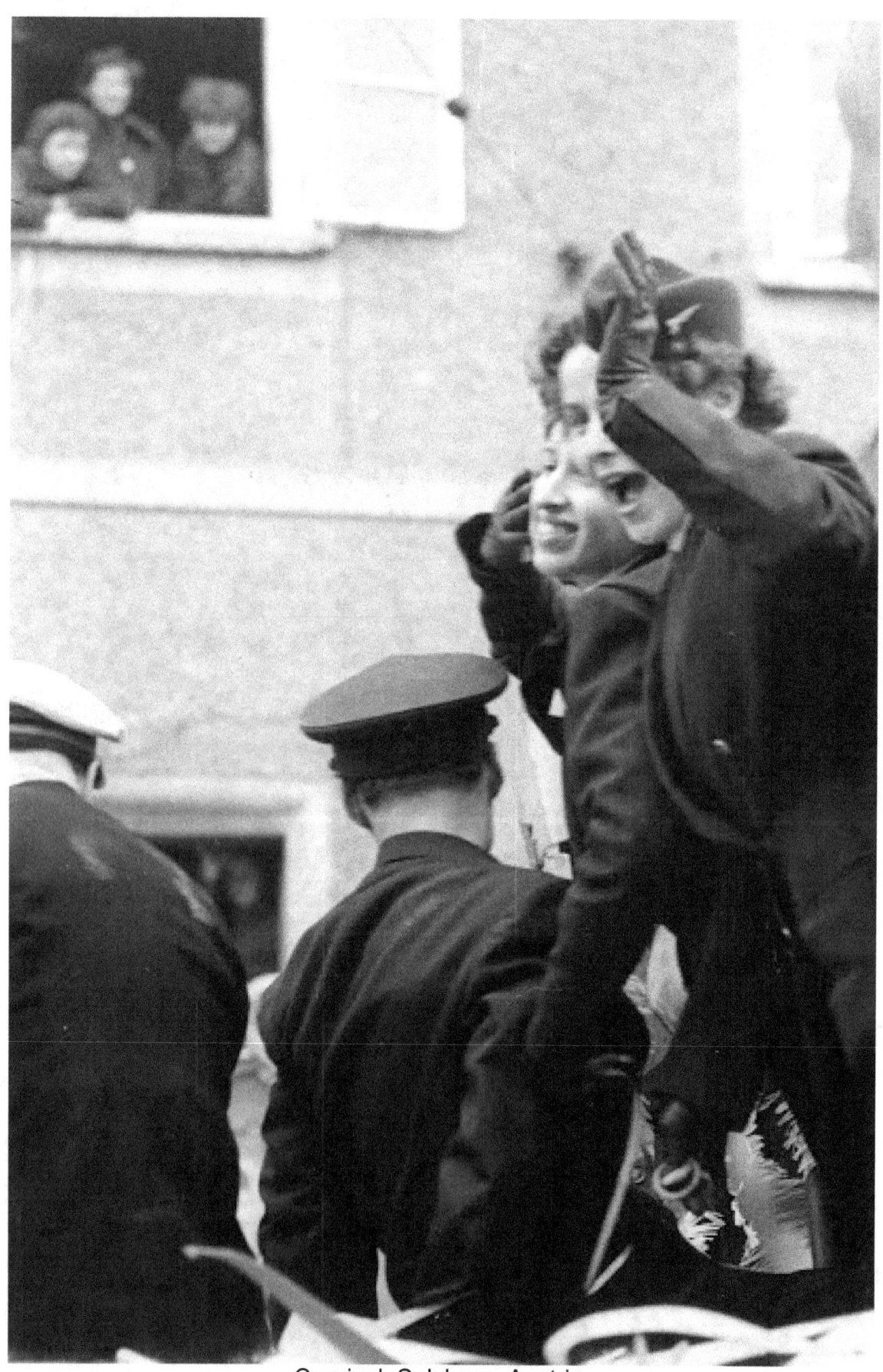
Carnival, Salzburg, Austria

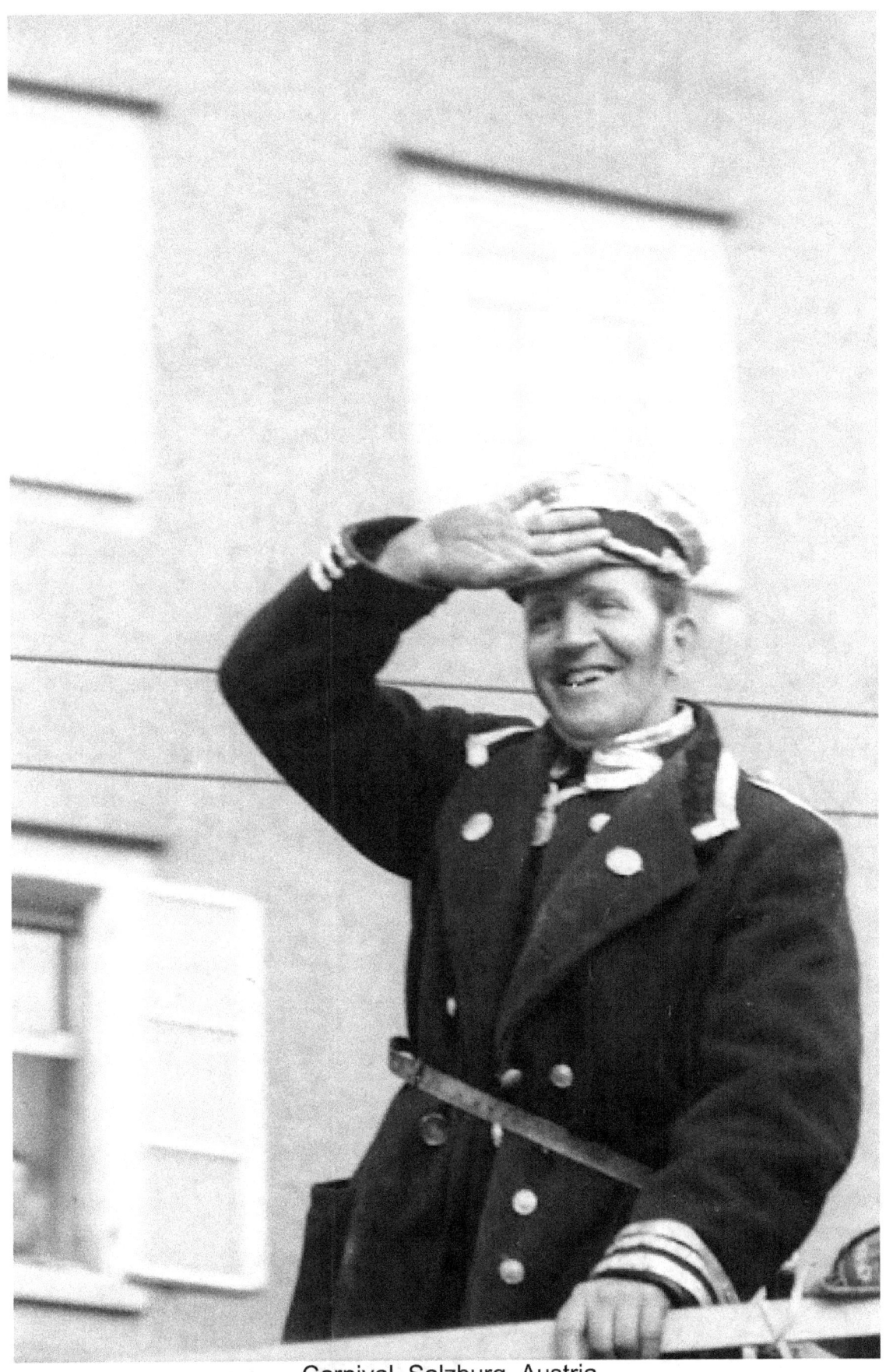
Carnival, Salzburg, Austria

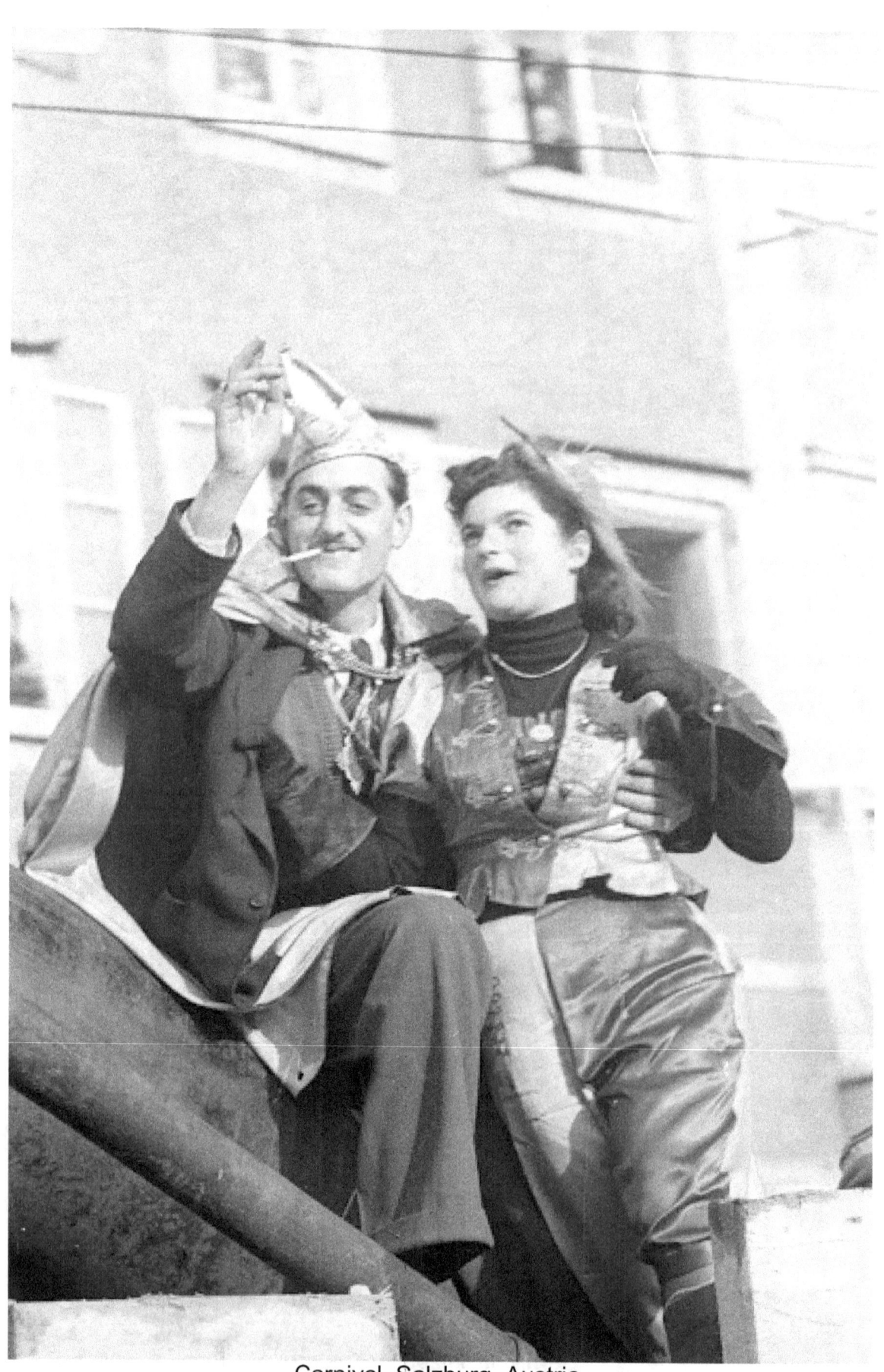
Carnival, Salzburg, Austria

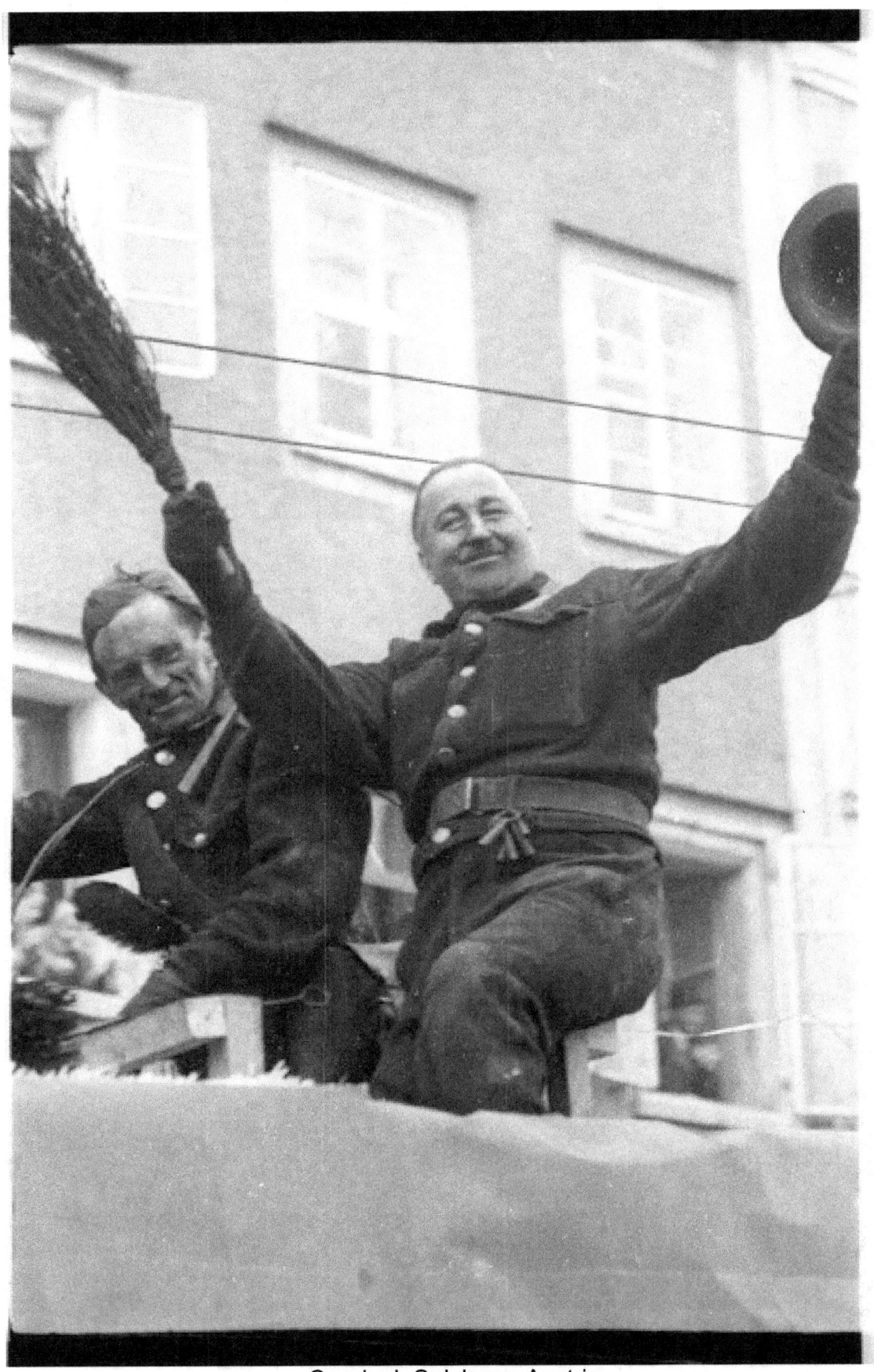
Carnival, Salzburg, Austria

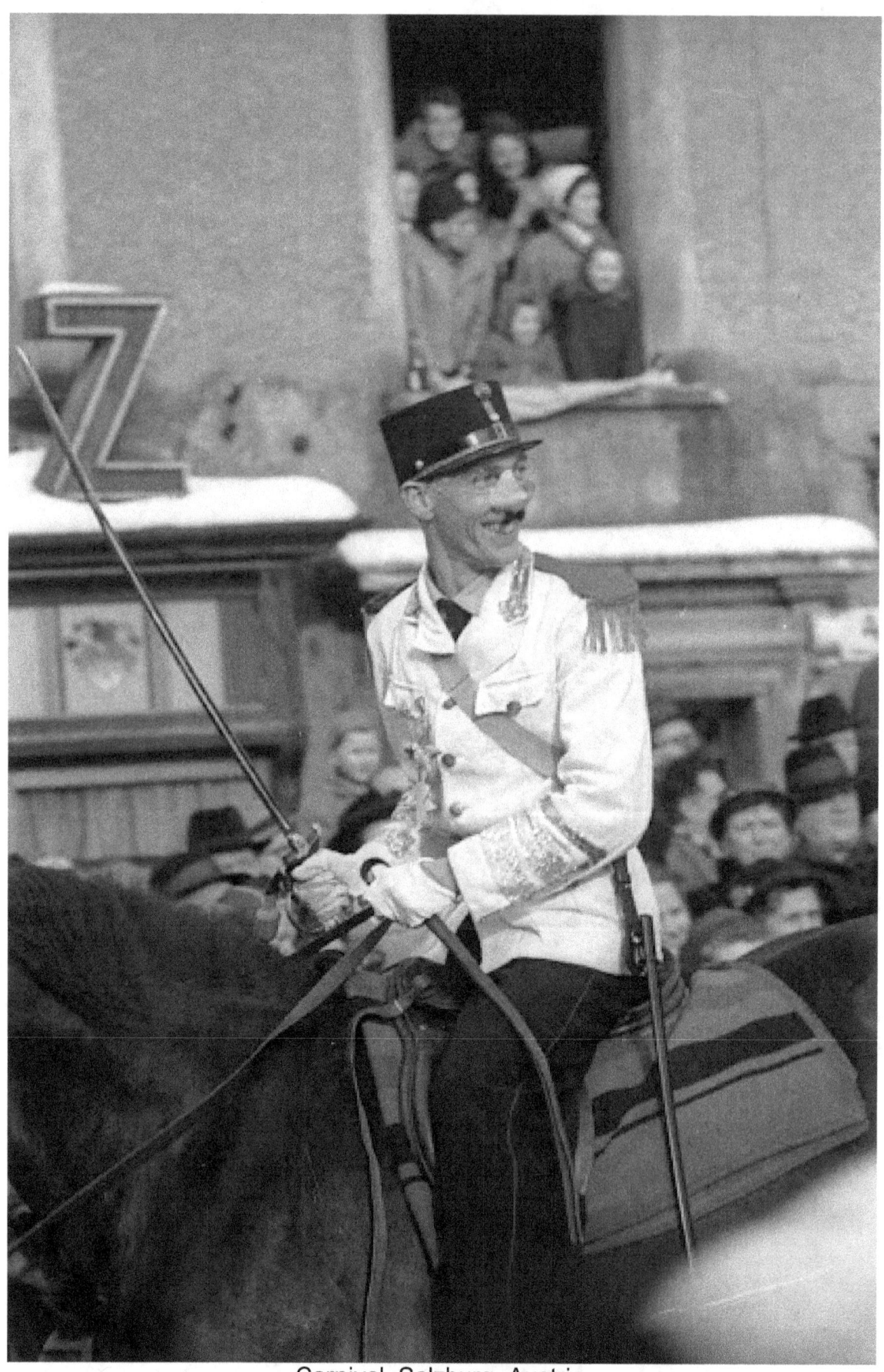
Carnival, Salzburg, Austria

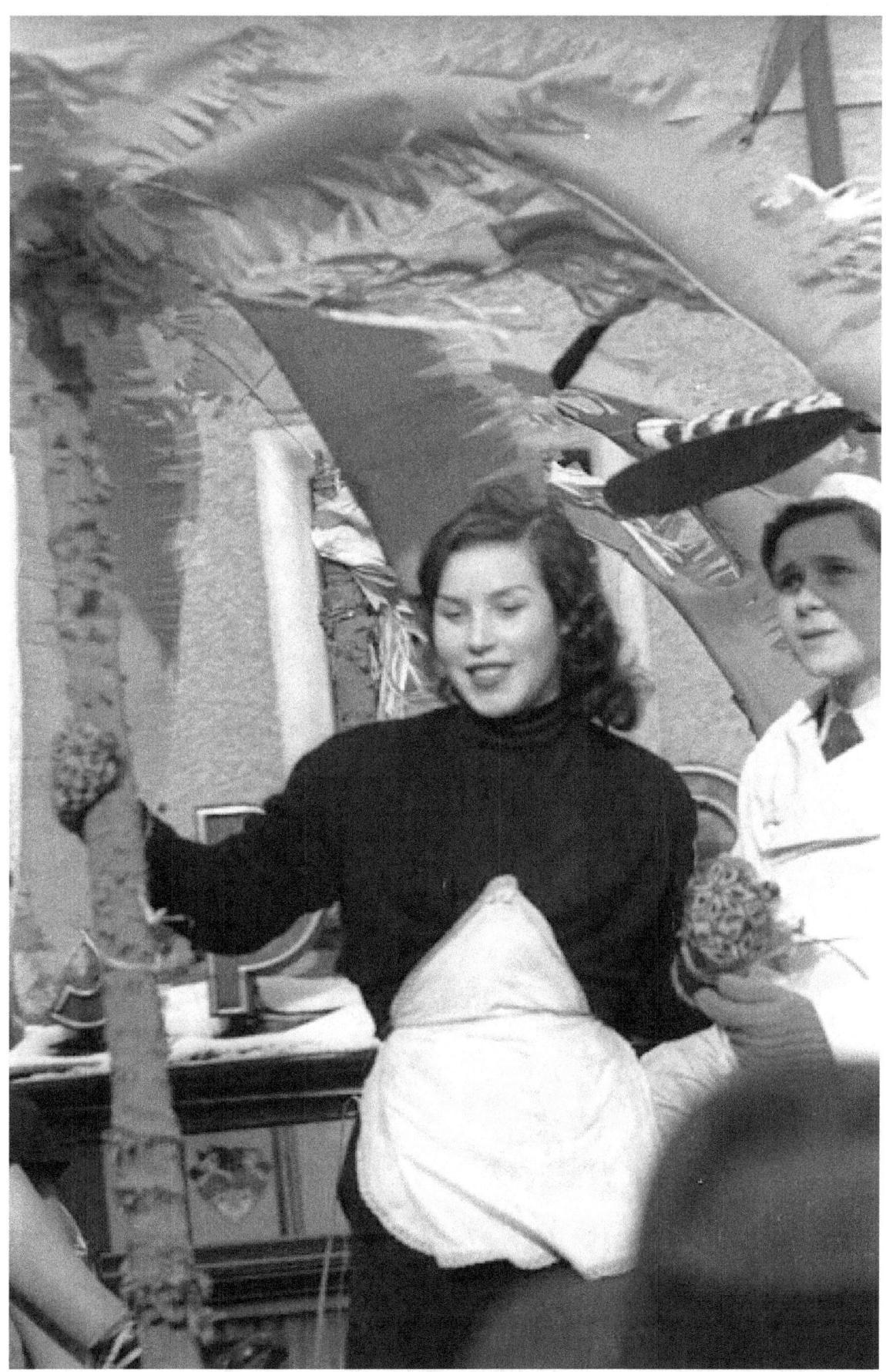
Carnival, Salzburg

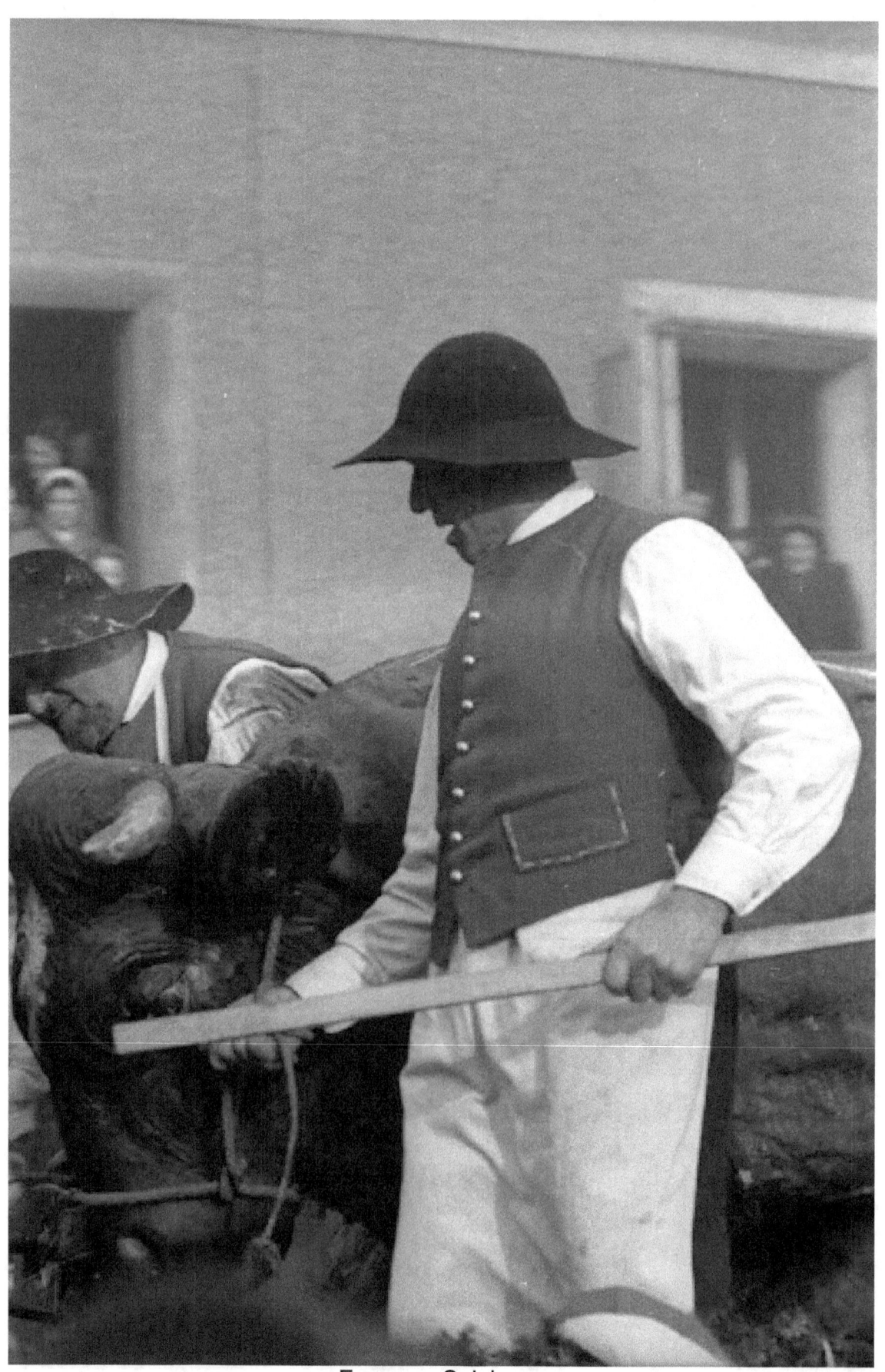
Farmers, Salzburg

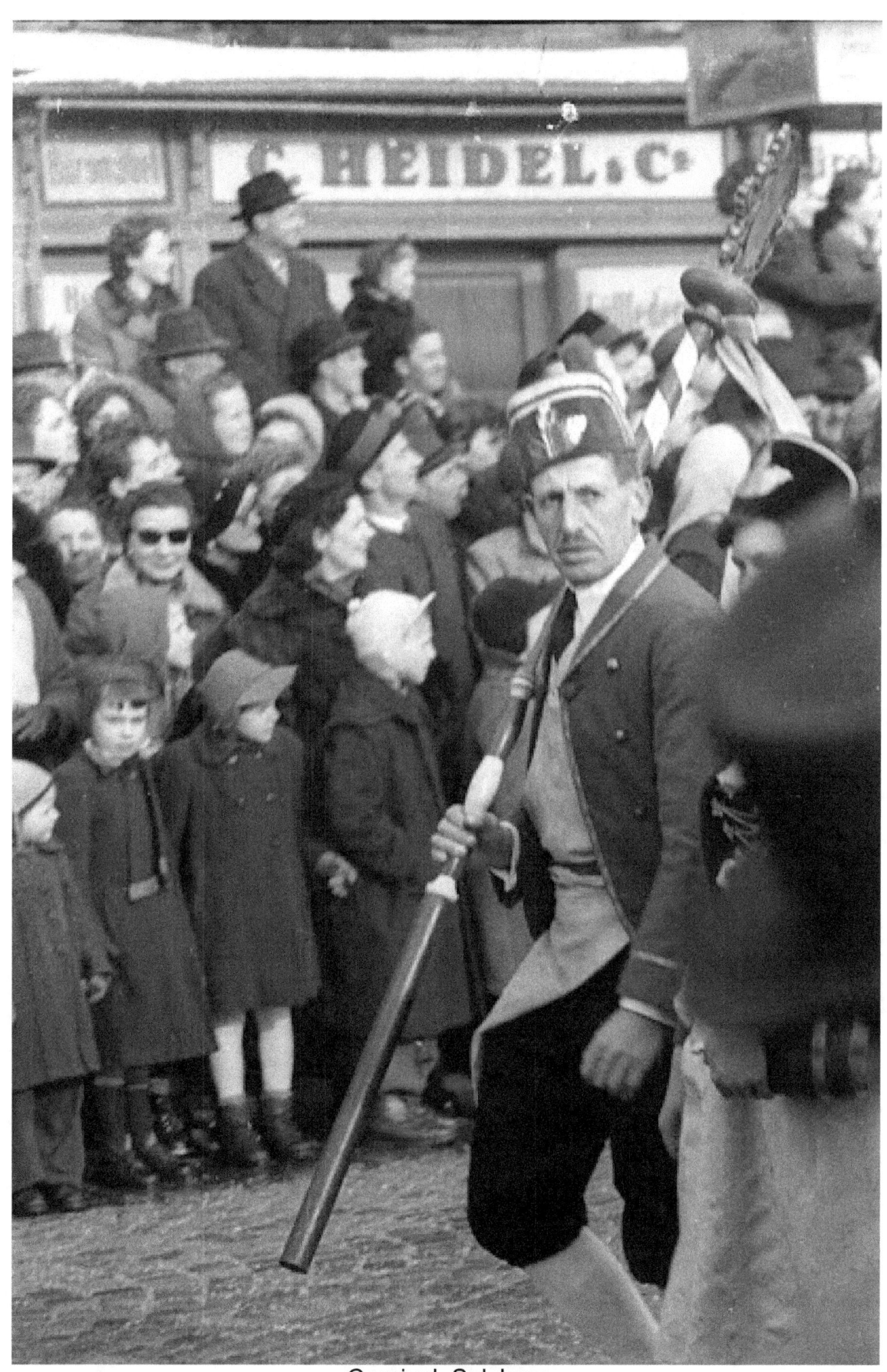
Carnival, Salzburg

www.ingramcontent.com/pod-product-compliance
Lightning Source LLC
Chambersburg PA
CBHW081435220526
45466CB00008B/2398